Oliver, Chantelle
Apocalypse the Memoir / Chantelle Oliver

Books may be purchased by contacting the author at:
http://apocalypsethememoir.com

ISBN 978-1-68222-148-8
1. Memoir 2. Zombie 3. Horror 4. Apocalypse
First Edition
Printed in U.S.A.

Apocalypse: The Memoir

C.S. Oliver

for my husband

that that was supposed to have frightened you – *Roky Erickson*

What I have in view is a much humbler, though perhaps, in the present state of science, not less useful object. I have desired, in fact, to show how the careful study of one of the commonest and most insignificant of animals, leads us, step by step, from every-day knowledge to the widest generalizations and the most difficult problems of zoology; and, indeed, of biological science in general.
- *Thomas Henry Huxley*

Those who hate you can't win unless you hate them. And then you destroy yourself.
- *Richard Nixon*

Truth is always stranger-stranger than fiction.
-*Lord Byron*

The substrate of really old memories is located not inside cells, but outside cells, in the extracellular space. The space between cells is not empty, but filled with a matrix of tough material that is difficult to dissolve and turns over very slowly if at all. The extracellular matrix connects cells and maintains the shape of the cell mass. This is why scars on your body haven't changed much after decades of sloughing off skin cells ... If I am right, then all of your memories/what makes you a unique individual are contained in the endoskeleton that connects cells to each other.
- *Terrence J. Sejnowski*

There either is or is not, that's the way things are. The color of the day. The way it felt to be a child. The saltwater on your sunburnt legs. Sometimes the water is yellow, sometimes it's red. But what color it may be in memory, depends on the day. I'm not going to tell you the story the way it happened. I'm going to tell it the way I remember it.
- *Charles Dickens*

Here it comes, Miss Crustacean.
Here it comes, our ideal.
Isn't it so pretty.
Crowned today in Ocean City.
Claws so comely and feelers so bitty.
- *Miss Crustacean Pageant Theme Son*

Birth: May 20, 1973.

The true story of summer 1988, exactly remembered.

Tara, Ontario, Canada, July 1988

Ring ring ring.

Indy, fifteen, choked down one more raw wiener. She was rehearsing for the Phil Donahue Show and staring at the army-green wall phone on the kitchen wall.

Chew chew chew. Ring ring ring.

The phone hadn't stopped ringing all morning.

Until today, it had been improbable for Indy to let the phone finish even one ring. The possibility of letting it get to even a second ring had been petrifying just days ago. Her stepfather, Dana (certainly a girl's name), promised to rip the phone out of the wall whenever he heard it ring. His constant threat carried such force Indy grew a superhuman instinct for answering the phone.

Indy could not live without that phone safely on the wall. It was her lifeline to Tammy. She'd wait until 8 o'clock (7:30 was Dana's bed time) to call Tammy. They would conspire in dulcet undetectable undertones about escaping their Tara prisons and plot futures of world travel. First stop: America!

Phone answering had been Indy's only religion.

It was no longer.

Today it was not impossible to let the phone ring twice or even, as it was now, to let it ring repeatedly for *hours*.

But this had been a week of impossibilities.

She massaged another hot dog out of the Schneider's shrink-wrap. She was sitting at the burgundy dining table inherited from her grandmother, and this compounded all the oddness because she had not sat and eaten at it, or any dining table, in three years. She always ate on a TV tray. Chew chew chew. Mr. Donahue, how do I explain the sheer horror?

Ring ring ring.

At least the ringing filled the empty space left by the silenced fridge. Dana had rescued it from the dump. The fridge had once produced more whining and neediness than a toddler. Indy and her mother had to defrost it every three weeks or they'd be chipping ketchup and mustard bottles from the back of the fridge with bread knives wielded like ice picks.

Indy's bare toes played in the remains of a puddle from the now fully defrosted fridge. She spoke loudly to the kitchen.

Are hot dogs miracles?

Since the power went off a week ago, she had been eating her way through everything in order of preciousness. Milk first. She had drained the last jug this morning and had to pick the last mouthful out from between her teeth like pizza cheese, a gross and perhaps bad sign. She had cooked all the chicken and hamburger on the propane BBQ the day the power went off. For a bone rack, she was proud how quickly she had downed three roast chickens and eleven burgers. Method? She pretended to be in an eating contest since she was, in a way. Only, instead of a stupid gilded plastic trophy, her prize was not starving to death. And no waste.

She did eventually get to the hateful rusty lettuce by artfully crafting it into a palatable soup with the last bottle of Kraft Blue Cheese salad dressing.

She was finally down to the best food ever, preserved meats: hot dogs, salami, mock chicken and the ham bejeweled with macaroni and cheese. The silent fridge was empty save for one

2

spoonful of relish and the Kraft Singles cheese slices she had saved for last, thinking them immutable. Wrong. She had eaten one yesterday. It looked normal but tasted like sand, reminding her of a Dairy Queen Skor Blizzard she had ruined by eating down on Sauble Beach on a windy day. She had gone there to dig holes in the sand and look for salamanders and had ended up pouring her inedible Blizzard into Lake Huron. She nervously tried a second Kraft Single and instead of the familiar waxy cheesiness all she got was another bright orange mouthful of sand.

Indy didn't waste. She was aspirationally MacGyver. It buoyed her heart when she discovered a new way to make best with what she had. And that, coupled with how much she loathed her own bone thinness, made food waste an anathema to her. Fifteen years old, just two inches shy of six feet and under one hundred pounds. No tits or ass, puberty had simply passed her by. So stick-thin her nickname was *Chicken Legs* on the school bus, *Titless* in typing class and, Dana's favorite, *Dumbo the Clown* for no clear reason. The newest attack in the cafeteria rotunda was to ask if she had AIDS. For no good reason at all, it made her think of her real dad. Foodless in Tara didn't mean she'd stop battling her body's inclination towards scrawny weakness. She'd beaten all odds by surviving; she could do anything now, and that included gaining weight.

Chew chew chew.

I LOVE HOT DOGS!

Indy enjoyed her new loudness, grabbing her flat chest that was really just ribs and sternum. She was shouting to no one because there *was* nobody, save for pretend Mr. Phil Donahue. He was the best listener.

There was no Donahue to watch because there was no electricity so no television. Phil would eventually want her story. Both tragedy and freak shows made for big ratings. Her favorite episode, the wildly popular hermaphrodite episode featuring Lynn Harris, fell, like Indy, more into the freak show

3

category. But they both endured a boatload of grief, too. Making both Lynn and Indy guaranteed ratings blockbusters.

Indy was living a real-life *tragedy.* She had seen no one for over a week. Everyone was gone. It was *sad.* She was *alone.*

Ring ring ring.

Where Lynn Harris the hermaphrodite and Indy really converged was on identity. Both burned with a need to re-invent themselves. To figure out exactly who they were. Lynn was searching for her true gender. The silver lining of Indy's *tragedy* was opportunity. She was not sure if she had to invent a new gender like Lynn Harris, but she at least needed to create a shameless, un-hated, un-bullied self. In the past week she had realized the possibility she could finally be the person she'd been waiting fifteen long years to be. The titless chicken-leg nerd in fluorescent green socks and gold faux alligator loafers agonizing over being picked last for volleyball again or paper toweling Luvs Baby Soft perfume off her biology textbook because someone emptied a bottle down her locker vents was no more. She had really sucked, had been a weak predictable bore. She was, thanks to *tragedy*, no longer the cafeteria table-clearing nerd. And nope, no longer the girl Cindy Brough shoved so casually into a locker for everyone in the halls at Chesley District High School to titter and point at.

Fuck you, too, Chesley!

She yelled easily overtop the jangling phone, nearly drowning it out.

You see, Mr. Donahue, I *used* to be a loser.

Chew chew chew.

To guarantee full metamorphosis from bullied nerd to hero she had banished her Old Name. She would never utter or think of her Old Name again. She was now Indiana or Indy for short.

4

Indy had been absolutely dying to come out. Hermaphrodite Lynn had explained to Donahue how exhausted she was pretending a gender, and Indy, too, was totally over being Old Name.

The timing couldn't be better. She had secretly been emulating Indiana Jones – from The Temple of Doom only – since she saw it at the drive-in. Or most of it – Dana had made them miss the last half hour so they would not get caught in exit traffic. She would gather hatchets, wrenches, water bottles, and a canary yellow extension cord for a whip, strap these onto the leather belt she'd found in a gutter at Sauble Beach and take expeditions out into the wilds of the Tara Sewage Lagoon a mile behind the trailer she lived in.

She had a formula for successful Indy reincarnation: first, she had memorized Temple of Doom in its entirety, all speaking parts and the movements in the Indiana Jones action sequences. She had watched the film on VHS nightly for forty-eight days in a row, a good round number. Next, she recorded it onto cassette and listened to it on her Sony Walkman on the school bus every day for most of grade 8. On the bus she acted out each whip crack, leap and plummet but only in extremely subtle ways that remained significant enough to burn into her muscle memory in heroic ways but not get her hit with spit balls or half-full Welch's drinking boxes.

Indy did not wear Indiana Jones' exact outfit but MacGyvered her own. Also, she was in Tara so there were particulars. For example, she didn't hunt historic artifacts; she protected the migratory waterfowl that hung out on the sewage lagoon on top of Tara's shit, including both literal feces and things like old condoms and tampon applicators. These applicators fascinated Indy because she had not had her period and was for sure the last girl her age on Earth who had not. The tampon applicators washed up on the shore around the sewage lagoon or were dragged there by seagulls. The used applicators mocked her, faded pink and blue beacons marring her heroic adult level crusades. When she came upon one she buried it, telling herself it was to protect the coots and black ducks from possible

5

choking hazards. After many such successful excursions into her own Tara Temple of Tampon-Burying Doom, a more regionalized Indy costume took shape: she wore her favorite red and white vertical striped Fame TV show pants for visibility (there were many enemy cross-bow water fowl hunters on the lagoon), her gold lamé blouse (the closest thing she had to Indiana Jones's khaki button down but with a touch of All My Children glamour). She hated hats.

Ring ring ring.

Chew chew chew.

Obviously, Indy had instinctively answered the phone halfway through its first ring when it had started this morning.

Hello, she'd said, her voice cautious but strong from practicing personal assertions and giving Donahue details for the past few days. The answer on the other end had been a distant, static-filled clicking. She thought it might be Morse code. Indy did not know Morse so she hung up.

Crank caller.

It rang again. She had repeated this answering hello operation, listening to clicks for more than half an hour, answering a dozen times. She grew more annoyed by the rudeness of who might be on the other end than curious about another living human existing so she stopped answering. It was an Indy-type decision, not Old Name style at all. It was hard at first because of her Dana-borne instinct, but she busied herself with Schneider's products and answering Donahue's eager questions, generally keeping her answering hands and mind otherwise occupied. She absolutely could not bring herself to rip the phone off the wall because it would still be, despite everything, a Dana victory.

I was in the greenhouse watering Dana's pot plants when it happened, Mr. Donahue. It felt unseeable but there just beyond my reach. Like something I knew ... but forgot.

6

She'd agonized over the description for hours and it still wasn't quite right, but it would do. For now. She liked the pause.

The air tightened, Phil, and I had to work my jaw to clear my ears. When I did, air burped like from opening a can of pop. My teeth glued together as if magnetized. Oh, Phil. I felt like lit tungsten in a new bulb freshly screwed in and switched on.

She had come up with the light bulb part over her final glass of (spoiled) milk. It was too wordy, but she didn't care.

It wasn't wholly unpleasant, Phil, so don't look so sorry. I ended up flat on my back though!

***

If she had passed out, it could not have been for long because the watering can had fallen over when she'd collapsed, but had only lost a few inches of water by the time she'd revived. It was no big deal. Hurt, not injured. She'd gotten hurt worse tumbling out of a gnarled crabapple tree trying to count and sketch baby kingbirds in their nest. When the mysterious thing happened, her hurt did not even register. Her entire focus was worrying about the hell she'd catch for knocking over two of the leafy green 'boys' with her Dumbo feet when she'd fainted.

Setting the pot plants right and smoothing out their dark soil, she also felt hopeful that her period had just started. One Christmas, her grandmother had gravely reported to her that at eighteen she had passed out in gym class and awoken to find she was at the start of her Special Cycle. At the time, Indy had been more curious about what people wore in gym class in the olden days, but now she wondered hopefully if she was finally Special Cycling too. She stuck her right hand inside her panties (the ones with the hot air balloons all over) and fingered herself.

Bloodless fingers. She sighed.

Indy finished watering the goddam pot plants then walked towards the chicken coops to feed the goddamn chickens. Her family didn't have the chickens for laying eggs. And they didn't have them to eat, although they did. The chickens she had to feed and water three times a day were in their yard solely because Dana believed that, on infrared, chicken shit looked the same as marijuana.

The chickens were camouflage. Needy, labor-intense subterfuge.

En route to the coops she'd found Dana, telephone menace and stepfather from hell, slumped lazily forward over one of his many privacy fences. His knees were on the ground behind him like a sinister Sesame Street letter S. S is for slumping, she thought wildly and giggled.

Dana had spent years turning his backyard into a labyrinthine maze of fences. He obsessively built, tore down, and re-built these fences according to a logic fueled by the Wondertwin powers of marijuana paranoia and OCD. He believed that people were always trying to see him and his activities, especially his greenhouse full of marijuana 'boys.' Dana diverged hugely from the stereotype of the pothead. He was manic in his work ethic, and rarely rested on the job. So seeing him slumped over his latest fence was jarring.

Indy paused. I wonder, she thought, if this is a joke. Dana was a curator of cruel jokes on her. For example, when she was five, he'd wrapped up a Winnie the Pooh (and Tigger Too!) Greatest Hits record inside a fridge box and put the present under the tree in November, well ahead of Christmas, hinting loudly and nightly about the great present Indy was going to get. The devastation she'd felt when she finally opened it wasn't because she did not getting a giant gift. She felt terrible because of Dana's loud peals of laughter as she' dug the Winnie the Pooh record from the bottom of the empty box. At precisely that moment, she'd fully accepted that one of the adults in charge of her, the one who called all the shots, found it hilarious to make her feel stupid and bewildered.

This slumping over a fence bit, thought Indy, might just be Winnie the Pooh Pt. 2. She had stopped trying to conceal her contempt for him; so he had figured out that seeing him dead would be roughly the updated equivalent of a wrapped refrigerator box Christmas present.

She decided to ignore slumping Dana. Fuck him. That, she thought, would teach him because his face was resting on the rough-hewn ends of the fence boards and that had to feel bad and only worse over time.

The happy news was the chickens no longer needed feeding. They were keeled over like Dana. Chickens could be hypnotized (she'd heard about that from the Mennonite neighbors), but even asleep chickens made chuffy breathing noises. They were silent but also goreless. How Dana had gotten them to play dead or be dead cleanly with no wounds wasn't clear, but he was inspired when it came to screwing with her. He might have suffocated each one. He was too cheap to have poisoned them.

Indy resented the chickens slightly more than the pot plants. She could understand that the pot plants probably helped Dana from burying them all under an avalanche of fences or from ripping every phone out of every wall all over Bruce County every day. Might also be how they were still alive or at least un-pummeled. But having to feed and water chickens merely because Dana believed that, on infrared, chicken shit was the same as marijuana was embarrassing. It made her feel like a chump, like being made to drink the Kool-Aid, a weak and sorry partner in his delusions. Especially because everyone in Tara knew that he had two greenhouses full of pot because he walked around town in a cloud of it and they had eyes. And yet, she had been too weak and un-Indyish to say anything or refuse to participate.

She peeked around the silent coops towards the fence. There was Dana, still slumped. Would he really waste the chickens?

She decided to risk it and walk over to him and see what was going on, Winnie the Pooh or not.

She got to five feet away and stopped because she knew. He was not faking it. There were no marks, no injuries. But she could tell he was really knocked out because he looked peaceful, and he was a man that never ever, not even in rest, looked at peace. His face always pulsed, fury giving him a constant flush.

What if he was dead? The air around her whooshed oxygen rich, clear. Real refrigerator box worthy gift not Winnie the Pooh record?

But Dana was probably only hurt. Heart attack. She shuddered to touch him. She did not know touching him. There was one photo of toddler her being thrown by him into the water at Sauble Beach, but she had no real memory of it, only a photo memory. And it was only *him* touching *her* in the photo, hurling her into a muted 70s-blue Lake Huron. Her own hands spread open, arching towards an even more faded sky in the photo, her orange water wings the only fully colorful thing.

She thanked her black rubber chore boots. Using the left boot she nudged him in his knee, roughly lifting it off the ground. The knee fell back. Inconceivable slackness from him.

Indy listened so intently she had to bite her tongue. She took a risk and leaned in. Hash-smoke-sweat. She looked up into his mouth. It looked like he was saying oh. Cringing, she lifted her hand up and held it like a flap one inch from his mouth.

Nothing was coming out of his mouth. No air. No breathing. Her stepfather, Dana, *not breathing*.

Could it be?

She knew for a fact that a non-breathing person was a dead one but could not grasp the truth of it. How could her soul tormentor, focus of all her fear and rage, be gone? How could

10

he be, as her mother liked to say about last years' chickens in the freezer, dead as a doornail?

She needed more proof. Wincing, she put her first two fingers against his jugular, like Mrs. Sweiger had taught in gym class after burpees to see how fit you were by feeling your pulse. She'd known Dana was not fit. She pressed her fingers into the meat of his neck, prickly with five days' shadow (razors were a rip-off). She swallowed to fight rising bile as she counted. One-one thousand. Two-one thousand. Three-one thousand. She got to thirty-one thousands and nothing. Not. One. Beat.

She felt feelings. There were familiar ones but mixed with ways to feel that she had no name for. Disappointment, too. But suddenly, for the first time ever, the idea of an unwritten future popped into her head. The fiercely tedious agony of tiptoeing around her life instead of living it drained like sand out of her tomorrow. And the next day and the next day opened up, like mysterious presents filled with hope instead of dread.

For example, she was relieved her mother would never have to snap off All My Children the minute Dana walked into the house to avoid his rants about how vile it and, by association, Indy and her mother, were. She was relieved too that she'd never have to sneak clothes into the house that her mother had bought at Woolco in Owen Sound by racing into the house while he was busy with his drugs. She felt foolish trying not to crinkle as she walked with a bag of socks inside her jacket, just so she could avoid a threatening lecture about how Dana still wore the same socks he had worn in high school and just layered them to cope with the holes. Without Dana, she could hang out with her mom now. She'd be able talk to her all the time like a normal person instead of an empty shell preoccupied with making sure Dana was either not around or not in an escalating rage.

But she felt disappointed too. She'd never get to kill Dana as she had fantasized about so often. More and more often, especially after the night he'd chased her around the house

11

with his fist raised to punch her because she'd told him he was never a father to her but instead a monster.

Indy felt strange. Instantly impotent were all the fantasies of him being gone or dead, along with the more specific scenarios of the perfect Dana murder. And here he was.

Or wasn't. And all her dreams had come true.

Indy started to shake in adrenalized realization of a past tense Dana. With the taste of her own lips on her tongue, she went to break the news to her mother.

Indy had zigzag jogged (the privacy fences made it the only way to cross the yard) towards the trailer she knew primarily as a prison. Dana had made it so airtight that she had developed terrible asthma from the mold growing in the gold shag carpets seeded by spores from the basement that became a swimming pool each spring filled by water from the Saugeen River.

The back door, the one with the sign that read *This House Guarded By Shotgun 3 Nights Per Week You Guess Which One* was wide open so she could already hear The Beatles playing.

Indy stepped through.

The White Album was blasting the secret skip in Revolution 9. There had been a scratch there forever but always her mother pushed it gently over the skip. Never Dana, because he hated The Beatles so he'd never heard it. He did not even know about the scratch and never would have stood for such gentle abuse of his phonographic needle. If anyone, even the Queen, pushed or touched and thus wrecked one of his $75 needles, he'd explained clearly that he would heartpunch everyone involved.

number 9 number 9 numb-

Indy knuckled the arm of the phonograph, sending Dana's beloved needle screeching across the already damaged record. Dana would be administering zero heartpunches in the future.

Mother? Karen?

She must be in the bedroom reading one of her detective novels. Indy fantasized that her mother was working on how to get away with the perfect murder and the boring mystery books were merely research.

Her mother was indeed in bed with a book. She always read leaning against pillows wedged in the cavernous small of her back that was a result of a thirty-degree scoliosis. She had a big hump. And so there she was, pillows squished into the small of her back. But she was not reading her book.

Her mother's legs and arms were flopped higgledy-piggledy, her neck rocked back against the pillows piled behind her. Her detective novel – A Dark-Adapted Eye – was open and resting cover down against her belly. Her face was wet with tea, the cup overturned between her humongous breasts with the Red Rose teabag balanced on her chin like a polite human version of a seal with a ball. She had been caught mid-sip. Her hazel eyes were open and pointed towards the creamy plastic tile ceiling.

Karen? Hey.

She reached to feel for her mother's wrist. Indy's hand hovered over her mother. Like Dana, this was another first touch. Unlike him, she couldn't even think of photographic evidence of any sort of touch with her. Indy searched her memory. Well, there was one from Toronto when she was about five and she was standing beside her mother as she sat in the ugly rocking chair. They were standing close, but she was pretty sure they hadn't been touching. They had both been smiling, though.

There was no pulse under her mother's dry unfamiliar skin.

She ran to the green kitchen phone to dial 911. She put it to her ear and heard silence instead of a dial tone. Indy yelled into the receiver.

We have an emergency here!

Mrs. Christie, from their party line, was on the phone as usual. Sometimes, when she wouldn't get off the line Indy would drop the receiver into the washing machine (the laundry was in the kitchen beside the phone) and turn the machine on. This was no time for such games.

Mrs. Christie? I need to call 9-1-1. This is an emergency.

Silence.

MRS CHRISTIE. 9-1-1! I HAVE TO MAKE A CALL.

No answer, no dial tone signifying that the old gossip had hung up the phone.

Indy hung up the receiver and bolted out the front door across the lawn to Mrs. Christie's chocolate brown house. It had horrible orange soffits, fascia, and an alarmingly orange garage and front door. Indy made her bony hand into a fist, and using the meatiest part of the side of it, banged on the door.

Mrs. Christie!

Indy had never shouted at a strange adult before. Well, she wasn't totally strange. Besides the party line, she babysat Mrs. Christie's five year old. He still wore diapers to bed and it was creepy diapering a kid that big, staring at his goofy penis. He was a good kid but probably deeply disturbed. She also hated how, through all the years when Indy waited for the school bus in her driveway, Mrs. Christie had done nothing to stop the brutal teasing from Jackie O'Rourke and Laurie Courtan, yet expected Indy to happily babysit her disturbed incontinent kid on a dime. Mrs. Christie had watched Jackie and Laurie march in circles around Indy scream-singing TWO IS COMPANY THREE IS A CROWD and RUBBER DUCKY. On top of that, Mrs. Christie had regularly camped out on the party line with impunity, further complicating an already fraught telephone situation for Indy when her lifeline to Tammy opened up at Dana's bedtime.

Indy tried the door and it was unlocked. She opened it. Mrs. Christie was face down on her ivory shag carpet. She had been drinking apple juice because it was soaking the shag around

15

her. Or maybe it was pee. Her skin was almost the same color as her rug, the varicose veins on her thighs like a map of a really amazing city, like Los Angeles.

Indy ran across the street to the Mennonites' house. She had never ever stepped foot on their property. When she cut the lawn on Sundays, the seven Mennonite kids would line up like a scene out of Children of the Damned and chant lyrically in unison: Old Name's going to hell Old Name's going to hell, until Dana sprayed them with the hose and they scattered. He'd cackle. Nothing made him happier than a good attack. This creepy behavior earned them their nickname: the Meanos. Today they were not acting so musical: their front porch was bookended by two of the teenagers, sprawled face up, eyes open. The girl sprawled in a very unchaste fashion, her knee-length underwear exposed beneath her rumpled skirts.

Ashlee. The little kids reminded Indy of her sister. She was a half-sister, actually, since Dana was Ashlee's real dad. Poor her. She was nine years younger than Indy. Indy had looked after her so much it felt like she had had a kid herself six years ago. Except she resented her because Dana, of course, treated her better and you wouldn't resent your own kid. For example, at that moment Ashlee was at horse riding lessons at Tammy's farm. Indy had wanted to be a ballerina so badly that every day she'd practiced her own made-up ballet, which Dana called flitting because he had refused to pay and allow her to be driven to any real lessons. He had also told Indy there would be no way she'd ever learn to drive. When she asked if she could take driving lessons at 16, he used his best Jack Nicholson face and said, Whose car are you gonna use, Dumbo? It would soon be time to pick Ashlee up from riding lessons. But the people who usually picked her up were dead. And Indy, Dumbo, couldn't drive.

Indy tried the door but the Meanos had, of course, locked it. No phone in there anyway because it was against their religion. She needed to phone someone and get a ride to pick up her sister. Oh, and probably do something about all the bodies in the neighborhood too.

16

Indy giggled. Despite all the drama, she felt really good. On point, like Indiana Jones being chased. She felt focused, Dana-free and alive.

After finding nothing but dead Meanos on the porch, Indy had gone next door to Laurie (RUBBER DUCKY) Courtan's house and found it open and their phone dead. As was Laurie. Laurie must have been having a shower because Indy found her crashed naked and wet, legs akimbo against the hot pink floral tiles of her bathroom, lips split open and teeth scattered like a box of spilled Chicklets. Her torso was upside down over the edge of the tub, her generally accusational eyes rolled comfortingly up to the whites.

Indy stared at Laurie. Her huge breasts were way less intimidating now upside down with rivulets of blood from her mouth running over them. She knew Laurie had been older than her by a few years, but judging by her mass of pubic hair, she must have been practically an adult. Laurie had terrorized Indy by riding her bicycle directly at her whenever they'd cross paths in the summer. Indy had never learned how to ride a bicycle. Probably because she did not have a bicycle, nor anyone to teach her. Laurie would lie in wait between their houses for Indy to come out to walk to downtown Tara. She would roll up on her, trying to run her down, causing Indy to jump into the marshy drainage ditches full of biting crayfish. Because of Laurie, Indy had started cutting through the backfields to town and had discovered the sewage lagoon. So it wasn't all bad.

Laurie's television was on, but it was just snow on both channels Indy tried, which were the only ones available in Tara. The skip pattern on channel 4 that sometimes came in from across the lake in summer was just snow too. Indy listened for a few moments, thinking of Poltergeist, to see if she could hear any voices, of children or anyone, but gave up quickly. The last thing she wanted to hear was Laurie singing RUBBER DUCKY from another dimension. Ugh.

17

Indy tried all the houses in her street and found them totally empty, save for Groady Roady's. He wasn't home but his house full of rabbits were. And they were all dead. Still cute, but dead. All the phones were out as were all the televisions. So she returned to her own trailer. Neither her mother nor Dana had moved. She hadn't seen a car at all.

Indy had tried to watch the snowy broadcasts for hours on her own television, holding the rabbit ear aerial aloft in her palm, flipping the dial until her back ached. She had seen and heard nothing.

Nervously, she tried Dana's Telefunken radio receiver too. She was forbidden by him from ever touching it. Whenever she did touch it, she had to memorize exactly where all the dials for station, volume, treble and bass had originally been. Really exactly. Or else, if he suspected her of touching his precious stereo, he would threaten to blow up the television and/or otherwise physically prevent her from watching Remington Steele Tuesday night at nine. As nonchalantly as possible, Indy turned the volume up on the Telefunken and listened. More nothing, not even static. She twisted the tuner dial and the silence spread across the dial. She began to return all the dials to where they had been – and then stopped herself.

Feeling giddy, her chest light yet tight, she spun the dials randomly and walked away. She turned back and shoved the entire stereo cabinet once so that it rocked back against the wood paneled wall gouging it. She grinned.

That night she had put all the lights on and used the front porch light to flash SOS, like she'd learned from her neighbor, Jen, who was in the Brownies. Indy had not been allowed to join Brownies because her mother said they were fascist and because it cost money and involved driving around, but she had still helped Jen sell the most boxes of cookies of anyone in the township, picking up some handy Brownie survival tips along the way. Indy even put on the pointless bug zapper light in the back yard in hopes someone would answer her signs of life. The sewage lagoon usually bred so many bugs the bug light went from totally clean to completely furred with bug carcasses after five minutes of constant neon blue zapping. But that night the bug light stayed blue and unfurred and totally silent.

After two days the power went.

Why had she survived? Had the loathsome pot watering ironically saved her, the greenhouse plastic some giant prophylactic against a freak airborne momentary mutation of AIDS? Was it going to happen again? Was she immune? Maybe she was already really sick?

Yet Indy had never felt so alive.

No phone, no information and no ability to drive to the big city, Owen Sound. And a daylong hike to even pick up her sister from horse riding at Tammy's. No power made it all seem more significant, or at least more inconvenient and dull for waiting around. Indy spent a few hours pacing the trailer. She crossed her gangly arms locking herself in a lonesome and bored embrace.

What would Indiana Jones do? He wouldn't be hugging himself. It was sad that everyone around was dead. But he would keep moving and so could she. She would not wait and hope for someone to save her because waiting for people (especially without TV) made her crazy. She was being like Willie, the lady Indiana was always saving in Temple of Doom, standing around holding herself and moping. Indy would save herself. She would find and certainly rescue Tammy and her little half-sister, Ashlee, along the way.

Operation Indy was born. Step One was to eat everything, even gross things like rust lettuce, so as not to let anything go to waste. Chew chew chew. To prove she had grit, the operation dictated a stoic resumption of daily chores. But the chores were different now. Not her regular maintenance of the anally clean surfaces and servicing Dana's drug delusions. Her new chores were finally personally significant and vital and included

19

removing the dead from the house. The dead, in this case, being her mother.

Everyone knew dead bodies caused disease.

Dana could stay outside where he was, a truly dedicated addition to his labyrinth of fences.

She had waited three days, and already the smell of her mother threatened to sap Indy's appetite and her goal of 0% food waste. Karen smelled like Ordain Morris's chicken slaughterhouse in October. Ordain charged just 25 cents a bird, half the price of sane butchers, or at least the butchers with zero walleyed kids (he had six of them). He let his google-eyed and mildly retarded sons help him, and that kept the prices down. The kids, who probably could not see well, never got all the feathers out of the carcasses, making for crunchy (in a not satisfying way) roasters. The barn was also a chicken bloodpool. Indy dreaded walking into the freezer room to retrieve their chickens because crossing the barn floor meant wading into inches of pale pink oil drainage from the birds. It was greasy and gassy and so slippery Indy had twice lost her footing and landed on her ass in the fetid goop.

The walleyed boys had clapped and clapped. Both times.

Indy's mother was shorter than Indy by a few inches on account of her more dramatic scoliosis. Indy had it too, but it was, she prayed, way less severe. Her mother made up for her lost height in girth, especially across the middle. And she had gigantic tits. She would not be able to carry her. Indy hunted around and found a wheelbarrow in the back of the Christmas Shed but she couldn't even get it through the door without knocking over the Christmas tree Dana kept erected year round. He had built the Christmas Shed to house the annual Christmas dinner because he did not want anyone, especially family, to taint his home. He hated them and the clutter and up and down redundancy of Christmas so much that he solved the situation by building the Christmas Shed. Indy kicked the tree

20

over (Dana probably would have enjoyed that) and dragged the wheelbarrow out and right away the wheel popped off.

Dana had gotten the wheelbarrow at the dump.

She'd have to drag her mother. Indy tied her American flag bandanna bandit style over her mouth and nose to block the smell and opened her mother's bedroom door. She'd moved. Upon closer examination Indy saw it was just that her abdomen had bloated to such a degree that her arms and legs had shifted. The teabag had fallen from her chin to the floor.

This was tough. With snowmobile mittens for hygiene, her mother's moldering flesh made it impossible to find true purchase on her ankles to drag her off the bed. Indy's mittened hands merely flayed her leg flesh, sliding down over anklebone. She pulled off the now skin-soiled mitts so she could grab more tightly, recoiling inwardly at the lousiness of the touch.

Her mother's skin did not feel like she had expected rotting human flesh to feel like. She'd seen enough long-dead things around the sewage lagoon to have expectations. Indy leaned in for a better look. Atop the skin of her late mother's ankle was a layer of translucent fibers, arranged in a way not unlike the scales of the pike she fished from the Saugeen River. Gripping her mother with her bare hands felt like holding giant stalks of sodden celery, stiff with cellulose. Her mitts had peeled off some scaly fibrous layers, not her human skin. She scanned her mother's body.

Karen's whole body was growing a strange second skin.

Indy tore outside.

Dana was gone. Or maybe not.

A Dana-sized capsule had taken his place. He was nearly invisible inside a translucent white cocoon. His hash-smell was gone. He reeked like the sewage lagoon on a hot August

21

afternoon when all of Tara hosted beer-based family get-togethers: warm puke and urine in a chemical treatment soup.

Indy got back to work dragging her scaly mother outside to the farthest part of the back yard and into the greenhouse, as far away as possible from Dana.

Indy could at least do that for her mother now.

That was yesterday.

Since then, Karen's scales had thickened and wept liquids and gases that withered the pot plants. It was neat. Her mother, pot destroyer. Or dryer. The pot was now dry and ready to smoke whole without having to be hung upside down in the basement. Even in death, her mother could not escape serving Dana.

This morning, the no ones had started calling her.

Ring ring ring.

Last hot dog. Chew chew chew. Total collapse of the society of Invermay, suburb of Tara.

She did not live on a busy road but there were at least five cars an hour on a typical weekday. She knew because boring days were all that Invermay ever had. On some of those days she would play Cars with Ashlee – a simple game: each person picked colors and got a point for each car of their color that drove past. It took hours to get past twenty points in total. From years of game play, Indy had become highly attuned to hearing a car approach so she could safely grab a glass of Dr. Pepper from the fridge and not have to trust her sister to give her a deserved point.

Since the initial neighborhood-killing event, not one car had driven by.

But what unsettled Indy more were the birds. The real birds, not the dead chickens. The red-winged black birds, bobolinks, meadowlarks and house sparrows had become impossibly silent. Birds just didn't do that in July. Bobolinks no longer bounced around the field beside the trailer, their fevered sproingy song gone.

The July air was silent of insect sounds, too. No cicadas rubbed, no flies buzzed.

The utter silence is what inspired Indy to talk out loud to herself. Probably not on account of loneliness, because she was used to spending all her time at home unspoken to. Perhaps she had to prove, in the absence of all diegetic sounds from birds to bugs, she was not deaf. Television and birds usually provided that.

I'm here!

Her voice stung but did not crack the silence.

Indy found the silence almost as interesting as all the dead, cocooning bodies in the neighborhood. She had visited all of Invermay and the outskirts of Tara over the last few days and found only cocoons. And an infuriating amount of rotted food. She accepted Tara was dead. But why everyone had decomposed in curious, poddy ways eluded her. She knew the people of this town were uniquely cruel, but did that cause them to defy biology in death?

On the bright side, the pods were less disgusting, certainly less of a water table-type health hazard than fetid bags of flesh.

Her confusion made her back ache. Why was she still alive? Would she soon succumb, too? Was there an infection she was in danger of catching? A pressure like a blunt knife settled against her right scapula. There were people she needed to still be okay.

Like Tammy.

Tammy and Indy had been best friends since Indy moved to Tara in grade 2 and joined Miss Streeter's 2-3 class in the round portable. They had not been friends at first. The popular girls had played with the new girl for about a week. Krista Steinecker – her parents owned the grocery store and so she

24

was Tara royalty – promised to be her best friend. It took less than a week for Krista to rethink that. Indy had no idea what she had done to make Krista hate her so fast. Indy wore denim and plaid every day in an attempt to blend in with Krista and the girls she ran with. She did do a book report on Stephen King's Carrie, pissing Miss Streeter off. She couldn't hit the t-ball either. She could only, with focus, whack into the black rubber stand causing the ball to roll casually off and usually towards her own feet. She'd never touched a ball in her life, let alone with a bat. Ball sports, her mother had explained, were ridiculous. Probably Krista preferred girls who read Nancy Drew and could play ball.

One day after recess, Tammy stopped beside her desk. Barely taller than the desk, her mouth so dark it looked like she had no teeth, she had said hi. After a week of playing together, Indy realized she had never known anyone so nice. She was also the funniest. Now she could not really remember life without Tammy.

Tammy was lucky. She hit puberty hard and early, growing breasts the size of melons by eleven. Big enough Indy could wear Tammy's bra cup on her head like a loose swim cap. Indy longed for breasts bigger than gentle mannish slopes. There was no cruel Laurie Courtan-ness in Tammy either. Instead, she made arguments and points against big tits, making Indy feel lucky to wear bras only on her head.

In grade 5, they began working together in the dark arts. They cast one singularly powerful and effective spell on their teacher, Mrs. Gowan. Tammy had gotten into Wicca, some kind of witchcraft, mostly because Indy had given her a deck of tarot cards. For Indy, lacking magical gravitas, the cards offered a cool new way to play solitaire. But to Tammy, the tarot arcana foretold.

Mrs. Gowan was malevolent. Her armed body held one unified warhead torpedo boob that, during choir practice, Tammy and Indy were obligated to stare into because if she caught you looking away from her while singing she pointed at you and you'd get The Strap.

And that was just the tip of the Mrs. Gowan, or Gow-Bow, as Tammy had christened her, iceberg.

When Gow-Bow launched into their noisy classroom she would ask the class politely if she had taken a wrong turn in the hall and come accidentally into the retard school. Then she would make them all miss noon recess to stay in and write lines pertaining to noise and non-retardation.

But Gow-Bow truly delivered her payload when she wrote student names *beside their grades* for each test on the very tippy top of the blackboard, ensuring that every student could see everyone's grades. How Torpedo Boob balanced up high to write the grades remained mysterious and was perhaps also magical. The kids who struggled and failed at school, in other words everyone in Tara except Tammy and Indy, were shamed. But mostly they were vengeful. Tammy and Indy slunk hard around the schoolyard, glued to the yard duty teacher. But with their names atop the grades marquee beside numbers 98 and 94, no amount of slinking could save them. The grade 5 war was on; the entire class of forty-one versus them, and their defeat was a lock from the hop. Verbal taunts, spitballs, tripping, itinerant guerrilla dodge ball and snowball grenades left nowhere and nothing safe, not even peeing in a toilet stall.

Indy's fury at Gow-Bow caused her to become unable to speak when called upon in class. When Her Torpedoness asked Indy a question, her only answer was silent red-faced tears. Mrs. Gowan had requested a speech therapist for Indy. Indy tried to protest, but all that came out was a garbled sob. Mrs. Gowan, percipient product of a Normal School, had mistaken Indy's monstrous teary seething for inability. But it all backfired when the therapist tested Indy's IQ and pronounced her a genius, recommending that she skip at least a grade. But Indy could never leave Tammy.

26

After the speech therapist, the magic sortie jackknifed into Indy's mind, perhaps dislodged by the Wechsler Intelligence Scale for Children test that included sitting in a supplies closet and calling out all the kinds of teacher detritus she saw. Skeptical as Indy was of magic and god and all the imaginary things people argued about that her mother called bullshit, Tammy's spells were the only untried method so far in their plight to make it out of grade 5 alive.

Tammy wasn't sure. She agreed it was at least a good test of her burgeoning magic powers. She made a list of necessaries. The worst being the seemingly impossible to attain hair off the head of Mrs. Gowan. Indy followed her out of daily choir practice after a particularly rousing rendition of Charlie Pride's "All His Children" in which Gow-Bow's conducting passion caused her to shake her balding head about. Indy saw what she needed. One loose static-charged grey strand caught in the worn fibers of her mint twinset. Meeting Tammy's gaze in a quick over the shoulder, Indy's rail thin arm shot out and plucked the hair off the sweater before anyone, except Tammy, noticed. With the hair and some of Gow-Bow's chalk and variety of oils, spices, and dirt, they were ready. Tammy took the items home from school and lit some candles on her makeshift altar (a faux-walnut desk with steel legs from the driving shed), and incanted. Indy, at home in the trailer, abluted herself in a bathtub at approximately the same time, but they couldn't be sure because it was too early and Dana was awake so they couldn't use the phone.

One month later to the day, Mrs. Gowan collapsed during choir practice and was hospitalized for weeks.

Tammy had done it. It was confirmed. She was magic. And from that day forward Tammy was a permanent lifelong beacon for Indy, no matter what life threw at them.

Indy dropped her head back and yelled.

Tammy!

People, such as Tammy and her family, were probably avoiding Tara because of what had happened. This Donahue-worthy tragedy. Village Die-off. The Cocooning of Rural Canadian Village. People avoided Invermay generally, and Tara was just a place to get milk and rusty iceberg lettuce at Krista's store anyhow. Owen Sound was the city of Romaine and yogurt. Indy had been spared, but no one knew that yet. Sewage Lagoon inoculation against cocoon killer virus was a possibility. Or maybe some more Darwinian cause.

Indy began to cautiously hope maybe, since her mother was gone, that Tammy's family could take her in. She'd run that scenario hundreds of times. They'd worked her hard when she visited, she'd help Tammy clean the house and make supper while her brothers fed the cattle. But cooking and cleaning for people who laughed and ate meals together enchanted her. And there was always so much fancy edible food to eat like New York Specials, Hostess chips and mashed potatoes that did not crunch.

A thrill went up Indy's spine as she realized she'd made the decision to leave Tara for good. She'd hike on over towards Arran Lake and Tammy's farm.

She had to go and find her sister out there anyway, because she'd be missing Dana and their mother and she was a homesick suck. Ashlee really loved Dana, and that was understandable because he was really her father and treated her occasionally with affection, although he still threatened her with taking away her horse riding lessons or Last Unicorn video when he was in the mood. Ashlee did not seem to mind the threats much. She'd even sit in Dana's lap while Indy could barely stand to be in the same room with him. But that was because Dana was not, and never would be, Indy's father.

Indy had been merely biding her time in the trailer until she was old enough to find her way back to her missing real father. No one spoke of him so Indy had pieced together his existence out of her own fractured memories of him. When she was younger she struggled to trust that he existed in the vacuum of information, but somehow the struggle just made her love him more. The futility of pretending she did not long to be with her real father—coupled with how unwanted Dana and her mother made her feel—circled every idea and decision Indy made like hungry turkey vultures.

It made her become certain that all that mattered in her life was finally reuniting with her dad.

Indy guessed her father was out of jail by now for kidnapping her when she was three. The only proof she had that he had been in jail is that she remembered police questioning her from a hospital bed.

She had told Tammy he was in jail when they were nine. And maybe she remembered more clearly at nine than now. She remembered he wanted to go to Las Vegas and become a lounge act – he played saxophone. Indy similarly had a real talent for clarinet. She couldn't remember what he looked like at all because she had never seen any photos. But she remembered he drank Molson Export beer and so, when she thought of him, she saw a tall ship like the one on the Export label. She recalled holding his beer as they drove around in his mustard yellow Datsun truck with a cap on the back, the self-same truck they'd made a home in during the kidnapping. Despite time and distance, she still loved him more than anyone walking the Earth, and dreamed of the day when she would see him again.

The love of a daughter for her father defied rational thought and for that reason alone she empathized with Ashlee's love of Dana. He was her real dad, so even though he was an awful father and human being, she knew that circumstances and facts don't dull that kind of feeling. She loved her dad, even though she didn't even know what he looked like, save beer imagery, and despite the fact he was probably a jailbird and maybe a really bad dude. So she rehearsed empathetic ways to tell Ashlee that Dana was dead without sounding the least bit relieved or happy:

Ashlee, I have news I hate to tell you. But your father has passed.

Indy flipped back the steel door of the well. With Ashlee's jaunty blue sandcastle bucket secured by pink skipping rope, she hauled up a bucket of water for her Last Supper in Tara. She filled and packed another Becker's milk jug of water, eight Mott's drinking boxes, and a package of Chips Ahoy she'd been saving for the road. She would set out at first light with her full complement of Indiana Jones tools and customized Fame uniform to give her sister the sad news, join Tammy's family, and call Phil Donahue.

***

For a while she slept deep and dreamlessly. The incessantly ringing phone failed to wake her.

Until the sound of metal on glass, like fingernails on blackboard, reached through her sleep and yanked her awake. Indy skipped right over groggy to alert, feeling each hair root in her head. She was that entirely alert.

Clean focused, all organs beating one ready rhythm, Indy flitted down the hall in her nightshirt with the giant Barbie B on it. From the front window she could see starlit pieces of the trailer's aluminum siding strewn pick-up sticks style round the yard.

The screech of another piece of siding being torn from the trailer made Indy wince. She retreated to her room to put on her Indy uniform and accessorize, hatchet in hand.

The front door was behind her so fast she didn't remember passing through. Before her was something so terrible she couldn't fit meaning over it. She pulled at her eyelids with her free hand to make sure she was not having a nightmare after this Donahue-worthy week.

She was awake and her eyes were open. Her mouth was open too. She turned her head just in time to avoid soiling herself with vomit made of well-chewed wiener chunks. She caught some of the puke by cupping her hands, hating to let any food go to waste, but had nowhere to stash it. She finally let it trickle through her fingers.

Déjà vu had made her upchuck. It *was* the Winnie the Pooh record all over again. She had been right after all.

Somehow, raging fifteen feet in front of her in the starry gloom was a wetly luminescent and totally naked Dana. He was back from the dead.

Dana was back, but he was not the man he used to be. He had been reborn into the world wearing an exoskeleton that seemed to both protect and mobilize his visibly rotting corpse housed within. Original Dana was visible but blurred slightly beneath thin layers of extra skin that glowed like an aura. The way light moved through him reminded Indy of the plastic that Dana used for the greenhouse. He had used many layers of cheap Home Hardware plastic precisely because it made it harder to see what was being grown inside.

As Dana moved, Indy saw his new skin was not the same flexible texture as the greenhouse plastic. It was bonier and articulated, like a crayfish carapace. As he walked, it clicked around and over his joints. She looked at his hands. In the summers, afraid to go to the bully rife Tara pool, Indy would wade scared in the Saugeen, catching crayfish to drop in Mason jars for examination before they could pinch one of her toes. Dana's hands resembled the toe-catching crayfish pincer: formed over his decaying fingers was one large upper claw, and over his thumb, a small razor sharp lower claw.

Dana had returned to her a horrible zombie crayfish man.

Dana creaked and crackled as he moved towards her. The faster he got, the more terrible the grinding, from his joints. The jaw was his crenellation, the only part of his body that

31

lacked armor. This purely human bone, puckered with decay, met its old upper lip only through the astronaut bubble carapace surrounding the rest of his old dead head. His bare purpled lower lips framed those familiar chronic weed-smoker spaced-out yellow squares of his bottom teeth. He worked his lower jaw hungrily up and down, tapping a senseless chattering rhythm against the upper carapace like a putrid Pac-Man, eating little worthless airbits as he clicked himself closer to Indy. As horrible as it all was, Indy realized she preferred these new noises to all his old threatening speeches. They were, at least, less predictable.

Rising sunlight struck Dana's newborn armor-skin, passing through his exoskeleton, but not his rotten middle. It formed a halo around his moldering remains. Indy found his furious eyes, angry even as they rotted. Eyes she had foolishly celebrated never seeing again.

Dana swung and let fly another section of the trailer's white aluminum siding at her head.

Indy ducked but failed to fully miss the siding. The sheared-off silvery edge removed her right ear with surgical precision. She heard the soft *plop* of her ear onto summer grass in mono because her right ear poured deafening blood. The hotness of the wound spread across first the side of her head, then neck and then shoulder. Her vision stuttered, blotting out her step-crayfish-father as he took another creaking step towards her.

Dana's jaw kept working up and down, clacking pot teeth against carapace, keeping rhythm with Indy's own racing heartbeat. Her eyes filled with tears. Blood trickled down her face. The longed-for Indy-style calm heroics fell away. How could her stepfather be back? How could she go on?

Indy dropped to her knees, backhanding the flow of blood and tears away. Dana clicked forward. From this close, just a body length away, she knew his next blow would easily finish her off.

Indy paused to regard her lost ear. It had come to rest near her right foot. It was so light summer blades of grass were holding it aloft. It looked so small, but then again, she'd never been so far from her own ear. Against the backdrop of its curves Indy replayed all the threats:

rip the phone out of the wall, blow up the television, heartpunch, rocket launcher, lucky to have a roof over your head

and trash talking

clown feet, ugly, useless, flitting

Petting her familiar hatchet that she had used to remove crabapple limbs towards amateur ornithological research and nest study, she tasted the snot and tears and blood on her upper lip with the tip of her tongue.

It tasted good.

The hatchet made a singular arc, real after a decade of mere speculation; mid-air Indy flipped it business end skyward and drove it solidly up into Dana's unprotected under-chin. It was the leftover, most familiar and weak part of him. Could it be a coincidence that in her daydreams it had almost always been his mouth too that she struck first? His only real weapon. And the worst. Her hatchet connected surely, making it clear through his chomping lower jaw and getting stuck in the upper mineralized shell that engulfed his entire head.

She had, at least, silenced his chattering.

There was an oozing-out around her hatchet. Dana's face deflated slightly like a winter balloon. Fish musk poisoned Indy's next gulp of breath.

With a quick jiggle, Indy removed her weapon, taking his entire lower jawbone with it. She bolted for the Meano side of the trailer.

She heard Dana clickclacking after her, a nightmarish engine that could. Cornering the trailer, she flicked her wrist to hurl his jawbone towards the Meanos' brick house. It hit the brick with a short *thonk* and dropped into their hollyhock flowerbed.

eeeeeeeeehhhhhhhhhhhhhhhaaaaaaaaaaaaaaaaaaa...

She felt Dana's new alarming sound in her bones before she heard it. A sound that he did not need a mouth to make. In place of a heart he had grown a rusted pneumatic horn. Indy felt like the British in a World War II movie running from a German bombing raid. Dana was not just a simple crayfish-zombie, he was also a mobile air raid siren calling loudly after her.

34

She noticed too late the crayfish-zombie version of Mrs. Christie standing in the driveway and smacked into her full force. Indy bounced off her while she stood resilient and unperturbed. Indy, knocked flat on her back, struggled to catch her breath.

Mrs. Christie's pincer creaked and she groaned upwards, pointing at Indy. Her jaw dropped and she joined Dana's wheezy siren call, in a slightly higher register.

Indy rolled hard away from Mrs. Christie and face first into the spruce tree Dana had traded for chickens. Its needles raised a constellation of blood on her face and made the spot on her head that used to hold her ear scream. Fresh tears blurred her vision. Dana's body resumed grinding and crunching towards her in his horrible crustacean suit. She stumbled, dodging around Mrs. Christie, towards the backyard.

Indy whipped her head back as if slapped, dodging Dana's claws. They breezed past her face but sunk into her long hair, yanking her head back. Panicked, Indy swung wildly until her hatchet met crayfish Dana's neck. Thus connected, they tumbled to the ground, Indy on top.

Dana was her survival-filled piñata; she'd wanted a candy one for her eleventh birthday but ended up with the free newspaper circular pin-the-tail-on-the-donkey game. See-sawing the hatchet out of Dana's neck as she had the crabapple tree, she chopped at him again and again and again, sobbing, working over the same spot in his neck.

Goo flew into Indy's hair and effort-contorted face. Dana's stiff pincers wrapped hungrily around her waist. He was finally hugging her, so hard it was crushing her diaphragm. She could hardly breathe. In one final desperate chop, she breached his neck's armor. His original rotted neck lay tender, dead, and squirming beneath.

Knees planted firmly on either side, Indy pushed out against his embrace, lifting her hatchet and holding Dana's exposed

35

neck taut with her left hand. This blow sunk smoothly through his throat, severing his head from his body but got lodged in the armor at the back of his neck.

Indy squeezed herself out the top of Dana's first embrace.

Dana needed further chopping to completely remove his head. A hank of sinew and armor still slackly held his shellacked rotten head to his horrid body. Four quick chops until she could kick his head away from his body. In zombie movies, ruining heads was how you ended them. His head roll stopped with a crack against Mrs. Christie's shelled feet. The sound seemed to spook Mrs. Christie because she lumbered off in the direction of the Sewage Lagoon.

Indy's body was smeared with Dana and sharp slivers of his carapace. A few shards as big as cocktail swords and others as small as ticks. It hurt. He cut into her. Faintly glowing fibers, tendons that weaved old grotty Dana to his new crunchy exterior, floated gossamer above his spasming neck hole.

Was he dead? Because twice wasn't the charm, Indy located Dana's head. His features were distorted, some parts still held by gossamer tendons: a Ken doll squeezed between angry fingers. Indy raised her rubber-booted foot.

Stomping on Dana's head made her feel unsteady, like she was on a tall ship in a rough sea. She had to use all her focus to stay upright. First one foot, then both feet. She watched to make sure she didn't miss and slip down into his mess. Tears and snot did little to clean the Dana gore off her face.

When she was finished, Indy used her hands to scrape Dana off. He was everywhere. The deep crevasses of her scrawny shoulder blades hid his gore. Her hair was soaking with him. Skimming off her forehead, careful not to drag his shards into her thin eyelids. She opened her eyes and stared at the dark spot on the lawn that was all that remained of his head.

36

Indy's eyes welled up with tears and it made the Dana stain blur in and out of focus.

Dana kept dying. Since he died days ago, how could he die again? A Dana stain on the lawn was still too potent, too thick. Indy rammed her fingers down her throat but could only dry heave. Another failure; her stomach was empty. Tears were not what Dana deserved but all she had to dilute him. They were not enough. Indy sighed, pulled down her Fame pants and hot air balloon panties.

Indy urinated on the Dana stain. Luckily, she had a lot of pee, perhaps enough for a terminal Dana dilution.

Indy watched as her pee pooled up around but did not mix with Dana. It did not, she did not, have the power to wash him away. Her hot yellow pee merely puddled in him. More tears fell into the hot pee mess.

The decapitation of Dana felt like entering a loop. He was everywhere. After breaching impossibility and coming back, she could never believe he was truly gone. She would surely have to kill him again and again and again.

Why was she sobbing? How could she cry for this monster? She had dreamed of getting rid of him! She was only thirteen the first time she'd imagined it on a heat lightning-filled April Fools' night. Indy had casually mentioned an imagined future to her mother, said she couldn't wait to go to university to become a doctor as she flitted brightly through the living room on her way to the kitchen for a Dr. Pepper, her worn science textbook under her arm that had the word HEAD written mysteriously in highlighter against the stack of its pages. Her mother had smiled and snapped her gum. Perched on the edge of his coveted record collection trunk in the corner of the room, failed DJ Dana summarized Indy's chances neatly:

University. Dream on, Bozo.

Indy had gripped her textbook like a life raft and let it carry her back the way she had come. Her burning face a storm-red moon over her Barbie Doll mansion, she pulled her favorite record, The Gambler, from where it was hidden behind the Barbie stage. Lovingly she pulled the record from its jacket. She had no paper besides her textbook and library books and she'd get in trouble for writing in them. So she used Kenny's record sleeve, writing overtop of his face like jailhouse tattoos. She even wrote onto the black background, her words disappearing except for texture. She was writing hard enough to rip through the thick glossy paper of the record liner, overtop of Kenny's lyrics. The force caused Indy's Paper Mate pen to leave inky clumps on the down strokes of the Js, Gs and Ys. The heel of her right hand was stained quickly blue, her fingers pressed bloodless white.

Indy climbed up on her bed, a free bed because it used to be her mother's bed when she was a kid, and leaned against the wide white wooden headboard, a headboard her mother, too, had leaned against as a kid. The springs complained, long ago worn out. Indy could only lean here and not against the faux wood paneled walls of her room because it would hurt. It would be like leaning against a bed of nails. On her walls were more than two thousand tailor pins she had painstakingly tapped into place using the back of her hatchet. She got the idea from the Midge Ure music video. The pins held in place cut outs from Soap Opera Digests and Tiger Beat magazine. There were also two life-size posters she had found at Woolco, one of Run-DMC and another of Matt Houston leaning casually on his raised denim knee. Indy had had to use the painstaking pins because anything else would ruin the walls and that would be a fast trip into Danaland.

Staring at thousands of pins, her hands hurting and ink stained, with Run-DMC as the backdrop, Indy imagined shutting Dana up by chopping up his head, mouth first. She would have to use the weighted maul she split firewood with to do it because she was too scrawny to split wood with just an axe. And a head was thicker than wood. She could maybe split his head in two, like cordwood and strap each half to her feet, messy split-side

38

down. Halfheads strapped on, she'd flit around, only truly it was not flitting; it was serious training for her ballet dancing which would fund medical school. In her mind, the Dana halfheads were wearing (half)grins, but these would wear gradually away with each graceful leap.

The writing and imagining made her feel better. It was working, but then her mother interrupted because she hadn't just been visualizing.

She had been stomping around on her mother's old bed. The squeaking and thumping had been hard and loud enough to shake her mirror, once her mother's mirror too, on the wall. It had caused Astronaut Barbie to fall off the edge of the Barbie and the Rockers' stage she was perched on, like Dana had been on his records trunk. Astronaut Barbie's space helmet had cracked. She looked down at her feet.

Indy's feet were planted in Dana and her own pee. The skin all over her body was on fire. It felt as though she was disintegrating. Even as a mucosal remnant, Dana still hurt. Indy jogged across the road to the Saugeen River.

Usually, wading into the Saugeen River filled her with worry about crayfish. They hid in the mud, under rocks in the river, waiting for your toes.

I just beheaded the biggest baddest crayfish on Earth.

She dove in without hesitation. Indy scrubbed her body. She washed her hair in the Saugeen, running her fingers through the length of it. The shallow river slowly soothed her stinging skin. She touched the spot where her ear used to be and the pain explosion caused her to slip on mossy rocks. She plunged backwards, underwater. When she burst out of the water, a longhaired boy about her age stood on the riverbank looking over at her.

The longhaired boy asked her if she was real. He collapsed to his knees on the riverbank, laughing or sobbing into his hands.

His long hair hid his face so Indy wasn't sure which. From the sound he was making, it could go either way.

The boy was Kris. He had been camping at Arran Lake with his parents when the thing happened. His parents, like hers, had collapsed, cocooned and been monstrously born again. He had been out in his kayak. Who, thought Indy, would want to camp at Arran Lake? Also called Leech Lake, it was full of bloodsuckers. It had once belonged to Tammy's grandparents and they had sold it happily, save the productive part beside it where Tammy still farmed.

Kris explained how he had waited at the lake, fishing to supplement camper freeze-dried food packs his family had brought. He had finally resorted to drinking the Leech Lake water when his bottles of water ran out. He had tried to use his father's car phone to call 911 but only got static.

You have a phone in your car?

He told her it was new.

Indy jumped because she felt a pinch on her toe and lifted her foot to see. Sure enough, a crayfish hung there. She yanked it off leaving a bloody streak on her toe and crushed the little thing's head. She trudged out of the river.

Indy studied the boy's shirt and touched his arm, remembering how Indiana Jones comforted hysterical Willie in Temple of Doom. Kris was wearing a dirty rugby shirt and Sperry Top-Siders. He had muscular arms that were sinewy smooth. He had long hair but not a hockey haircut: business front, party back, like everyone in Tara. He had Michael Hutchence from INXS's hair, one even length all around his head. Indy had never seen a boy with music video hair in real life. He had bad acne along the ridges of his lion-shaped face. This imperfection was a relief to Indy. He held himself so confidently you could not help but feel he was a perfect. The opposite of her. He stood up even as he slumped. This was the kind of boy from the kind of family that went on vacations. To mountains. And

40

Europe. And apparently to Arran Lake. He'd been to art shows probably. And his family camped, meaning they actually liked to spend stretches of time alone with each other in tents and cars. A family that spent money to buy kayaks and phones for cars with no fear of the day when there would not be enough money for life, causing life to stop. His parents probably sent him to every lesson, no flitting needed, and made sure he had all the normal life skills like riding a bicycle and throwing a ball and probably even skiing and skating and...

Do you know how to drive?

Of course I do. I'm 16.

Then we have to go back to Arran Lake. Now.

Kris pulled his arm away from Indy's touch. His breath hitched as he spoke.

My parents—

I know.

You cannot know. My dad chased me out of our camp!

I cannot not know.

You don't understand. He tried to hurt me. I ran away. I followed the river. We can't go back. We need help. He's sick. My parents aren't well.

You think I cut off my own ear?

Indy turned her lack of ear towards him. At the same time she pulled her hatchet from her Fame belt loop. She held it out for Kris to examine.

The thing that hurt me? I killed it with that hatchet.

41

Indy remembers how her pee failed to dilute the Dana stain.
Liar.

My best friend Tammy lives beside your lake. Her dad has a
rifle rack hanging over the chest freezer in their foyer. We need
those guns. I can't kill more than one at a time with my
hatchet. Can you?

***

Having the job of driving Dana's 1972 green Ford LTD
seemed to soothe Kris. It was good because Indy had not been
able to block Kris's view of her front lawn when she had gone
to the woodpile to retrieve her maul. Dana's decapitated body
left Kris shaken. Luckily, he did not seem to notice the lawn
stain.

Pulling out of the driveway, Indy shifted the rearview mirror so
she could see the trailer.
Her mother was in the front yard standing over the Dana stain.
It should have been hard to say for sure from this distance
because it was a crayfish version of her, hard and glowing on
the outside, grey and decomposing on the inside. But it wasn't
hard because of her mother's distinctive hump. Her crayfish
self had inherited her scoliotic slouch. Her fleshy lower jaw
was busy chomping, and that was familiar too because she had
always been chewing gum. Usually a terrible purple soap-
flavored gum, called Thrills.

Kris busied himself with talking and very slowly reversing the
massive car out of the narrow driveway. Indy kept watching
her mother in the rearview.

Where do I turn? This car is real old. Is it a classic car? I've
never driven an antique. Do you think there's a cure? Do you
have any water? I'm so thirsty.

Indy produced an apple drink box. Indy popped the straw in the
juice for him. She looked into the mirror again. Kris stopped at
the end of the driveway and ridiculously searched for the
LTD's turn signal.

42

Instead of helping, Indy watched in horror as her mother picked up her lost ear, pinching it delicately in her handclaws. Her undead mother lifted Indy's ear to her chomping mouth and popped it in, like a piece of Thrills. Indy was held captivated as her mother pulverized her ear, turning it easily into nothing.

Indy used her hand to make an ear shape over the congealing hole where the ear her mother had just eaten had been.

Kris downed his apple juice two gulps. Indy handed him another.

Usually I hate apple juice. It's full of pesticide.

Indy nodded and offered him a Chips Ahoy cookie.

These are terrible for you. I don't even know your name and you are feeding me.

Indy did not hesitate.

Indiana, but everyone calls me Indy.

Turning onto highway 21, Indy and Kris saw it would take longer than the usual fifteen minutes to get to Arran Lake.

The stopped and crashed cars forced Kris to slow the car to a crawl. The gigantic LTD was no help. It was wide enough for tall Indy to stretch flat out across the back seat. Kris's sweaty hands slipped nervously on the worn, green steering wheel. At the turn to Tammy's dirt road, they saw their first stranger. Lumbering from the crabapple scrub to block their way, a broad shouldered crayfish-zombie appeared. He was dragging a long-dead calf, its entrails following them both like a cruel bridal train.

Kris hit the brakes. Indy held onto Dana's firewood maul she had brought with them, and slammed her foot onto what she believed to be the gas pedal. The Ford LTD grill connected with Mr. Crayfish, making a wet crunch. He buckled in half, a clumsy bow. His putrefied internals exploded onto the windshield, blotting out the view. Kris searched for and turned on the wipers. He screamed. The wipers dragged up the calf head, eyes milky and tongue lolling. Kris hit the brakes again. It slid off with a thud.

Go left.

They were on the dirt road to Arran Lake and Tammy's farm. The road was clear.

I think we just killed that guy.

Indy looked again in the rearview mirror. The guy, who was no longer 100% pure guy, dead or not, was still following them.

Indy studied the fields so she didn't miss Tammy's driveway. Everything looked the same out there in the countryside. Just like all the crayfish people looked the same. They all looked like Dana.

The Indy girl was weird. He could hardly believe he was with her. He had never spent time with anyone like her. All morning, Kris had been contemplating drowning himself in the river, filling his pockets with rocks like Virginia Woolf. He had, in fact, walked closer to the shore to begin to gather stones when he saw her.

She wasn't like the girls he was used to seeing at private school parties. It was only partially the clothes. When he met her she was wearing bizarre striped pants; the schoolgirls always had uniforms. She looked like a ballerina reflected in a fun house mirror: very thin and sort of elegant but also shocking. And though she had the physique of a twelve-year-old boy it came with the height and presence of a grown up. In the car, she just stared in the rearview mirror and absently plucked at her missing ear.

Indy didn't talk so much as give orders. She told him to make a right. They drove up a long driveway, lined in cedar trees.

Just keep driving until you reach the back of the house. Try to pull up right beside the rear of the house. I want to go in the door there.

Kris did his best to maneuver close to the door at the rear of the house. Indy popped out and disappeared through the door. She returned five minutes later with a grocery bag that said *Knechtel* in orange on it, and a large hockey bag.

No one is in there, but let's drive to the barns.

Indy spoke into her lap because she was rummaging in the bag.

Drive!

They pulled up through the farm, between three large buildings, some barns, and a big garage. At the garage, Indy told him to stop.

Indy hugged Tammy's dad's Heritage & Richardson 12-gauge that she had first fired the previous summer at some Levis to make them look fashion forward. She loaded the H&R with a shell from the Knechtel bag and stuffed more shells in her pockets. She jumped out of the car and shouldered her way through the drive-shed door. This was the only outbuilding that was not for animals. It had furniture and a water spigot. It might be another place for a normal human person to hide.

Tammy! Ashlee!

The answer was not even the usual pigeons flapping from the apex of the rafters, the familiar sound that echoed through the massive steel structure on each of Indy's other visits. The interior gloom was shot through by rods of late afternoon summer sunlight shining through holes made from hunting those perpetual pigeons. Tammy's dad would fill a burlap feed sack with the killed birds and string them up hoping to scare off the rest. Indy could see two dark sacks still hanging from the rafters. And a harvester and a Massey-Harris. She sneezed. She was allergic to just about everything in there.

Indy returned to the car. There was no Sparky, the farm's official greeter dog. And no barn cats and not one head of cattle in the surrounding fields. A breeze troubled the poplars at the property line. Their leafy rattle was the only thing cutting the silence until she used her voice.

Back to the house. They always have good food. I'm starved.

Indy was right. They found Hostess Sour Cream 'n Onion chips, and pickled eggs in the cellar. And pickles. And homemade apple cider. Indy's heart lifted when she noticed every bag of salt 'n vinegar chips emptied and scattered messily on the floor. Her little sister's favorite kind. Kris set the table. It made Indy feel bad because she missed the table's denizens: Tammy and her family. They were the only people Indy had easily eaten at a table with in her life. They would make fun of how skinny Indy was, but it was okay because they'd make fun of each other too.

She doubted Kris would understand so she ate in silence. Kris did not.

What do you think happened? Should we go to Owen Sound? My house is there. It would be safer.

Indy stared at the pickled egg about to go in her mouth. She bounced her legs to feel the reassuring weight of the H&R resting there, her toes toying with the maul at her feet.

Sure.

She glanced into Kris's bright brown eyes but could not bear their hopefulness for more than a second.

Indy was mid-swig of her cider when an air raid siren interrupted their meal. Only it wasn't really a siren, it was a song.

Indy handed the shotgun to Kris across the table. She hefted her maul in one hand, close to its head.

Can you shoot that?

Gun club, St. Andrew's.

Kris's eyebrows knit together, but Indy saw his forearms flex.

From the living room four-foot-square picture window over the wooden console television, the two-armed teens watched as a crayfish monster moved towards them through the dusk.

It's my dad looking for me.

48

Indy doubted finding loved ones was a priority for the creatures, but maybe. Whoever it used to be, its disturbing cry continued. It creaked and groaned forward, jaw working hard. Out of the near-darkness, more shapes emerged, easy to notice in the dark because their shells gave off a firefly glow. The entire herd stopped to chomp angrily at them on the other side of Tammy's living room window.

Indy recognized Tammy's smelly neighbor, the goat farmer and his sons.

Mom! Dad!

Kris was crying. His undead mother clutched something that looked like a doll but was not.

And then Indy saw. Her best and only real friend Tammy. Tammy was glowing.

The mix of Hostess chips and pickled egg rose roughly up her esophagus. Indy tried to master it and failed. Her final meal at Tammy's table sprayed across the window temporarily blotting out the horrific scene. But the meal had been too thin, her stomach acids too active, and in seconds all that was left was a greasy transparent smear and Tammy's undead gaze.

Tammy and Indy had sprawled under this same window in front of this same console TV for hundreds of hours. They were horror movie addicts. The Hellraiser series had been their favorite, but living in Tara, one took whichever VHS tapes were available. Tammy's mom had no idea what they were watching because she did not follow popular culture and would fall asleep every night to Tommy Hunter or Highway to Heaven right after supper.

Tammy's mom had rented Night of the Living Dead for them once because the guy at the Emporium where she rented the movies said it was his favorite. They did not watch the whole thing because it was in black and white and so boring compared to Cujo or Poltergeist. The make-up had been totally fake and it was too easy to kill them, so it was not the least bit scary or good. Eventually, the two girls found it hard to find any movie that actually scared them, although they kept trying.

Indy was finally terrified.

In the window above the TV where she and Tammy had been bored by Night of the Living Dead was a terrifying Tammy. All their critiques and dreams had been answered. Zombie Tammy and her friends were not weak, softly rotting groaners like the Living Dead. These crayfish-zombies were a vast improvement. They were hardened, glowing, and communicated to each other in an alarming pneumatic language. Tears streamed down Indy's face. Tammy would have loved this new version. It was so much scarier. And in color too.

Kris's dad tilted forward into the window, his armored head crashing and easily shattering it in wrecking ball fashion. The creatures' armor made them immune to the glass. Fleshy Indy and Kris turned too late away from the living room glass explosion. Kris's dad tumbled into the living room onto the console television chest first. He reached for Indy as she turned to flee. His pincers caught her, clamping stiffly around Indy's back. He hung suspended mid-air between Indy and the television. Indy struggled to get away but was not heavy enough to even drag the rest of him off the television.

Kris stood back and leveled the shotgun at his dad.

Stop, Dad, please.

Indy, arms pinned, pulled as far away from his chomping jaw as she could. His pincers loosened slightly and she twisted around, but they sliced her skin. She wanted to turn and face him so she could at least see her death coming. Up close she recognized a very full Kris-like lip, even with all the decay.

Kris's dad had her hair and was mouthing it in, pulling her head closer and closer to his gnashing jaw. Indy had the handle of her maul in her hands but her arms were too pinned to her sides to make use of it. He squeezed harder still. She could not breathe.

BOOM.

Kris's dad lost his head. Tammy's living room got a new décor, an edgy horror update to the classic farmhouse chintz. Indy got a mouthful of gore instead of the air she had been gasping for. Indy spit into the hole where the head had been, sort of putting it back as best she could for distraught Kris. Despite having no head, the claws did not loosen. Indy had to squirm out the bottom, shredding her golden shirtsleeves, leaving a bloodied lamé thread spider web dangling over her bare shoulders where her sleeves had been.

Indy dropped to the dusky rose carpet, nearly, but not quite, pulling herself away from under him before he collapsed on top of her. The dead weight of man plus carapace knocked the wind out of her again. Once more she had to squirm away.

Using her knuckles, Indy gently swiped her eye area free of the mess of Kris's dad and her own sweat and blood. She looked around the living room. Kris was frozen in place, shotgun still aimed in her direction.

Kris fired again.

Indy hoped the shot was meant to connect with the goat farmer who had climbed through the window too and not her. It was hard to know because private school gun range expert Kris missed both Indy and farmer. Indy used momentum from a 180-degree swing to plant her maul into the goatman's neck. He crashed sideways.

Indy tossed shells from her pants' pockets at Kris. She screamed, IN HIS HEAD IN HIS HEAD, and the once goaty, now crayfishy man's head burst. A shrapnel shard of him sliced a deep line across her forehead. A foul shower of dead brain rained down on them.

Indy could not see. Fresh blood from her own head wound, and carapace and guts left her blind. Hands dripping in fluids, she rubbed at her eyes with her bare shoulder, leaving gold lamé streamers on her cheeks.

Kris's mother had pitched herself into the living room too and was groaning and creaking to a standing position. She had held tight to the doll-thing and it dangled still from her pincers.

The doll-thing that Kris's mother was carrying was not a doll at all.

The doll-think was Indy's sister Ashlee.

Ashlee was still wearing her huge Last Unicorn barrette. She was not glowing or sporting a new crustaceous skin. She was simply dead. And nearly as abused as she was decayed. She had no arms and her childish face had been peeled and pummeled. Indy was only truly sure it was her because of that Last Unicorn barrette, pinning back her thin blonde bangs she was trying to grow out. Her nose was chewed off and her chest was flayed down to the bone, nearly bare of flesh. Her exposed ribs and sternum gleamed whitely in starlight through the rusty gore that described her torso, a sad mimicry of the glow of the crayfish-zombie who now held her now like an overused toy.

Indy did not hesitate. She wheeled around and knocked Kris's mother's head off-kilter in a single glancing blow, snatching Ashlee away from her claws. Because she had been holding the child by one rotten leg, the entire leg and hip gave way. Ashlee's innards sluiced out.

Indy hugged Ashlee to her, retreated to the kitchen and placed what was left of her – torso, head, one unicorn hairpin and one leg – on the kitchen table, on top of the plates and remains of supper. Taking Tammy's father's 20-gauge, she returned to the living room in time to see Kris fire point blank at Tammy. Her shell chest imploded, vaporizing her shelled breasts. Her voluptuous bosom became a grey mist. Tammy kept creaking forward, unperturbed by her loss. Indy thought, *I'd be devastated.* And then, wildly, *I finally have more chest than she does.* She giggled. Then sobbed. Only then was Indy able to feel shot in the chest too. It felt real. She palmed her own bony chest to check.

Indy watched as Kris pulled the trigger again and obliterated the head of the only person she had ever felt loved unconditionally by. Tammy crashed forward like a felled tree and Indy had to sidestep out of her way.

Indy finished off Kris's mother and three other crayfish-zombies. She missed only once. Kris had stopped firing. He sat huddled in the corner of the living room beneath a Jay Norris catalogue lamp that rained oil raindrops onto a plastic Venus de Milo. His head was in his hands. Again. Only this time corpse gore had made his long hair stringy enough that Indy could see through it. He was bawling.

Kris could not think about his parents and the Indy girl in one thought; they did not fit together. From just her expression you would think she was in history class listening to a lecture, but this was not a lecture. She was paying careful attention to what she was doing.

Kris moved to the kitchen. Against the backdrop of the dawn coming through the kitchen window, Indy was dunking her head in the sink. Her spidery arms were ballet-folded in an arc over her, framing the sun's rays as she poured water from some bottle over herself. As her head rose, dawn was caught in the liquid, making the scene beautiful, despite everything they had just been through. Indy turned and the moment snuck off. She opened her eyes a slit.

Kris handed her a towel from the counter.

We have to clean ourselves up.

Kris nodded. You missed something on your neck.

Indy handed back the now-damp towel. He delicately rubbed her neck and upper shoulders. He felt so emotional. He was a competitive snowboarder and at the top of his class in all things, especially math. But math seemed irrelevant now. Snowboarding, family too. It was all dead.

Kris felt Indy shudder through the damp towel. All the reasons she had to shake tumbled around in his head even though she was most likely just cold.

Tell me about your family

That is my sister. I changed her diapers. Her dad never did, not even one time.

Indy sounded annoyed.

Kris dropped his head to his hands again, his trademark stance of radical surrender and confusion, forgetting that he was still holding the wet towel. He felt Indy move close. She took the wet towel from between his head and hands. She used the coolness of it to soothe the back of his neck, tickling the hairs there lightly.

Kris shivered. Indy leaned down and in. They were the same height so her lips easily reached the base of his skull. She spoke into his skin and bone there.

We have to leave here. It's time.

Kris wondered, and didn't dare ask, where they were going.

Safe in Tammy's dad's red F150, they ran the back roads towards Owen Sound. Kris talked non-stop. Indy listened politely. She was bewildered by why he got so choked up describing his hometown. When he was driving he could not hide his face in his hands so she figured he hid behind this constant laugh-filled chatter.

Kris edged the truck, still talking emotionally, around an abandoned combine. The straw and cow manure-caked tires squeaked against the sides of their vehicle as they passed because Kris got too close.

Indy did like how he used *we* and *us,* even knowing she would stay just long enough to get her belly full and play voyeur inside an actual doctor's house. She nodded and looked at Kris. All the while thinking how to leave as fast as possible for Las Vegas.

She looked at Kris, his mouth moving, hands pointing and gesturing. He had been so gentle doctoring her ruined ear, pulling shards of what was certainly his own parents' out of her head and back. It had been so soothing. She imagined massage felt like that. It was the kindest touch she'd ever known. She could not recall ever being touched so soothingly by anyone except Tammy. But that had just been a guessing game where you draw letters on each other's back.

The day's events had changed everything. Her only guaranteed loved one, Tammy, was gone. So far, being Indy had been very confusing. She'd cried and puked more as Indy than she ever had as her old weak self. But she had found an all-new ability to protect and belong instantly with Kris. Her future felt unstuck and it was unspooling before her. She was basking in the thrall of these changes.

Kris, on the other hand, looked gutted. His careful and hemmed-with-love day-to-day life of kayaking and family closeness had been mineralized then shattered. Indy was responsible for the worst of it, of forcing him back to face and destroy what was left of his parents. She was not sure if the next time he dropped his face in his hands would be because he was so utterly sad or because looking at her made it all worse.

The last few days had ruined Kris's life and granted Indy hers. What her new name and victorious exodus from the pot and chicken farm meant to her was something she wished she could tell Kris. She did not dare try.

Indy sat with her secrets. She had never felt more alive.

There was no question about what came next. She would return to her only real family.

She would return to her father.

Indy did not so much decide to go to her father as feel set upon the world with that one task. All past and current events in Tara were mere preparation for what would certainly be a brutal and death defying trip. She had been pent up and waiting for a decade, everything passing through the lens of the day when she'd finally see her father and prove he was, *they were*, real. She couldn't tell orphaned Kris of her thirst for father in Las Vegas. How could someone like her get something someone like him would never have again? He'd be disgusted.

I bet your house is nice.

Kris laughed brightly and explained how he had a trampoline and a harpsichord and a piano, and Indy stared out the window thinking of Las Vegas.

Kris slammed on the brakes and Indy lurched forward against the waist-strap seatbelt. The big truck fishtailed, riding the ditch.

In front of them, balanced on the double centerline, was a girl. A gingham dress-wearing, non-glowing, non-shell-skinned girl who was utterly unimpressed that their truck had successfully avoided running her over.

Before Indy could stop him, Kris was out of the truck and running towards the girl. Indy cautiously stepped onto the running board to watch.

Are you okay? What are you doing? Get up!

The almost-killed girl got up. She was sawing at her hair with a Swiss Army Knife. Not with the scissor attachment but with the plain blade. She had chopped enough so the left side of her hair was hacked as short as Mia Farrow's in Rosemary's Baby while the untouched right side was shoulder length. A sideways mullet. She ignored Kris and focused on cutting another fistful of her hair.

Kris yanked her hair out of her hand, maybe to get her attention. She slashed at him with her blade. A red line blossomed through the front of Kris's rugby shirt.

Kris recoiled, pressing his hand to his chest.

Haircutter horked at Kris right on top of the cut she just gave him. She bolted away into a cattail ditch, arms pumping, dress billowing, and disappeared through the wood-line a field away.

Kris walked back towards the truck, a gobbet of the haircutter's phlegm dangling jewel-like against the July sun from his chest, mixing with the blood from his cut. He wiped it all off and it mixed into the stains already on his shirt from the mess of the apocalypse.

We can't let her go off alone. She's the only other real person we've seen. She's not safe out there.

It looks to me like she is good at defending herself.

58

Kris stared after the girl.

She's as fine as we are. We can always come back for her.

Indy was speaking into Kris's hair because his head was once again tilted into his hands. She hoped he wasn't hating her. She hoped he couldn't hear the lie in her voice. Indy stretched her long arm out and rested her hand on top of his head, petting him. He eventually lifted his head and smiled a sad smile.

Kris steered the truck back into a lane. He took a deep breath and Indy readied herself for more babbling. Instead, it was an accurate observation.

It looks like smash-up derby.

The crest of the hill ahead of them, in exact alignment with the bullet-ridden Owen Sound *Welcome* sign, was car Tetris. Some cars were crashed, some parked, and all were abandoned. A white Tercel was charred as though it had been hit with a flame-thrower. They were not going to be able to drive further this way, not in this truck.

We'll have to go back and take different roads.

But Kris was not listening to Indy. He was slowing down, mouth agape. He shut off the engine and opened the truck door. Indy grabbed for his departing elbow and hooked it with her fingers. She pulled Kris back into the truck.

A gunshot echoed and a spider web pattern spread across their windshield. Indy yanked down on Kris's elbow and they both dropped their heads down to the faded red bench seat of the Ford. It smelled of sun baked grease and buckwheat.

Hey, loser. Stop shooting at us!

Indy was still holding Kris's arm so she squeezed it to shut him up.

59

The shooter answered with another shot. This one released the windshield down onto them. The same shot continued over their heads shattering the back window too.

Indy and Kris crouched frozen on the truck bench seat under a blanket of glass shards and buffeted by a breeze blowing through the newly ventilated truck. Indy's fingernails dug into Kris's elbow, yet he took another deep breath to yell.

You LOSER.

Someone hopped onto the truck bed, rocking it gently. The broken glass squealed under their footsteps. Just above Kris's head, a rifle poked through the broken back window. It swiveled and took aim at Indy.

Youse two there!

Indy followed the barrel slowly up, squinting against the sun. A dry and intensely wrinkled face, framed by a filthy camouflage baseball cap and a fall of fuzzy grey hair grinned back.

The old man had a ZZ Top beard braided into two pigtails. His irises were the juicy blue of someone who had seen at least eight decades of grief and misery. One cheek was round with chewing tobacco. The stains in his braided beard said it was not a new habit.

The old man spit brown juice into the bed of the truck and spoke to them down his rifle sights.

I seen youse two last night.

As Kris spoke, the rifle pivoted in his direction.

You could not have, mister. We were over near Tara last night. We are just headed home and to the police—

60

The bearded man's shrill cackle shut Kris up in a way Indy's elbow squeezing could not.

The old man's grin was made more hideous by oversized dentures bunged up with tobacco mess. His laugh slipped into an emphysemic sputter. He horked another wad onto the truck bed.

I finished off more'n a few of them monsterified cops. It's not Owen Sound anyhow. Welcome to Eldontown. Eldon is me. I'm as done with all you brats as I am with those deep fried monster folk. Both kinds not welcome in Eldontown.

During the lecture, Indy sank her weight onto her haunches. Before Eldon could pivot his rifle back towards her, she launched forward, broken glass flying off her torso, and yanked his rifle out of his hands.

Eldon lost his balance, flailing back onto the truck bed. He smacked his head on the tailgate. Indy had Eldon's rifle. She flipped it around, got out of the truck and aimed it at Eldon's prone body. She looked across at Kris who was out of the truck too, shotgun ready.

Whose town is it now, loser?

Eldon wheezed. He palmed his hat back to wipe a trickle of blood from the top of his head.

Friggit. I've bit my tongue to boot!

It seems like we got off on the wrong foot. Hello. I'm Indy and this is Kris. You must be Eldon. Sure we'd love to share your supplies.

Got me beat. I got more than enough.

Eldon wobbled momentarily, then hopped off the truck, marching them over the hill towards Eldontown.

61

The Eldontown City Hall had, until recently, been the showroom of the Fyreplace Christmas Shop. Eldon had been taking down and splitting spruce from the Christmas tree farm behind the store and using the wood in the showroom wood stoves to heat water and cook. The wood was wet so it popped and smoked badly, giving the Fyreplace Christmas Shop a war-like ambiance.

A Christmas store is decorated year round for Christmas. The Owen Sound version had catered to those obsessed with Christmas and fire. Locals shopped in the festive fireplace showroom for decorations and wood heat appliances even in July. Flinching at the décor and tearing up from the smoky air, Indy struggled to not lose sight of Eldon.

Eldon collapsed with a groan into a giant red and gilt throne. A Santa Claus throne to be exact. A smaller, elfy green velvet tufted chair sat across from it. He hoisted his booted feet onto it. The room dripped red and green foils. Glitter-coated Styrofoam pheasants and pale pink plastic angels hung suspended from plastic nooses overhead. Filth smears darkened the only windows that had not been broken. The broken windows had been repaired, as though by a child, with shaggy white faux fur, the kind used to wrap a tree base that is supposed to look like snow. One entire end of the showroom was lost behind a wall of supplies: Evian, cases of Pepsi, Twinkies, Kraft Dinner, Campbell's soup and Cottonelle. It was a Santa's stockpile of pragmatic gifts. With Eldon holding court from his Santa throne, all filthy pigtail beard and Carhartt overalls, the scene overwhelmed Indy in a way the crayfish-zombies never could.

She fought for breath in the smoky, festive room. She pretended the tears streaming down her face were from the wet wood smoke.

Christmastime was *the* benchmark for misery in her life. In a childhood of lows, it was the bottom.

Dana became berserk with strangers in his house. Strangers were defined as any human being other than himself and maybe, on a good day, Indy's mother and his daughter, Ashlee. He mostly pretended Indy did not exist. The list of those who required at least three solid prep days of rip-the-phone-out-of-the-wall type threats and rocket launcher themed discussions was thus vast, basically everyone, and included his own and Indy's mother's family.

He hated everyone and lived in mortal terror of anyone seeing his pot plants at any stage of growth. He had started them as seeds in Corelle bowls lined with paper towels in the hall closet beside the furnace. Often around Christmas, he planted and kept them beside his stereo in the living room because the greenhouse did not have enough of a heating system for precious baby plants. Out of this hatred and paranoia, the Christmas Shed was born.

The Christmas Shed was an obscene fruit of Dana's loathsome loins. Like the Fyreplace Christmas showroom, the Christmas Shed was left festooned with tinsel and garlands year round. The Shed, however, was not for catering to Grey County area Christmas fans. It was for the preservation of Dana's trailer from the taint of seasonal clutter of decorations and people who might see his baby pot plants.

The Christmas Shed was built to house the people who had to visit on Christmas Day in order to sustain the appearance of normal family to someone. Indy was never sure who, since she was sure deep down everyone knew the whole thing was nuts. Immediately following the thirty minute tearing open of cheap homemade gifts, everyone would sit side by each in plastic chairs around the shed and loudly scarf Indy's mother's trademark crunchy beige sour cream mashed potatoes, and her grandmother's perfectly rested turkey. Then leave. Immediately.

Except Indy. She had to stay. Dana naturally presided over the family with war stories from his nuclear power plant job. He described the Pakis he would be soon heartpunching and revised again last year's list of who he would kill with rocket launchers once he could afford them. Stockholm syndromed, so hypnotized by decades of his tyranny, everyone echoed his maniacal laughter using their own titters to mask the increased fork to mouth pace. Indy ate deadpan and languorously, condemning her pussy family who threw the Pakis and Indy under the bus to save themselves.

Family would leave immediately after pie, and before their taillights vanished, Dana would start explaining exactly what sort of assholes they were and how he couldn't believe he'd survived another horrible Christmas around such low life scumbags who should just fuck off and die. Scared, Indy had to agree, throwing herself under the bus. Besides, they had left her there and he was clearly a madman.

And those, *those*, were the *good* Christmases. The fun ones. The worst had been the Christmas of 1982.

Indy had a real bad cold. She got it from her mother who was even sicker. A full deep breath was impossible despite draining all the household inhalers. Dana said Karen got it from being stressed out on account of fucking Christmas coming up, thank-god-he-built-the-fucking-shed-at-least. Ashlee was not even walking yet, so she stayed attached to her mother in bed, scratching her eczema body raw. Indy wrapped and re-wrapped her tiny bloody knuckles in cortisone and gauze. She picked large dandruff scabs from Ashlee's thin blonde ringlets to pass time and distract herself from her own labored breathing.

On Christmas Eve, Indy woke early to heavy footsteps pounding down the hallway. It was Dana carrying the added weight of a second adult body.

With her wooden chest holding just enough air for her to stay unfortunately conscious, Indy slid out of bed. Dana and her mother and the car were gone.

She went to Ashlee and comforted her and she would not be comforted without her mommy. Since it was Christmas, there were nothing but hokey feel good movies on television. No distracting horrors or thrillers. So, for the next twelve hours Indy drank back-to-back mugs of lemon NeoCitran to calm herself down enough to not smother. Occasionally she would be pulled from her haze by Ashlee bawling. She was always breastfed so she was hungry. Indy fed her Gerber yams microwaved for 22 seconds for supper. Indy ate another mug of NeoCitran.

It was December 24, 11:30 pm when Ashlee finally fell asleep or knocked herself out from screaming. Indy nodded off again listening to WBZ Boston skip patterns of conservative talk radio *without* earphones. One small thing to celebrate: making noise because Dana was out of the house.

Christmas morning, Indy knew her tolerance to the magic lemon drink was high because, despite being barely fifty pounds, she woke early even after downing a four-packet mug at midnight. There were no presents under the Christmas Shed tree. She didn't even have to go check.

Luckily this bothers no one, thought Indy. Ashlee doesn't know about Christmas so doesn't miss it because she is seven months old, and I've known there was no Santa since before the Winnie the Pooh incident because the black boy she kissed at pre-school told her so after he showed her his penis.

Should I put something under the tree for Ashlee anyway? But just standing up made her cough so bad she was sure she was not up to going outside to the Shed. Her coughs and a wet diaper, or both, woke Ashlee. Indy braced herself against the kitchen wall, her hand beside the green wall phone, wondering if Tammy was up yet.

Dana burst through the door behind her and spoke in a voice Indy had never heard him use.

Karen is dead.

Indy nodded and everything got blindingly bright. She needed to raise her hands in front of her face to shield her eyes. She tried to see Dana through the brightness and her hands. He had brought a cloud of pot smoke in with him, pinching off even more of her air. She coughed.

Dana strolled casually past her, towards the hall, and because she couldn't see to get out of the way, he knocked her off balance, maybe angry she was so close to the phone. She stumbled back two steps, smacking her hip into the washing machine. It rang like a distant bell.

Dana slammed his bedroom door at the end of the hall. Even though it was plastic –
everything was – the entire trailer quaked.

Blind, even though her eyes were open, Indy stumbled halfway down the hall feeling along the faux wood panels for the plastic doorknob that was her half-sister's door. When she found it and opened it, the brightness burned out. She could see enough to change Ashlee's diaper, rubbing extra Penaten cream on the folds of her labia because they were inflamed. Tears splashed on Ashlee's baby gut, and Indy had to touch her face with the back of her hand to see that they were indeed coming from her own eyes.

I like the rain because then no one can see me cry. – Pam

Don't fish for complaints. Some people might think you're shellfish. – Bazooka Joe

Eldon was relaxing in his Santa throne. Indy and Kris, cradling weapons, moved towards the dreamy junk food stockpile at the end of the room and started pulling. Kris exchanged his shotgun for Evian, Indy balanced Dr. Pepper, Twinkie and weapon artfully. The room tinkled because the breeze blowing through the faux fur window repair agitated the Christmas ornament-covered ceiling. The decorations rubbed up against each other. Indy collapsed into the elf chair across from Eldon. She swallowed half her soda without taking a breath. Her gun, a lapdog.

I would never sit there if I were you.

Indy noticed Eldon's two front teeth were sideways like blades.

Well, you are not me.

Indy crackled her Twinkie wrapper for emphasis.

Thunder growled in the distance. Eldon jumped from his throne and cracked the front open. The thunder grew. The thunder was not from a storm.

Kris was peering through the faux fur gaps in the windows. Indy didn't get up but pet her gun.

Eldon leaned into the front door, holding it open with his back. The non-storm source of the rumble arrived. It was a tank.

The tank parked in the Fyreplace lot beside Tammy's dad's truck like it was a normal vehicle, dwarfing it. Eldon burnished his stiff old man hands, pulling himself up to his full height. He crossed his arms over his puffed-out chest.

A girl jackpopped out the top of the tank. She was wearing the white shirt and woolen plaid skirt of a private school girl. She had rolled the skirt up so that it was incredibly short.

She climbed down from the tank. Her shapely legs, in black tights, had curves that Indy's did not. Indy and Eldon stared and Kris looked away. She stomped into the Fyreplace. Maybe she was stomping because of her Doc Marten's that were weighing her feet down. Or, maybe she stomped because she was angry; it was impossible to tell. She laughed as she looked at Indy, like Woody Woodpecker. She also had, what would be on any other face, an unfortunate nose. And yet her other facial angles struck an uneasy but surprising balance with the nose. She finished giving Indy a once-over, her eyes finally came to rest on Kris. He waved meekly, raising his hand barely to shoulder height, like he knew her.

You go to school together?

Woody Woodpecker laughed again. She slapped a hand over her ha-ha mouth, shaking her head.

As if. The uniform is a joke, silly. Everyone knows *him*. He's snowboarding-champion-private-school-boy. Mr. Perfect.

Pam, how do you drive a *tank*?

She beamed. She shifted her agitated gaze to Eldon who had resumed his throne.

One thing I can do that you can't, *privateschoolboy*.

She slapped at the tinsel above her head.

Kris flopped his head forward in his trademark move. He raised it and dragged his palms along his cheeks. He enunciated slowly as though speaking to an idiot.

69

You losers will go to jail forever for stealing a tank.

Welcome to the rest of your life, Kris. Me and my tank. We will never go to jail because jails are over. I can pulverize zombies for days. What can you do? Whack them with your polo stick?

I play lacrosse, not polo.

Eldon rummaged around in a pile of garbage at his feet and produced a sheaf of thermal fax papers stained with what might be blood or grease. He threw them at Kris's head, but they didn't reach and instead unspooled through the air in front of him.

You think you know everything, know it all?

Indy didn't move, only tightened her grip on the barrel of her gun and sucked the guts out of another Twinkie. She watched Kris gather up the fax streamers. He had to pluck the ends from between the wings of a plastic angel. Indy already knew Kris well enough to see he was trying to be expressionless. He instead achieved a look of barely contained panic. His shoulders twitched out of sync and his face appeared to be breaking out in new pimples before her eyes. Indy felt really bad for him. She hoped she was mirroring his expression of worry, tried shifting her shoulders a bit. She licked Twinkie icing off her fingers. She feared for her father's life, but knew beyond doubt he was waiting for her in Las Vegas. She could feel him.

Indy stood up for another Dr. Pepper. The adrenalin of the past 24 hours was burning out, leaving her feel like an empty firecracker. She didn't trust Eldon or Pam and never would. She trusted Kris, but he was taking this apocalypse deal too hard.

Pam sat in the green chair Indy had vacated across from Eldon. Indy piled two Evian water bottle flats on top of each other and sat beside the stockpile at the end of the room. It felt safer there. Further from the densest Christmas decorations and Pam.

Chew chew chew.

Pam giggled nervously. She pulled up a golden leather pouf and slapped the top, pointing at Kris. He wandered over dazed and sat, his eyes barely leaving the fax papers.

Kris finished reading. He searched the room, in a panic, until he located wall of food sentinel, Indy.

These papers are from the government.

Eldon snickered. The snicker devolved rapidly into a phlegmy cough.

They say New York City had more than 5 million casualties.

Kris stopped talking because he was crying. He didn't even have time to drop his head into his hands. He probably did not want to ruin the precious faxes he held there.

Pam leaned over to Kris. She put her arm around him dramatically. She moved her lips an inch from his ear, but still spoke loud enough for Indy to hear.

We are *the last people on Earth*. You guys are lucky to find us. We have everything we need right here. And a tank, too.

Eldon's mouth had become a tight line. With the pigtail beard it looked as if he had just swallowed most of a little girl. He nodded.

Pam started listing off all the places they still had to loot, all the things they could do like get the generators out back going, once they'd cleared Eldontown of zombies. She explained to Kris how she could even teach him to drive the tank.

71

Kris stared down at the papers in his hands, mourning, Indy imagined, his lost world of snowboards and loving family dinner conversation.

Pam. They aren't zombies.

The Christmassier end of the room gave the supply end of the room their full attention.

I mean, they are undead. But – and I'm an expert on this – they are not any zombie I've ever seen. In a movie, I mean.

Okay, *privateschoolgirl,* if you're so smart, what are they?

Indy smirked at Pam's assumption. She thought Indy was fancy enough to be a private school girl. It may have been guilt by association with Kris, but it was still empowering. Indy confidently explained the situation as she knew it to be.

Zombies are just mindless, soft dead people. These things are dead people wrapped up in hardened skin. Like crayfish have. One thing I am not sure of though is who is wearing who.

Indy crammed another Twinkie into her mouth and chewed. Eldon pointed his pigtails at Indy.

The facts is crayfish-zombie or what, we still gotta get them before they get us.

Pam's arm was still around Kris. Kris decided to do some rereading. Indy stood.

I've been here long enough.

A thrill caught in Indy's throat as she spoke. She had a plan. A plan that had been inside her all of her life. Destiny. Amidst the glittery ritualistic leavings of a newly dead culture she revealed herself.

I am not staying here. I appreciate all this. But I am on my way to Las Vegas.

Kris, still gripping faxes, shouldered out of Pam's half embrace and stood.

Yeah, me too.

Indy flushed. Her heartbeat blossomed on her cheeks.

Why? We have a tank. It's no different there, just hotter.

What do you know?

Indy saw the shape of a Molson Export tall ship form among the spaces between the plastic angels and sparkly birds like a Rubin vase, sailing away from waves of Christmas.

Did the faxes say anything about Las Vegas?

Nope.

Exactly. Vegas is an island in the desert. You can see everything coming. We're blind here.

Indy drove the point home by gesturing calmly at the vestigial Christmas clutter around their heads.

Well, I've always wanted to get married in Vegas. I could drive us in the tank.

Eldon was shaking his head no.

You are not the boss of me!

Pam sprang at him. For a moment, Indy feared Pam had turned into a new kind of monster and was about to munch on Eldon's ear. Instead, she only hollered and spit gibberish into it. He threw his hands up to protect himself and staunch her wet diatribe. Finally, he gave in.

73

Whatever. Nevada is millions of miles away each one of 'em zombie miles. Or crayfishes and whathaveyou miles. You'll come back to me in tears.

Pam resumed her Eldon assault, this time wrapping her legs up around his chest tipping his Santa throne so Pam was on top of him, pummeling his face, chest and shoulders with the heels of her hands.

Indy and Kris shared a glance that said all it had to.

***

Indy offered to take first watch even though she was exhausted. With a handful of Bazooka Joe chewing gum, she sat armed and cross-legged atop the tank. Indy dropped into a familiar melancholic, vigilant trance, chewing and scanning the horizon for movement. It was like when she had to go into the kitchen for water or food and she'd have to listen and watch for Dana in case he appeared. She unwrapped a new chunk of gum. It seemed a waste because it was too dark to read the comic so she stuffed it in her back pocket.

It was Pam's turn to take over. Instead of waking her, Indy silently passed Pam and her garish makeshift bed of tree skirts and flaccid inflatable elves towards Kris. She shook him awake. He was curled up asleep beside the flats of Evian she had used for a chair earlier. They moved across the Christmas showroom to the door. It was impossible to be silent because the air they displaced was enough to make the tinsel talk softly from the ceiling. Eldon was gone.

Leaving empty handed from this mound of supplies caused a physical ache in Indy's ribs, but Kris had assured her his home, where they were headed now, was fully stocked because his mother kept a huge pantry. Of course, Indy added silently, they were rich.

74

It will take us about twenty minutes to jog to my place from here, Kris whispered as they moved back across Springmount Road where Eldon had attacked them earlier.

NO.

Pam screamed from behind them. She exploded from the Fyreplace and flung herself into Kris.

Don't leave me behind. I love you.

Kris held onto Pam because she had dropped her full weight into his arms.

We will be back for you, Pam. You stay here with your grandfather. We'll come back with even more supplies.

Pam didn't move.

Really.

Pam stood slowly up. It had begun to rain lightly.

If you don't come back, I'll find you. You'll be sorry.

Kris nodded and backed away from Pam and the Fyreplace. Indy followed. As the Christmas wonderland disappeared behind a rise in the road, he whispered, *run*, and they did, down the hill towards town.

Even though it made running harder, Kris took Indy's hand.

T hrough the darkness and drizzle, Indy saw movement near the Woolco entrance and squeezed Kris's hand.

Indy pointed across the mall parking lot. Barely audible over Indy's winded breathing was the pneumatic call of the crayfish-zombie. The shelled things glistened under the Woolco sign in the early morning drizzle and fluoresced softly as was their nature. They were assembled in a way that reminded Indy of the Raiders football team awaiting a coach on the field, in staggered but purposeful rows, not walking but swaying.

Kris whimpered. Indy let go of his hand and aimed her H&R. She did not need a tank.

Kris folded Indy's hand back into his and pulled it gently away from the trigger so she would instead run again. Not fight. Indy gave in. Kris ran like a deer. The fatigue in her lungs and awkward gait from carrying the shotgun made it very hard for her to keep up.

Kris kept her hand tightly in his as he took the shortcut past Harvey's, through the West Hill Secondary School back parking lot towards the Raiders football field and tennis courts. The field was full of what looked at first to be lazy players. Up close, Indy saw they were dismembered limbs and pulverized remnants of crayfish-zombies. Indy rolled her foot over painfully on an empty shotgun shell and landed hard next to the severed upper half of a normal human girl wearing a baby blue Raiders tank top, the pirate head logo speared neatly by a human-sized crayfish claw. The team spirit and claw-filled-girl's matching legs were nowhere to be seen. Kris pulled Indy up and over the remains of the half girl and then they both tripped over a gouge in the field the size of a tank tread. They helped each other up this time, gathering speed to quickly

76

round the four tennis courts and enter the rich people neighborhood. Indy was running so hard she wondered why she wasn't wheezing like Piggy from Lord of the Flies.

Kris's house was the fanciest house Indy had ever been in, but she played it off. Symmetric pillars regally framed his front door. It was brown brick, no aluminum or tar paper anywhere. Inside, everything was wood and wool and pale and tasteful like the houses on All My Children. Indy stopped to examine the family portrait over the dining room table. It was Kris and his parents dressed in black pants and turtlenecks like a family uniform. They were arranged on the deck of a tall ship. Their faces were airbrushed so they looked perfect, like The Cosby Show only white. Kris's acne was even gone. Indy could barely recognize his parents.

Why do you have two dining tables?

Kris didn't answer but disappeared to the back of the house and the laundry room. The laundry was a pharmacy. His dad, an anesthesiologist, got free samples of drugs. Painkillers, experimental and otherwise, pretty bandages, cold pills, cough syrups, antibiotics. Especially precious to Indy were the Ventolin inhalers. She had not taken any with her and, after the sprint to Kris's house, her lungs could go at any time. She took two quick puffs just to be safe. Before she had inhalers, when she had an asthma attack, the only thing that would help her breathe enough so she could sleep, besides NeoCitran, was watching a horror film. Since she was living inside a horror film now, it made sense that she was breathing easier. Maybe the apocalypse had cured her. To be safe, she stuffed all six inhalers from the closet into the Gregory backpack Kris was filling, along with an impressive array of sample packs of drugs.

His house had a music room, impressive and useless.

You have two pianos too?

Kris answered by plinking one of the keys on the uglier piano. It resonated baroquely.

I told you. It is a harpsichord. It's on loan from a museum. So not two pianos. Just one.

Indy hunched over the museum thing and played Here We Go down the Row.

In the basement was the pantry, four times the size of Indy's bedroom. Former bedroom. Canned goods, something called kirsch, flour, nuts that Indy had never seen, like macadamia and enough almonds to bury her feet in. She grabbed a handful and sat down on a case of Canada Dry.

Wow.

Yeah. My mom loves to cook. So she keeps – kept – a stocked pantry.

Beside the pantry was a tidy windowless bedroom with a fluffy bed and antique desk. On the desk were bird skeletons, carefully arranged by size from wren to robin. Since Indy considered herself an amateur ornithologist, she knew what they were and was impressed. Indy touched the wren bones.

My dad liked to look for dead birds and boil them and assemble their skeletons – I can move them if you like.

Don't bother.

This is our guest bedroom, it has no windows. So if you wanna sleep, it will be safe while I keep watch.

Indy almost protested. Instead she collapsed down into the bed and was asleep before Kris left the room. When she woke ten hours later, Kris was eating corn chips and sardines in the basement recreation room, sitting on the floor in front of a Danish style couch. Their shotguns and shells framed his meal. He had lit a few pretty candles too. She stretched and joined him, although she had never eaten a sardine in her life. In fact, Indy had never seen a sardine and only knew for sure what they were because the top of the can said Pastene sardines.

Indy sat on the couch behind Kris and stared into their distorted reflection in the blank television.

Kris was kneeling in front of the couch and eating as he worked on a black and red pencil crayon drawing. He was coloring in infinite tentacles, from an unseen octopus, that reached out of the picture to grab at you.

You were joking about Las Vegas.

Indy finished chewing a mouthful of chips. Her disappointment flickered briefly on her face and she wanted to see if he noticed. She licked sardine grease off her fingers.

No.

But we have everything here.

Not everything.

If you go, you will die. If I go with you, we both die.

Indy blinked and looked back at the television and chewed a sardine.

Explain it to me?

It won't make sense to you because it makes no sense to me, Indy thought.

My father is there.

But you know he will be dead.

I've never met him. Or I have, but I don't remember. He looked after me until I was three. I'm pretty sure anyway. The

79

only way to know is to find him. All of this that has happened means I can do this. Means I have to try. What is important is that the only thing I have ever wanted to do on Earth is go to Las Vegas and try. I love him?

You don't believe any of that and none of it is true, Indy finished wordlessly.

Why did he stay away?

He wasn't allowed to see me. I had no pictures of him because my mother hated him because he is probably a bad man. See?

I don't see, so I hope you see, Indy whispered.

Her face flamed. She did not want to, but could not stop one traitorous tear from slipping down her hot cheek. This was the only time she had ever spoken plainly of these things. Or tried to. She was dizzy and out of her body. She wondered if she was still asleep or maybe had finally succumbed to her own chrysalis.

Kris climbed up onto the couch beside Indy and easily put his arms around her shoulders, gently pulling her to him. He was holding her and it was another first. Instead of calming her, it fueled her anxious thoughts and heartbeat. Why, Indy thought, won't this feel better? They sat that way, comforter and uncomforted, for a long time while Indy thought.

She came up with not one picture or fact about her father. She saw the tall sailing ship on the bottle of Export beer and nothing more. Beer ship father. The only information Indy had came in hint form. Each time Dana drove them through the town where Indy's father had once lived, they made her lie prone and hidden on the floor of the car like a prison escapee. He must be very bad. From the floor, Indy had felt bad too. Guilt by association. There were only these kinds of things, not words or facts.

With one exception.

80

Even at only eleven, her best friend Tammy had been fantastically and bravely curious. One summer she had asked Indy's mother flat out where Indy's father was. Her mother, folded up in the living room chair with her knees squishing her big boobs, bounced her legs a few times and told them he'd run away to Las Vegas. Then she'd asked if they wanted some blue or red Freezies as she popped another piece of purple Thrills gum in her mouth.

It was the first and last time she'd ever hear her mother acknowledge that she'd had a father. At that precise moment, like the click of a lock, Las Vegas became her beacon. She watched sunsets just to know she was looking west, and then glanced slightly to what she hoped was south, feeling comforted knowing she was looking in his direction. The daily process gave her the strength to endure Dana's rants and her mother's ambivalence. They'd hated her father, had driven him away and hated her and had obviously tried to drive her away too. At the time, she'd sworn that, one day, when she was finished school and had the resources, she would go to where she belonged: to Las Vegas. To her father.

Indy's thoughts slowed back down. She was being hugged by Kris on an elegant couch in a rich person's house. His embrace tightened. Indy shifted her head slightly so she could see the tentacle drawing Kris had been working on.

You are crying for a parent you do not know, and I am crying because I knew mine.

He was crying now; they were both crying. Tears commingled on cheeks so it might have been that only one of them was actually crying. They tilted gently down together, never losing the connection of their foreheads, onto the Danish couch. Indy saw their tears were darkening the perfect wool upholstery. They leaned into each other, silently weeping for what seemed to Indy like hours, hypnotized by the relief of shared, if perpendicular, agonies. When Kris pulled away, Indy was surprised by her own disappointment. But he only pulled away

81

far enough to rest his face nose-to-nose with Indy. Indy stared, but his eyes remained closed. His full lips, so like his father's, were less than an inch from her own. Her mouth ached. She could smell nothing but his clean natural smell with just a pinch of fetid zombie crayfish stink underneath. The ache in her mouth moved up her facial muscles to her cheekbones, like the first chew of Gatorade gum. They were sharing air. It dried their faces. Kris opened his dark eyes, but he was so close it hurt to focus on them so Indy closed hers. No one moved and the ache in her lips, her cheeks, spread across and down the back of her skull. Eventually her lips felt his.

Indy held her breath and shuddered, providing the friction to deepen their kiss.

The clatter of broken glass and the air raid siren of the crayfish-zombies ripped Kris and Indy apart. Indy was up, shotgun in hand, scarfing a mouthful of chips before Kris even sat up. She took the carpeted stairs three at a time and stopped at the closed basement door to listen. Kris showed up behind her. It was impossible to tell how many were in the house. It sounded like thousands.

A voice, a human voice, joined the pneumatic din.

LIAR!

Pam was screaming at them over the zombie song.

I brought some friends!

Pam yanked open the basement door and Indy fell flat onto the pretty kitchen tile. Pam looked like a character from Top Gun in mirrored aviator sunglasses. She helped Indy back up. Pam moved her face as close as Kris's had been just moments before. Indy held her breath against Pam's foul smell. She was throwing hot and stink like a kerosene heater crammed with fish heads. From so close, Indy could see, peeking out along Pam's hairline, glowing scale-like filaments framing her face. Indy froze.

They had not been there yesterday.

Pam whispered.

I've found better friends.

Pam pushed her Maverick sunglasses up onto her forehead. She stared deeply at Indy. Or at least, her eye sockets were aimed in her direction. Indy could see all the way into her eye sockets because they were free of normal human eye meat, yet they were not entirely empty. Pam's eyes were synesthesia made manifest: growing in barber pole arrangement from the fleshy inside of her sockets were cilia, pulsing rhythmically. Indy, locked into this asymmetrical staring contest, forgot to breathe. Until her own heartbeat became deafening.

Indy realized it was her own heartbeat that Pam's new eyes were keeping rhythm with.

Indy's arms moved faster than a bird wing in flight. She swung around and jammed her shotgun into one of Pam's horror eyes and fired.

Kris threw himself over Indy to protect her, covering both their heads with his long hair and sinewy arms. A hot mist soaked him first, followed by a dagger rain of bonier things. They were drenched. Protruding from the wetness were the softly glowing hair-like things that had been Pam's eyes. They burned and itched terribly. Indy crawled out from under Kris, reaching for the basement doorknob, coming far enough into the kitchen to see three crayfish-zombies chewing something at the kitchen counter. She pulled the door shut. Within seconds the bony scrape of them was against the door, like impatient dogs.

At least, Indy thought, we are done with Pam.

By the time the things Indy had blasted out of Pam's eye sockets had been plucked from Kris's arms, there were enough crayfish-zombies scraping at the basement door to make her need to raise her voice to be heard.

Is there any other way out of here?

Kris nodded and took the stair down sideways and three at a time. He led her through the basement past snowboards, hundreds of copies of National Geographic and a corner entirely devoted to making semi-precious stone jewelry. Finally, passing even more sporting equipment of varieties Indy could not easily name – a lacrosse stick? – they reached stairs leading up to another door.

This door goes to the back yard. If we make it across the field to the woods we can hide. Figure out where to go. Maybe to my grandparents' house on Balmy Beach road. They have a sailboat.

Those things we pulled from your arms were Pam's eyes.

Look, there are probably people somewhere working on a cure.

All the teenagers who specialize in biochemistry? Or is it all the eighty year olds who haven't yet retired?

Indy kneeled on the stairs below Kris. She put her hands on his shoulders. She looked into his eyes in a way she hoped looked affectionate because it was. But it was also an eye exam.

I want to find my dad. Before anything happens to me.

Kris nodded and smiled sadly, leaning down towards Indy. A strange feeling passed over her but was gone before she could name it. The basement door they had left crashed open. Kris unlocked their current door, heaving himself into it and dropped into a dead sprint. Indy kept up more easily this time. They fled Kris's yard, past two more things Indy had never seen in real life: a hammock and a trampoline. They leapt over a thigh-high line of boxwoods into the one-acre empty field behind his house.

The dry summer grasses of the field re-opened Indy's old cuts and forged new violations. There were no bugs. No grasshoppers dryly charging her face as she disturbed their perches. Halfway across the field, Kris took Indy's hand and they were running like that across bright gold, hand in hand, when a bomb exploded over their heads.

The runners dove into the brittle grass sea. Indy, spitting toothpick bits of grass out of her mouth, rolled over and cautiously peeked up.

The tank turret was wheeling in their direction. Indy only realized her hand was still in Kris's when he pulled her to her feet. They ran. Risking a glance over her shoulder, she saw the tank rolling on its tread after them. Another explosion knocked her hand from Kris's, and off her feet. It also must have knocked her out because when she woke Kris was standing over her and talking to someone. Indy could not hear because her ears were ringing. She noted briefly cassette tape-sized shrapnel protruding from below her hipbone, deep in the meat of her thigh. She yanked it out.

Eldon was addressing Kris from the hatch of the tank. He was gesturing wildly. His pigtail beard grazed and caught the top of the hatch as he spoke. The main gun of the tank was aimed at Kris. When Kris spoke, Indy finally began to hear.

We don't know where your granddaughter is. We left her with you.

Eldon vanished down the hatch.

85

Kris looked back to Indy and shrugged. He took Indy's hand.

Eldon popped back up from the hatch of the tank. Cradled in his arms, mostly headless, was Pam.

Eldon's face turned upwards, his mouth opened wide and he screamed a plaintive but wholly human scream. Finished, Eldon dropped Pam's lifeless body back down into the tank. The setting sun slid out from behind the clouds and lit up the dry yellow field.

WHICH ONE DID THIS?

Kris opened his mouth, but before he could speak Indy summoned her well-rehearsed yelling voice.

I DID!

The next events pulled time apart. Each moment sank dreamlike, unstoppable. The main gun of the tank vanished behind a fireball. Kris slammed into Indy, his torso knocking her breath and her verticality away. Only once she was prone on the ground, crisp grasses again on her tongue, did the sound of the blast register, like a memory.

Kris had landed face up, heavily on top of her. It was hot under him. It felt safe. She felt his blood before she saw it. Where their tears had been, not long before, she felt his bloody wetness. She languished there in the ignorant closeness for too long.

She dragged herself out from under Kris. Searching to see where to staunch his blood flow, she found an un-pluggable fist-sized hole in his chest. A hole meant for her. Her hole.

Time congealed around Indy's considerations. She stared into Kris's bloody hole. Eventually she bolted. She made for the opposite side of the tank, trying to outmaneuver and blind Eldon with the setting sun. She heard the turret wheeling.

Reaching the rear of the tank, Indy charged, her long arms reaching the hatch door. The turret quieted. The heat of the machine warmed her as she scuttled up behind Eldon. She had lost her shotgun somewhere in this latest battle, so all she had for a weapon was herself, fuel-injected by rage. Her hands curved into crayfish-inspired claws and she hooked them neatly into Eldon's face pigtails from behind. She yanked.

Eldon's hands flailed behind him, striking poorly. He tried to scream but the angle of his head relative to his neck squeezed it down into a gurgle. Indy grunted, dragging him from the tank by his beard. She pulled him more than halfway out. His hands continued to flail. Indy dropped to her butt on top of the tank and wrapped her legs around his neck.

Indy hugged her thighs together and dug through Eldon's beard for his chin. It felt gross, his filthy beard gathered in her palms, like using the kitchen tuffy to scrape Shake 'N Bake goo from the rusty cookie sheets her mother used. Eldon's hands beat the air behind him. One or two weak backward flails connected painlessly with her upper thighs.

A disappointingly soft pop preceded Eldon's arms dropping lifelessly down.

Indy cautiously released Eldon's chin from her grasp and spread her thighs. His head lolled back at a disastrous angle. Indy pulled him fully out of the tank by his forearms and shoved him over the side. She jumped down beside him and gave him a kick. And another.

She sprinted back to Kris.

Kris was there. The hole that should have been hers was still there. Indy kneeled beside him. In mere days, he had made her feel safe enough to speak of her father in ways she never had been able to, even to herself. And he had awoken in Indy a longing for things she had not known she even lacked. Physical touch. Hand holding. Hugging. Harpsichord and sardines, hammock and trampoline. Her first affectionate touch since sitting on her father's lap as he drove around, his Export beer in her toddler hands.

Kris had unquestionably, variously, thoroughly saved her life. Indy leaned in to press her lips to his. His lips were still warm, almost as warm as the tank had been. She traced her tongue along the outline of his thick lips, tasting sardines, memorizing their feel.

Indy sat back up, and though the sun was mostly down, the air was glowing. It was too soon for stars. Disoriented from the final kiss, it took Indy a moment to recognize that far up in the sky above her were more fireflies than she could possibly count. Enough to screw up dusk. It was spectacular. She rested her hand on Kris's forehead lightly, absorbing his receding warmth.

Lost in the romantic moment, Indy failed to defend herself as the tower of fireflies fell upon onto her, slicing stinging razor wounds into her body, through her clothes and hair, into her back and scalp.

This was not a swarm of fireflies.

These were crayfish-zombie insects. All the varieties of insects, undead and sporting razor thin carapaces that glowed and cut.

Indy leapt to her feet but could see nowhere glow-free to run. There were weaponized grasshoppers, wasps, no-see-ums and mosquitos everywhere. All the dusk insects swarming around alighting on and slicing into her with their X-Acto blade wings and bodies.

She squeezed her eyes shut for fear of losing them. She staggered forward as slowly and calmly as she could. They tangled in her hair and swarmed on her back. She held one hand out ahead of her while swatting things with the other. Her swatting hand was wet with what she assumed must be blood. She swallowed her screams instead of a mouth full of blades, pressing her mouth into a tight line. Failing any other solution, Indy broke into a run, hoping to outpace the crayfish insects.

In four quick strides her front foot caught on something meaty. She flew headlong into cooling tank metal, knocking herself out.

Indy was awake before she opened her eyes. Her first thought was that she was dead and asleep in her very own cocoon, nestled inside thousands of layers of papery whiteness. She accepted her death and was snuggling into it and her skin answered with agony. Her stinging flesh cartographed new body territories. Unknown parts of her that heretofore had sent dismissible mediocre signals to her brain were now charted and needy. Is this being undead?

Indy opened her eyes.

She was in a huge vaulted room. The white warmth embracing her that she took for cocoon was a beam of sunlight pooling around her from a high and long window. The air was perfumed with Murphy's oil soap. Indy tilted her chin up. Behind her hung a teak Jesus, as skinny as her, but twice as tall.

Indy sat up slowly and gave her surroundings a name: church. She was on the dais of one of those new-fangled churches with ugly nineteen-seventies architecture. No historied stained glass, instead mindless blue industrial carpets. The pews were made of the same stuff as Jesus.

Indy had only been to church on a couple of occasions. Her mother had explained to her that church was something only people on TV did. Her only real world visit had been in grade 5 for a Christmas choir with the infamous and vile Mrs. Gowan. Indy had shown up wearing her Michael Jackson dress: a faux black leather mini dress with a silver mesh breastplate. When Mrs. Gowan spotted her on stage, she froze, her dry-lipped mouth caught between a sneer and a scream. She turned the color of the holly berries in the pattern of her muumuu. She did not speak, but pointed to the church doors and held her arm aloft until Indy started towards them.

Ring ring ring.

The sound of someone imitating ringing, not the sound of an actual phone, snapped Indy back into the present. It was ridiculous.

Ring ring ring.

Indy turned away from the scrawny Jesus towards the pews.

A teenager had materialized in the back row. He had his hand held up to his head the way you do if you are mimicking someone talking on the phone, with his baby finger as the receiver and his thumb as the earpiece.

The boy repeated the ringing sound again and nodded at her, saying in a gesture, please pick up.

Unsure of what else to do, Indy turned her right hand, swollen with angry red inch-long cuts, into a telephone receiver mirroring him, and held it to the ear she still had.

Hello.

In a high-pitched silly woman's voice, her caller answered.

Fin-all-ee. Never thought you'd pick up. I have a collect call coming in all the way from hell. From a pigtail-bearded Old Tank Driving Man. Will you accept the charges?

Indy stared.

Well, will you?

Uhm. Yeah. Yes. Yes, I accept.

The boy cleared his throat, bent his head and when he lifted it he spoke, in a voice that was more Foghorn Leghorn than Eldon.

I say now, I say is this that young lady who done me in?

Indy was unsure if this was interrogation or trial. She shrugged then winced at the pain along her shoulder blades as cuts grazed against tattered shirt.

I guess.

Do you guess or do you know?

It was me, yes. It was.

Then I got two words for you: fuck—

Cutting the boy off mid-curse, a cherub-faced girl with sleepy looking eyes and huge bangs sat up in another pew.

Scott! What did I tell you about talking like that in church! What would Pastor say?

Scott immediately hung up his hand phone.

Since you ran him over with your car I guess he'd say gurgle gurgle click.

The girl, ignoring Scott, skipped down the aisle to Indy. She wore denim overalls and mint-green Converse shoes with GLASS Sharpied on one, and TIGER on the other. She had the most impressive poufy bangs Indy had ever seen. She held out her child-sized hand towards Indy.

I'm Tiffany but you can call me Tiff. You've been passed out all day!

Indy was still holding her phone hand up to her face. She dropped it and stood. She loomed over Tiff, having at least seven inches on her, plus another two feet from the dais. She held out her hurt phone hand.

I'm Indy.

Oh, what a neat name. Like Indiana Jones?

Indy nodded. Her face flushed recognition.

Welcome to my church, Indy. What Scott is trying to say is thanks for stopping Tank Man. He killed most of our Bible verse memorization group at the grocery store.

Scott appeared behind Tiff.

He fired that effing tank at us for half an hour.

Tiff shot Scott a dirty look.

We screamed at him to stop and told him none of us were the possessed devils, but he couldn't hear us.

Oh, he could hear you.

We watched you charge Eldon after he killed your friend. It was glorious. We prayed for something to come between us and the evil. And here you are.

You saved me, though.

We just drove up and pulled you into our car. Tiff bandaged your head.

I did first aid for the Apostle Retreat in Burlington last year!

Indy raised her hand to her head and felt fresh fibers of a bandage across her lost ear.

You just can't go out at sunset anymore. You must be hungry, Indy. We haven't got anything too gourmet but we've got more than enough to share.

Tiffany hopped cutely up on the dais, passing Indy to open a door on the left side of Jesus. Scott, taller than Indy, stepped

93

easily up beside her and offered his hand. Indy shook her head and stood up awkwardly, changing the timbre but not the tone of her body, cutland.

Hope you know how to say grace.

Indy had never said grace in her life. She'd had only seen it on TV. Religious assholes, as Dana always said, deserved a fucking heartpunch.

Tiffany had gone into some sort of office and was sitting behind a desk that dwarfed her. Indy sat stiffly across from her in an orange plastic chair. Scott sat beside Indy. The desk had food. Pepperettes, Ritz crackers, Triscuits and a jar of Skippy. Indy's stomach roared loud enough to make Tiff giggle.

Scott offered Indy his hand again and she took it. Kris had been the last person to hold her hand. Tiff reached across the table for her other hand. Both teens bowed their heads and closed their eyes while Tiff murmured stuff about Jesus Christ.

At first Indy thought Scott had vinegar on his hands. Where their skin touched felt molten. It wasn't the cuts on her hands because the hand Tiff was holding felt slightly sore but in a regular way.

Indy looked and saw Scott's hand looked normal and dry. And strong and clean. She looked up and his piercing eyes met hers, sucking all the air from the room. Indy could not look away from his eyes while Tiff's prayer to her god about safety and food came to an end and Tiff let go of her hand.

Amen!

Scott let Indy's hand go and the spell broke. Her appetite had vanished, but she lived by her eating doctrine, so she loaded up a Ritz with a wad of Skippy. She struggled to put words together, sinking back into the quicksand of Scott's gaze. She could feel it searing into the bandaged side of her head. The bandages were no protection from him.

Do you know what happened?

Nope. We were planning on driving south to our sister church, but that Eldon dude trapped us in here.

Indy's head had become tungsten and Scott's every word and gesture, the current. Tiffany was still talking.

At least Eldon was God-fearing, unlike those possessed. He didn't try to blast us in here. Just any time we stepped out the door. I've been praying every day for His guidance and I think that is why He sent you, Indy. We're finally free to get to safety.

Indy, too afraid to look again at Scott, stared into Tiff's cherub face and thought no god sent me. God did not send me.

I know some things.

You do?

Scott leaned in close enough that Indy could see him in her peripheral vision. She struggled to calm her breath.

New York. It is the same. But millions of people. Worse.

Tiffany's face lit up.

I had a dream the world was ending when I was a little girl and us apostles would get to realize our predestination. That's why our entire youth group survived when no one else did.

But I am not part of your group. And Eldon.

Eldon was just our test. You saved us so we could save you. It's simple really.

But I've seen other survivors our age not part of your apostles.

95

Well, where are they now?

Indy said nothing.

Exactly. Gone. All part of God's plan.

Indy ran her hand across the church bandage over her lost ear.

There's something else.

If anything, Tiffany's smile widened.

The only other girl I've seen who was normal—

Scott swallowed hard.

Changed yesterday. And it was different. Her eyes disappeared.

Tiffany's smile shrank. Slightly.

She probably just wasn't baptized or something.

I've never been baptized.

Tiffany jumped up, squirting joy.

That's it. I can repay the favor you did us by saving you! There's a baptismal pool behind the altar.

Um. Can I pee first?

Scott sighed, smirked.

Of course. No peeing in the baptismal pool!

Scott held out his tingly hand. Indy grabbed it eagerly.

I'll show you our bathroom.

Numb, a marionette on Scott's strings, Indy stood. She let him pull her. She felt like she was giving in and it was profoundly comforting. She just let go. Scott horizontally controlled her through the door of the office and guided her down oiled teak steps. Halfway down, he produced a tiny Maglite, letting go of her hand to twist it. Indy ached for his hand until he took hers again.

At the bottom of the stairs was a pair of restrooms with swinging doors. One said Son, the other, Daughter. Scott, through tiny movements, guided her into the Daughter room. On the wall across from the bank of sinks hung a corny painting of an angel that looked very much like Tiffany, only with feathers in the wings instead of the bangs.

Scott put his Maglite in his mouth and lit candles with matches from the counter. He lined them up along the mirror behind the sink wall until his flashlight was moot. The musk of Ivory soap was heady. The toilet stalls were closed, but piled up inside, a line of milk jugs full of water was visible. Done with the candles, Scott emptied water jugs into the sink furthest from the door. Indy stood, hypnotized, transfixed and entirely relaxed. She sighed.

Having filled the sink, Scott took both of Indy's hands. She rejoiced. He removed her bandages as if they were fragile textiles and dropped them beyond candlelight. Dipping a fresh white washcloth into the water he moved her hurts, starting with her head, towards his cloth.

There was absolutely no pain.

Scott attended each gash left by razor-skinned insects. As he cleaned, Indy shivered with pleasure. His hands faltered on her pencil thin collarbones, lingering overlong.

Indy shifted her gaze anywhere, to the candles, to the taps, to their monstrous shadows. Scott set the washcloth against her ear. Or lack of ear. The same spot already cleaned once by Kris, then Tiff while Indy was unconscious.

97

Scott was no longer silent. He was no longer using the cloth; he was using his lips. With each kiss, he was saying, *and this will make it better, and this will make it better, and this will make it better.* She gave in and met his gaze to implore, please stop, to say loudly, no more, and instead his lips silenced her. Indy did not know who she was kissing – Scott, Kris, a zombie, and she did not care. Her wounded lips re-opened. She shared the taste of her blood with him.

Scott snaked his arm around her waist and turned her to face him. With the thumb of his other hand, he stemmed the flow of blood their kissing had opened on the slices through her lower lip. Indy brushed his hand away and kissed him hard, and more.

Scott's lips pulled back across his teeth in agony. He fell down onto the bathroom floor, writhing. She got to her knees beside him.

A glowing, fist-sized lump was attached to the back of Scott's neck like a succubus. He was clutching frenetically at it, hands slicking up with his own blood from where it was eating its way into him. Indy seized a candle and jammed it flame first at the glowing thing. There was a sizzle as the light extinguished, but no relief came to Scott, only more darkness and screaming. Indy removed her boot and gripped Scott's head to her flat chest in a headlock. She wore her boot on her free hand and beat at the glowing thing with the heel of it until it broke off.

Indy released Scott and he shrank away under a sink, nursing his neck. She bent to work pummeling the glow-ball. Scott joined her, his own shoe in his hand (a deck shoe with the cryptic word GWAR written on both toes in Sharpie). He stopped to focus his Maglite on their quarry.

It perhaps used to be a mouse. And now it was, like almost every other living thing, an all-new rotten version of itself. Dead yet defended, weaponized and mindless.

Indy put her boot back on her foot.

Scott grazed his fingers along her spine.

They both slid down to the tile floor and made out; it was the only thing that made sense.

***

Searching for Tiffany to warn her about the, as she would say, *possessed* mouse, the couple found her at the baptism pool behind the curtains on the dais where Indy had first woken up. Too obsessed with Indy's impending baptism to hear bad news, or even look at the gruesome gouge on the back of Scott's neck, Tiffany asked if Indy was ready.

Ordinarily, Indy would not have been. But this was no ordinary time. There was something thrilling about a new ritual because her old torturous rituals – Christmas, pot watering – were over. Besides, Indy thought, I need a bath.

Yeah. I guess.

Indy pulled off her soiled, mostly destroyed gold lamé blouse, revealing her white Sears undershirt. She kicked off her boots and socks. She hesitated, but then unbuttoned her ruined Fame pants and climbed up and over the wooden stairs, wading into the pool. It was about the size of an eight-person hot tub but perhaps a little deeper – just below Indy's non-existent nub breasts. The walls were scratched Plexiglas, like the dolphin pool at Marineland. The water was bright blue like Scott's eyes. The water was neither hot nor cold.

Indy waded into the middle of the baptismal pool.

Tiffany, not removing any clothes except her Glass Tiger Converse, joined Indy in the middle of the tub. But, because she was so short, she had to bob on her tiptoes to stay above the water line. Scott's eyes were riveted to Indy's chest.

99

Tiffany recited some stuff.

Don't you know that all of us who were baptized into Christ Jesus were baptized into his death? We were therefore buried with him through baptism into death in order that, just as Christ was raised from the dead through the glory of the Father, we too may live a new life.

Indy and Scott exchanged glances. According to Tiff, Jesus might be the original crayfish-zombie. Indy couldn't remember anything from the Bible about him having armored skin, but she had never read it, only watched cartoons like Davey and Goliath and sang religious songs in choir. That detail might be in there. Lost in her own musings, Indy was taken off guard when Tiffany dunked her underwater.

Indy splashed back up sputtering and coughing. Scott's laughter echoed.

***

Fresh and clean in all possible ways and wearing only a towel, Scott and Tiffany led a dripping Indy to the Alliance Church Thrift Store on the third floor. The special that day was everything 100% off. Indy's uniform was in ruins. It was more appropriate for bird watching than an apocalypse anyhow. She had to come up with something more appropriate. She settled on a pair of well-used Levi 501 jeans, a wife beater that was a little too small (from the children's department) and a golden sparkly button down shirt that fit like a glove in the torso but was, of course, too short in the sleeves. She even found a Northern Reflections backpack to carry the things Scott had recovered the day of her rescue.

Indy daydreamed about staying with Scott and Tiff as she tried on clothes. Of helping them destroy all the zombie mice and rats in the church and kissing Scott some more. Then she thought of Pam. And her father. She had to go.

The three sat down in the office again for, what Indy knew, was their final dinner. Indy scooped another wad of peanut butter onto another cracker and wondered how to tell them. Tiffany was so proud of baptizing Indy. It was as though she had become the church pastor. Scott kept 'accidentally' knocking into Indy and sending jolts of electricity up her spine. Indy decided the easiest, if not kindest, thing to do would be to steal away in the early hours of the next morning.

Indy did not know how to drive. When asked at their Last Supper together what the trick to driving was, Scott had explained to her how an idiot could do it. The '79 VW Rabbit Scott used to save her from the zombie bugs was parked in the Alliance Church lot. The car was pale blue, upholstered in brown vinyl and the keys were kept in the ignition because he'd already lost them in the huge church twice. Indy started the car no problem (she had already tried that when she was a little kid), but forgot to put the car from P into D. After revving the engine noisily a couple times, and fearing Scott and Tiffany would hear her and awaken, she remembered what Scott had described, and made a disgusted noise. Slipping the car into D, Indy at first jerked forward and then smoothly accelerated out of the lot.

Indy took side roads out of the city in the direction she knew to be west, hoping to avoid the twin dangers of car wrecks and crayfish-zombies she had witnessed on the main roads. The Alliance Church was in the outskirts of Eldontown, so it didn't take long until she reached the highway.

The highway was a disaster. The tininess of the car did not fully mitigate Indy's inexperience. She scraped up against almost every car and truck she passed, leaving streaks of pale blue behind her. Passing a red Honda Civic, a shell creature that might have once been a German shepherd, lunged at the car tires, losing its head underneath. After a sweaty forty-five minutes, Indy picked through the last of the apocalyptic pile up and found her way out onto a mostly clear highway 21. Fewer people drove these roads, so when the die-off came, nothing stopped the drivers from driving neatly off the highway, crashing into barbed wire fences and ditches. She drove under thirty-five miles per hour, as Scott had suggested new drivers do, until she got used to driving, and in case she met something she had to steer around or brake for. Only occasionally did she see a car that seemed to have rolled to a literal dead stop in the middle of the highway, door open and papery tatters of cocoon fluttering in the summer breeze.

She needed supplies. About half an hour outside of town, she remembered a Gulf gas station in the middle of nowhere. It was far enough from any village or town as to be ideally empty of any kinds of violent monstrosities. Forgetting exactly where it was, she drove by the Gulf station and had to brake and try backing up for the first time. She almost steered herself into a ditch, but was able to right herself by figuring out how to move the wheel opposite to what her instinct was when looking backwards. She parked as close as she could get to the door.

Only a month ago, she had been at this Gulf station with her mother and bought a Skor chocolate bar and a Dr. Pepper for breakfast. When Dana wasn't with them, her mother let her get treats. She hoped there would still be food there.

Opening the door with the barrel of her shotgun, Indy got hit by the stink of rotten milk. The ice cream cooler, with a sign proclaiming MORE FLAVOURS THAN BASKIN, had, of course, gone out and so had all the creamy contents. The Baskin-busting varietals had leaked all over the floor and made the greenish sticky mess Indy was standing in. Otherwise, it looked just as she remembered, only gloomier without the overhead lights. The Pepsi cooler at the back of the store was still partially stocked. The candy bar display under the cash register was picked over but, fantastically, the Skor bars were untouched. And there were Pepperettes.

Indy stopped short. Lining the shelf behind the till where the cigarettes should be, was a collection of … something. Not food. Not drinks. Indy took a few cautious steps forward to get a better look, her footfalls making sucking sounds as she tracked melted ice cream. The mystery things looked like a messed up fishbowl collection. As Indy got closer, she detected their soft glow against the gloominess of the back of the store.

It couldn't be.

103

Organized behind the till of the Gulf store, seemingly by size, was a collection of crayfish-zombie heads, cleaned entirely of their rotten human remains. Even worse, they were cut neatly, as if by saw, where the upper jaw enclosure had been. Changing them from contained Barbie Astronaut helmet into misshapen, open-ended fishbowls.

Beautiful, aren't they?

Indy swung around and took aim with her shotgun at a boy, not much older than ten. His hair was so tightly ringletted, it looked like handfuls of bedsprings. He was filthy and naked except for a pair of acid washed denim overalls at least two sizes too big for him. A paintbrush poked out from the front pocket.

You can shoot if you want, I don't mind.

Are there others?

Yes. Well, sort of. My brother Paul has become an armadillo and so I locked him in the cellar. You can see him if you want.

Take me to him.

Indy followed the boy across the ice cream puddle back out of the convenience store and around the side of the building. He stopped in front of a pair of rusted hurricane cellar doors, angled towards the earth. The doors had been chained and padlocked. Cautiously, Indy leaned in and listened. She could hear breathing.

Your brother?

Sort of. We called them all zombies at first. But Paul figured they aren't real zombies. Not like in the movies, you know?

I know.

All that extra hard skin. They creep up on you like the armadillos that lived in the parks around where I was born. When I was little I'd have nightmares about monsters under my bed. My mom would say, it's okay, it's just your imagination; in the real world there are no monsters. Then one day, I was four, playing in the parking lot behind Piggly Wiggly. I got chased by this cat-thing, but covered in pus-colored armor, clicking when it ran. It had mean beady eyes. I ran into the Piggly and told Mom I *saw* a monster in the parking lot. I took her outside to show her and she said silly, it's just like I said. There are no monsters, that there is just a 'dillo. So when she woke up again after being dead with armor that clicked when she chased me, I knew. I knew my mom was just an armadillo.

Indy put her hand on the boy's shoulder.

My brother was okay for a while. Stayed with me and we learned how to chop them up. Some folks used to eat armadillo, he said, but we wouldn't eat these. Still, we tried to make them useful. Until his eyes fell out and he locked himself there in the cellar and explained never let him go. I thought maybe because he was just blind but he explained he was worse than blind. I don't know *what* to call him.

Brian leaned face first against the rusty doors. He spoke into them.

He always was a good brother. The best. Smart. Smarter than anyone. He never did too good at school, but who cared. He'd investigate important things, not teacherly things. Like, last year he turned our basement into an ant farm so he could study their society. Until Mom found them and fogged the whole works with Raid.

He was good at fishing and hunting and collecting. He said these zombie 'dillos were no different than squirrels or other vermin, only more it was more crucial to understand them on account they can kill you where a normal 'dillo can only nip, and taste right in soup. At first I thought maybe he collected

105

the heads to make sure they were dead, or just so we could keep track like pelts and skulls. But he was making another important study.

The boy reached under the counter and pulled out a small black notebook and handed it to Indy, open to a folded page. Brian pointed halfway down the page and told her to read it:

The infection seems to make our largest organ, the skin, mineralize and become somehow chitinous like a lobster or other cephalopod's carapace yet even stronger, bioluminescent like a firefly beetle. At the same time the skin seems to become prime, growing without limits while the host rots within. After tests I even witnessed regrowth of damaged limbs that began with the external shedding of damaged areas and the emergence of fresh carapace beneath. Internally, mucosal membranes have also mineralized but to a lesser extent. This may lend itself to the wheezy pneumatic calls in a cicada-like fashion, I witnessed one creature vomit what at first appeared to be a thick cellophane sack but upon closer inspection seemed to be the j shape of a human stomach.

By now I'm good at breaking open and cleaning the heads too, just like I used to scrape pelts and fish skin. Only I use a soup ladle first to get the worst of it, then a teaspoon and a nail file and finally paint brushes for nooks and crannies. And then a good scrub and rinse. Everything is useful. Not good eating, but these 'dillo heads are useful so we shouldn't waste them.

Useful *how*?

The boy pushed himself enthusiastically away from the cellar door.

Let me show you.

He skipped back into the store, and Indy watched him clamber up onto the cash counter. He reached up onto the shelf of 'dillo head bowls and pulled the smallest one down. Carefully, he inverted it so that the mouth of the bowl was over his head like a halo and pressed his ringletted head into the opening of it until it popped on. He was wearing it just like a helmet.

Won't wearing that make you sick?

My brother said we've all been infected anyhow. So if we aren't sick, it's because we are immune. At least until, well, until we aren't.

Indy thought about the monstrous mineralized skins that had rubbed up against and cut deep into her. On her, in her mouth, and mixing through her blood. She was indeed already exposed and dirty.

The boy stood before her grinning from inside the monster head.

It's a shelmet!

The boy reached for another, larger shelmet and handed it to Indy. Reluctantly, she squeezed it on. She held her breath and squeezed her eyes shut. The smell was not fishy at all. It did smell mildly of lemon and vinegar. Indy opened one eye at a time. Everything was blurry and out of focus, like trying to see out of someone else's prescription glasses.

I can't see anything.

I have to customize it for you.

The boy pulled a Sharpie from his overalls pocket and bent forward on his haunches. He drew circles on Indy's shelmet over her eye area like he was making a jack-o-lantern. He colored in her eyes to the point where she was blinded. Indy pulled the shelmet off.

Now I just haveta drill out the eye area. Customized!

Indy mirrored back the boy's wide grin. But beneath her smile was rot. She couldn't leave this boy here alone. But how could

107

she deal with him all the way to Las Vegas. The odds of survival were less dragging a kid. Never mind how much her progress would be hampered in her race against time until she was killed or the eye disappearing sickness finally took her from her father forever. Stopping for twice the food and water, or trying to run with and save him in an attack while saving herself was daunting. All the ways she looked at it, it was going to be hard enough to survive and find her father on her own, let alone with a kid.

What's your name?

Brian.

I'm Indy. Do you have anywhere I can take you? Other family?

Yep. In New Orleans, or Lafayette. A grandma I haven't seen since Christmas. She gave me a Hot Wheels racecar set.

Nobody closer?

The boy looked puzzled. He jumped off the counter and grabbed a Pepperette, biting the end off and spitting it out on the floor like a cigar. He brightened.

Heck, yeah! I got a granddad in Detroit. I never met him since I was small, but my mama sent him my photo every Christmas.

A foamy relief tempered by the knowledge that this relative, too, might be dead. Or worse. Detroit was on her way to Las Vegas.

Brian, how would you like to see him again?

Brian spun around on his heels and squealed.

Mid-spin Brian stopped. He looked worried.

Listen.

Indy's relief at having found a solution to the Brian problem wavered.

I need you to do something for me.

Indy nodded her head slightly.

My brother explained to me how even though Mom and Dad were walkin' around still, it wasn't really them. They're dead and gone and you can see them in there, sort of, but it isn't like they used to be on account of how they look all rotten and ropey, like the Tupperware of Caesar salad I left in my desk at school one time. I could recognize that it was salad, but I wouldn't want to eat it. I could recognize Mom but I wouldn't want her to hug onto me like she used to, or read to me or nothing like that.

Indy tried to push her hair behind her non-existent ear.

Paul said our parents weren't really even dead. Like, dead but in prison, locked inside armadillo skins. I argued that maybe one day somebody from the TV, or back home in America, would figure out a way to put everything right. Peel them like bananas maybe. But then Paul said you can't fix rotten. Mom was grey when she used to be golden. Her eyes didn't recognize us. Her jaw just worked up and down, up and down all day saying nothing.

Brian, what are you asking?

Ok. Well. Paul, he set our parents free. I need you to set him free.

Indy bowed her head.

And Miss Indy?

Indy smiled, impressed and surprised at such politeness coming from a boy. Brian took the smile as agreement.

109

I know it's asking heaps, but I need you to take his head off. Just to be sure he's gone. He asked for that specifically.

Drawing her hatchet from her Levi's loop, Indy laid her hand on Brian's head, feeling grown up. It was a good feeling. She breathed an affirmation that said she did not find it unimaginable that the boy needed her to take off his beloved brother's head.

***

Well, hello.

Paul smiled coolly because it was impossible to smile warmly without eyes.

I guess my brother sent you.

He tossed his head, shifting his thick curly mass of hair, coiled bedsprings like his brother's, away from his face. His eyeholes glowed.

Indy knew she had to do this fast. He could call for backup like Pam had. But it was weird. Besides the lack of eyes, he seemed very normal and nice. Cute even.

I'll just tell you – do it quick, because I'm fighting, but I want to chew your entire face off.

Paul paused, cocked his head, and fell on Indy. He rammed his tongue down her throat, and cupped her face with his hands. She opened her eyes briefly and searched his sockets. Twin plum-skin colored holes, tissue knitted with bioluminescing veins and pulsing hairs. Their pulses matched her heartbeat exactly. His fever-shot tongue carved Indy's mouth open. He tasted like spring in Tara, the Saugeen River's swollen season.

Indy broke first; Paul stepped back. He licked his lips. Indy sniffled and swallowed hot bile.

Indy emptied her shotgun into Paul's chest as politely as possible.

He was knocked down. She put him between her feet and rapidly hatcheted his, as Paul himself would have explained, imprisoned head away from his imprisoned body. Oily blood pooled around his head. His arms scraped through the air, glancing a couple of times off Indy's outer leg. Indy was thankful for the protection of her new and improved Alliance Church uniform. Unlike crayfish-zombies, Paul's head was simple to cut off. Like normal movie zombies.

Indy repositioned his severed head atop his neck, as though trying to repair his mortal wound. She kissed his cheek. She said sorry. She sproinged one of his ringlets.

This was the first time Indy had completely beheaded someone not wearing the crustacean armor. Eyes closed, he looked merely human – the human who had thought through the ideas and made the arguments for Indy to do this finally final thing to him.

Indy and Brian spent the night within the protection of the store's four by four walk-in freezer. It had been built to hold the Baskin-beating back-up ice cream tubs. Inside the milk stink assailed them. Yet the rankness of fouled milk was perfume compared to the dangerous smells of crayfish-zombies. Or 'dillos. They made their bed atop a floor tarred with a rainbow of ice cream sludge.

Brian and his newly beheaded brother had set up the bedroom inside the freezer by placing cardboard over the sludge and sleeping bags on top of that. Once the door closed, nothing could get them. Two Mason jar candles lit the space once the door was sealed. Safe from all forms of crusty monstrosity, human-sized to insect smallness, Indy fell asleep instantly. She had not felt so safe since the night in Kris's basement. She might have slept for a week if it had not been for Brian playing with her hair the next morning.

Indy opened her eyes to see Brian inches away, searching.

What?

I'm checking. Paul told me I could only trust kids young like me or old like grandma. Especially not teenager girls.

Brian?

Yeah?

Do my eyes look anything like his did?

Not yet.

Past dawn and the danger of 'dillo insects, Brian and Indy filled twelve jerry cans with gasoline from his family's pumps. They loaded them into the Rabbit, keeping a shotgun on the roof. Brian outfitted Indy with his dad's revolver and holster belt from their time living in Louisiana. In return, Indy gave Brian her hatchet. They packed the back seat to the roof with bottled water, Pepsi and Canada Dry, Snickers and Skor chocolate bars, Hostess chips and homemade meat sticks.

My mom made the best meat sticks.

Indy patted his arm and he turned into her, draping his arms around her shoulders and back. He squeezed.

Indy pulled the boy closer.

Brian was the one who broke the embrace to point across the road.

A 'dillo dog! I saw it yesterday too.

Indy opened the car door and shoved Brian in. The 'dillo dog was noisily working towards them from about twenty feet away. It moved stiffly in that 'dillo way, head low and dead even with the back. Indy aimed carefully with the shotgun and fired. A grey mist replaced the thing's head. The body took a few more steps and then fell over in a creaking heap.

Indy opened the driver's side door, handed Brian the roadmap with the route to Detroit traced out in red Crayola, and dropped into her seat.

Ready, navigator?

Indy hoped her confident smile was convincing. She leaned back and her head came to rest against the shelmet Brian had fit snugly over her headrest.

Am I ever!

Brian popped in his favorite tape: Mary Poppins. She was singing A Spoon Full of Sugar. He sang along.

Indy knew the words but she just hummed softly. Driving was so new, and the way so potentially lethal, she had to focus all her thoughts on keeping the Rabbit on the road.

You know what, Indy?

No, what?

That shelmet behind your head?

Uh-huh?

That one. It used to be my mom.

Chapter 14: The Body, Mirrorland

I dance to the clicks of their skin. – Magic Andrew

A wiry smooth-faced teenager with hair the color and shape of flame, recited nonsense poetry between precise hackings at 'dillo heads. He was using the largest maul Indy had ever seen. It was almost as long as nine-year-old Brian was tall.

Indy and Brian had taken the gift of Ontario land settlement patterns – easy to follow grid-work concessions – and shifted roads when tractor crashes or combine jackknifes hindered their progress. They avoided every settlement larger than a hamlet. Dog-like 'dillos and birds with double wing-sets like dragonflies menaced them but could not penetrate the Rabbit. The dog-like creatures scraped uselessly against the vehicle body and then were behind them. The birds, impinged by carapace, flew like fat chickens in brief clumsy gallops at the car, only to be ground to mealy pulps under their wheels. Only because the car kept driving could Indy assume no vital car organ had been ruined by the attacks.

Testing herself as a driver, Indy sped up until suburban Windsor swallowed the concessions. Eventually, the roads became congested enough to slow her down again. Indy had had to get out of the car to push a rusted Pontiac out of their way. She opened the driver side door to shift it into neutral causing a cocoon remnant blizzard. Indy shook off cocoon dandruff, disgusted.

Her rib bones felt the 'dillo alarm before she heard it. Her jaw itched with the vibrations.

Racing back to the car, she saw a group – Brian called them a disaster – of shell monsters stumbling across the field towards them. Indy counted the rounds in her pockets, and in the box at Brian's feet. Eighteen. Her heart sank. There were far more 'dillos than rounds. If she never missed she could probably finish off the last couple by hand. Brian leaned across the driver seat with his mother's head – now Indy's shelmet – in his hands.

Put this on.

Indy snugged into her shelmet and looked out her newly carved eyeholes in time to see the strange redheaded boy running flat out at the disaster wielding his gigantic maul.

Indy fell in with him, and when she was close enough to aim, she stopped, slowed her pounding breath and calmly began firing. Her first two shots were low, serving only to slow the lead creatures down and blast massive leaks in their carapace. The redhead took full advantage and popped their heads open like cruel water balloons filled with congealed oatmeal.

Indy was impressed. She got close enough for him to shout mid-strike at her.

Hello. I dance.

And then, upon direct connection with a shelled head, he finished his poem to her.

To the clicks of their skin.

Over and over, this was his refrain. Indy dropped a few by gun and one by hand. In the end, they were both sweaty and heaving. The redhead was smiling despite being splattered with reeking goop. Indy was glad for the protection of her shelmet, sparing her hair and hooding her eyes. He lowered his maul and pulled a shard of carapace out of the tender nook of his clavicle. He did not even wince. He held his bloody hand out to Indy.

I'm Andrew, but you can call me Magic.

Wiping her sweaty hand off on the hip of her Levis first gave Indy a moment to pause and think. She looked down at his gore-soaked hand. She finally chose to take it in her own. She squeezed as hard as she could.

I'm Indy. How'd you do that?

Practice practice practice. Just above the ear line is a weak spot. Like a flaw in blown glass. If you connect, you get lucky. I call it their G-spot.

Indy blushed hard, so hard she knew Magic Andrew could see it even through her shelmet. She pulled it off. She craned her neck around to check on Brian and hide her flushed face, shaking her hair out so her missing ear was covered.

Magic Andrew stepped into her sight line and ran his filthy hands through his startling red hair, perhaps to clean them. He stared intensely at her with his human eyes.

What the hell did you have on your head?

Indy explained to Magic as they walked back to her car and Brian.

This is my shelmet maker.

Did you get any heads?

Not wanting to disappoint Brian, she ignored his question. Razor sharp dusk was only a short time away. They had already averted one disaster and Indy was too spent to face another.

You two are welcome to stay at my cabin. It is made entirely of wood, no nails at all. So we can trust it.

Indy took a deep breath. She stared back at the carnage behind them. They seemed to be on the same side so far. She accepted Magic's slightly odd offer to stay at his metal-free cabin.

116

As they packed up what they needed from the Rabbit for the night with Magic, who was standing just out of his earshot and watching for 'dillos, Indy asked Brian what she thought of him.

He's good at killing 'dillos.

Yeah.

Yeah, but I don't know if I trust anyone who calls themselves *Magic*. Here, I don't think I could ever use it anyhow.

Indy sighed deeply and slid the hatchet she had given Brian back into her belt loop within easy reach. Magic was not what they needed right now. Sleep was.

***

On the half-mile hike from down a dirt path to the cabin, Indy began to feel more and more the girl virgin victim in a horror film. Magic explained on the walk that he had been born in Toronto but his parents had retreated to the woods off the grid long before the apocalypse. Magic Andrew's cabin was made of logs. It was rough, like a hunter's cabin and not made for year-round living, but for temporary shelter while stalking deer. It had never had electricity or plumbing. It had a woodstove and unlit Christmas lights strung everywhere. He explained it had been a rogue Dukhobor cabin – a Russian immigrant group usually only found on the west of Canada who were skilled at building stuff with no nails. Magic had grown up using wood energy for everything, so his talent with the maul had been earned: he had borne the sole responsibility for chopping wood since he was old enough to walk. My dad, he explained, was the captain here, and I was the crew who followed orders so they could all survive.

There was an outhouse. Magic Andrew explained his outdoor bathroom had the Best Toilet View in the Universe. In other words, no door, and facing the woods. He explained his cabin was the safest place on Earth because his parents had planted concentric circles of trees emanating out from the their hearth and had these rings blessed by a monk.

Inside, the cabin was dark and smelled familiar. Indy was unsurprised when Magic plopped down on a red velvet couch and tilted green sticky contents from a jar out onto a wire spool coffee table.

Where do we sleep?

Magic gestured upwards without taking his eyes off the joint he was rolling.

Indy took Brian's hand and led him up the slippery wooden stairs, holding on tightly because there was no railing. The second floor was covered almost entirely by three large bare mattresses. Likely from the roadside or dump, Indy deduced, from the density of the stains. Three skylights made the upstairs brighter in a weak starlit way. Flung helter skelter on top of the old mattresses were matted sheepskins of varying sizes. Indy led Brian to the closest bed and they both lay down. Brian leaned in close to whisper.

I think we should take turns sleeping.

Don't worry. There's no way I can sleep.

A smell more disturbing to Indy than the fish-borne rot of the 'dillos floated up the stairs. Pot. The front door thumped. Moments later the sound of an engine started and the strands of multi-colored Christmas lights glowed on, turning the cabin festive.

Indy's heart leapt upwards. Magic Andrew had started a generator. Monk blessed rings of trees aside, making that much noise would attract some sort of unwanted attention. Crazed semi-human, hungry former-human or some horror that would hurt them.

Another sound joined the generator. It reminded Indy of her stepfather's fence building. It was the grind of a power tool.

Brian, stay here and sleep. One of us should.

Indy silently descended the stairs. The cabin artwork was now more visible. In the Christmas light, Indy catalogued the details of dozens of paintings and drawings. Each piece was of a different size and composition, but all were unmistakably of the same subject: Magic Andrew himself. The art at the bottom of the stairs depicted Magic with a halo made from a crown of thorns. All the artwork depicted Magic with crowns suspended over his head, some of thorns, some of gold, and still others, pot leaves. One was a crown of eyes and hatchets. One was a thick weave of bright white bones.

Indy had been raised atheist, but had watched enough Sunday morning television to know that these paintings of Andrew were him as Magic Jesus.

From the cabin door, Indy could see a cloud of white dust coming from a wooden outbuilding behind the cabin. Slipping her hatchet from her belt, she approached the outbuilding door. Inside she saw Magic, in a cloud of white that reminded her of baby powder. He was stooped over a vice that was connected to a large wooden table. In the vice was a piece of something white about the length of a butter knife. He was using a drill to bore out the center of the knife-sized white thing in the vice.

The drill noise and dust obscured her approach, and Magic did not yet seem to notice Indy. She fretted about how to let herself be known without startling him when he spoke.

So you've come to watch.

Indy flinched. She was pretty sure she had not come to watch but ascertained that he liked the idea and decided to go with it. She dropped her hatchet into her belt loop on the back of her pants.

119

Yes!

She watched for an excruciating thirty heartbeats.

I wonder, is it safe making all this noise?

Magic Andrew stopped drilling. The only noise that remained was the drone of the generator working away somewhere below them.

Magic looked at Indy and then down at his work. He unscrewed the vice and freed the white thing he had been drilling and tossed it at her. Her brand new shell-monster honed reflexes did not disappoint and she caught it mid-air, if only by the tip. She turned it over in her hand so she could feel it and look inside. It was a familiar texture. It was a bone. He had been drilling out the marrow and polishing the outside. Indy resisted the urge to fling it back at him.

I'm making chillums.

Indy had no idea what that meant, but felt sure it had something to do with smoking pot. She dug deep to find some enthusiastic tones.

Neat.

Yeah. Waste not want not, I always say. Take a look and help yourself if you want to pitch in, I have an endless supply.

Magic gestured royally towards the corner of the room.

In the corner there were dozens of burlap sacks, stuffed to the brim. She opened the top one and untied the twine bow that had been keeping it closed.

A flesh-free human skull stared vacantly up at her. Not a 'dillo head. Not a rotted, long-dead human skull retrieved from inside a 'dillo head. No. Just a normal human skull, like the useless one on her shoulders.

120

In all of her 'dillo hunting, Indy had not encountered any hard carvable human bones. They got brittle, like an octogenarian with osteoporosis, as they rotted away in there. As though the human corpse inside was being used like yolk.

Dread fell like a wet wool shawl onto Indy's shoulders. She was not sure what was going on but every nerve in her body was screaming *run*. Killing and evading the shell beasts was one thing, but she had watched Magic Andrew drop dozens of them with a gifted dexterity that had, well, seemed like magic. It had impressed her. She was not sure if she could best him. She knew she could not. She needed to run.

I am supposed to protect Brian, Indy thought, but my lack of care might have killed us. She had been so tired and eager to accept a safe place to sleep because a night in the car seemed so uncomfortable. Worse still, her stupidity might have gotten them turned into a horrifically fancy way to get Magic high.

She refused to become marijuana paraphernalia.

Leaving the sack of human bones, she wished Magic would start drilling again because she knew he could hear her heart pounding in her chest. She set the human bone chillum thing down on Magic's table and crossed the room to the door in a single movement. She had to get Brian and get out of this nail-free, blessed place.

Indy's ears had closed up. All she could hear was the sound of her own blood working.
She fled the outbuilding, hatchet handle swinging from her belt loop and slapping her ass as she ran. She found Brian in bed asleep.

RUN.

Brian only blinked. Indy slapped him roughly.

NOW.

Indy had never felt anyone press a penis into her so, despite Andrew choking her to death, she was caught up in that sensation. His body weight flattened her diaphragm; his leather hands engulfed her neck. She writhed under him, slapping his trousers and shirt. The room filled with human bone dust. I survived my childhood. I survived 'dillo attacks and Eldontown – to be killed by Magic?

Waves of unconsciousness lapped at her until she was drowned.

She woke with a falling sensation and jerked hard against her sock-bound ankles and wrists. She felt a chill against her legs and opened her eyes to see that she was prone on the bed wearing only her shirt and Willy Wonderful balloon underwear. Magic was kneeling at the foot of the bed, squinting as he lit a joint.

I am going to hold you down and force you to smoke, okay?

It doesn't make any sense to ask permission to force me, Indy tried to say. Her voice was too hoarse from the choking he had administered, so it came out as mumbles.

She repeated herself with little improvement.

Magic sucked on the end of the joint to make the plant matter catch fire and held the smoke in his lungs so long Indy hoped he had given himself brain damage bad enough to forget his assault on her. He finally exhaled and blew the smoke in her direction. He pulled his dusty shirt off over his head. He was wiry and looked made of only bones and steel wool. His chest was a tattoo of a cartoon pelican giving the thumbs up. Indy fought tears. She did not want him to see her weak. He stood up, joint in his mouth, and dropped to his ripped Wranglers knees. He undid them. He was commando. Indy had never seen a naked boy or man other than John Lennon in her mother's only Playgirl magazine she kept on the bookshelf in the living room. It featured a series of photos with him and Yoko, posing on Astroturf.

Magic dropped to his hands and knees between her feet and crawled up her. His face was slack. His penis, unlike Mr. Lennon's in Playgirl, was pointing at her. He was dragging it up Indy's legs, bouncing it off first one of her calves then the other. He buried it in her thigh meat, grazing her balloon rider underwear. He paused at the point where her legs met, pushing between her thighs at the spot where the balloon riders sank below sight onto the gusset. He lifted his hand to take a drag of his joint. He continued upwards along her abdomen, bouncing from her ribs to her bony sternum.

Indy pressed herself into the mattress to get away from him. She was trying to disappear. Using his thighs, Magic was able to pin her bound arms to her body. He dug his knees into the soft meat of her forearms. He sat comfortably down on her sternum, compressing her ribs into her lungs and making it nearly impossible to breathe once again. Indy saw sparks as her already shallow, painful breaths receded. He deliberately poked his erect bright pink penis into her face, slapping her lips, her nose. Indy shut her eyes to block him out and twisted her head around to avoid it. He grabbed the top of her head by a handful of hair, twisting it back to control her face and mouth. Hair-wrenching her neck up off the bed, he jammed his penis into her mouth. She pressed her lips tightly closed, even though it made breathing impossible. He pinched her nose. Spittle flew from Indy's tightly pressed lips and snot glistened from her nostrils. She opened her eyes wide to plead with him and instead witnessed a bead of clear liquid drop from the end of his urethra to her chin. Moments from unconsciousness, Indy's mouth flew open. She took one gasp of air and Magic shoved his cock down her throat. She gagged and vomited stomach acid and swallowed it back down, along with the length of his cock.

Magic unpinched her nostrils and took a deep drag on his joint. He hunched down so he could blow the smoke into her.

123

It smelled exactly like her stepfather.

She bit down as hard as she could.

Magic Andrew crumpled back as though gut-shot.

Indy's mouth was filled with the savory taste of blood.

Magic curled up at the foot of the bed, hands a cradle for his bitten part.

Indy felt burning. It was Magic's lit joint on her chest. She sat up and rolled over, knocking it off. Face down, she swung her legs off the bed and came to stand on her knees, balancing awkwardly and squirming against her bondage.

How could you?

Andrew was hunched protectively over his genitals, his face reflective with tears.

I'm handicapped, you know? See this? That's blind! I'm blind in one eye.

Indy scanned the room for some way to cut her hands free. She had no idea how hurt Andrew was, how long he would remain incapacitated, and was pleasantly surprised that her bite had disabled him further.

Upstairs, there was nothing to cut her bondage. The wood stove downstairs would burn through it. Indy got to her feet and kangaroo hopped to the stairs. The slippery railing-less stairs were treacherous. If she hopped wrong, she might break her neck or worse, live but be hobbled enough to be further raped by Magic. At least her socks were off her feet affording flesh traction. Her first hop was almost her last as she overshot the top stair, slipping painfully from its edge to the second step on the meat of her heel. Air hissed out of her damaged windpipe through clenched teeth. Focused only on the next level down, she took the next hop quickly, fearing for balance. When she reached the final stair she could not take the final hop to the ground floor.

Brian lay crookedly against the last stair, his leg at a sickening angle. Indy lowered herself to her bum beside him, and losing no time despite overwhelming fear for both of them, lifted her feet over him. Using the last of her strength she stood again and made three quick hops to the wood stove. Turning around so her rear, and hence her bound wrists, faced the stove, she pressed her restraints against it. She could smell the cotton burn. And herself, too. Her underwear, mostly polyester, superheated her ass. Over the sound of the fire and roar of the generator, Indy thought she could hear footsteps upstairs. She yanked against her restraints, cursed and pressed into the iron stove harder, cutting off all instincts to yank herself away from blistering burns. Instead, she searched for comfort in the searing heat.

Yes.

Soundlessly, the socks that had been holding her fell apart. Indy bent to untie her ankles. Her infant-sized wrists were already blistered. It did not really hurt. She searched the room and spotted Magic's gigantic maul underneath the sofa. Dragging the maul, Indy ran for the stairs. She paused to lean over Brian's broken form just long enough to feel for a pulse.

He had one.

By festive light, Indy pulled Magic's maul up the stairs, bumping menacingly against each step.

Magic Andrew was administering to himself on the far side of the room, his back towards her. With no hesitation and only her face revealing the effort and strain involved, she hefted Magic's own maul over her head in a graceful arc as she crossed the room in two leggy strides. It connected exactly with the apex of his fiery red Magic head.

Indy had hit Magic's G-spot.

The sound the impact made was the same coconuts made when she used to crack them open against the tarred gravel blacktop in front of the trailer in Tara by climbing the telephone pole and hurling them down.

The maul got stuck. Indy had to wiggle it a little to release it. Magic's head rocked along with her wiggling, back and forth.

Indy had cracked Magic's head open. Not a big crack. Not yet. Blood only trickled from it.

Magic spun around, meeting her gaze with both of his eyes, even the handicapped one. One hand held his limp penis. Dragging the maul overhead again, Indy stopped short. Magic's eyes filled with fear and he was trying to talk.

Fuh!

It was as if by opening his mouth a tap turned to *on* in his throat. A glurt followed by a stream of blood poured forth from his mouth ruining his diction and obliterating his message. He kept trying.

Fuh Fu Fuh.

Indy grew bored waiting for him to make sense. She shut Magic up with an energy efficient chop to the left side of his neck, severing arteries and meat all the way through to the spine. Finally, he fell over, the weight of his upper body cranking the angle and deepening the wound on his neck until his head was all but removed and caught under him. He was still holding his penis. In a death grip.

Not so Magic now.

But she felt bad. Magic was the first entirely human person she had beheaded. First 'dillo, then Paul, now Magic. A worrisome progression. But all in the name of survival.

Brian moaned from the bottom of the stairs.

Dragging the bloodied maul after her, she returned to Brian. He was struggling to sit up. He was not bleeding anywhere, but one of his legs was wrong. He looked sickly and sweaty under the Christmas lights.

Indy comforted him. She pulled him gently off the last stair and arranged him as evenly as possible on the floor. His left leg was swollen. His forehead had a welt, and that seemed to be it. It was enough. Indy grabbed a filthy red velvet pillow, complete with crusty and unraveling gold fringe, and placed it under his head.

I am going to have to set your leg.

Indy had broken her arm when she was nine, about Brian's age. She had been tap dancing in her basement. Tap dancing was a concession. Indy had always planned on becoming a prima ballerina because of her favorite record, Tina the Ballerina.

Tina practiced every day, and one day traveled to gay Paris to see the ballet. When the prima ballerina fell ill, Tina was ready to awe the audience. Indy hated her life, but knew she must prepare for gay Paris-type moments. So she created a practice regime, dancing every day. Her ballet moves were gleaned entirely from the Tina album sleeve and her own experimentations in the basement of the trailer. Indy would run across the basement floor and, grabbing the poles that anchored the trailer to Earth, whirl around them, legs akimbo.

Since ballet was useless, expensive, and all classes were inconveniently located outside of Tara, lessons were impossible. Nonetheless, Indy begged her mother for dance lessons. Miraculously, in her eighth summer she was allowed to take one program of tap lessons in a town closer than Owen Sound. When it was over, Indy's mother convinced her she had completed training and could now continue on her own. The truth, and Indy knew it, was that Karen did not want to drive on Saturdays because it made Dana furious when she went anywhere useless. Or anywhere at all.

Indy, refusing to let her Tina-shaped dreams die, combined her ballet with her new tap dancing tricks.

One grim morning during tap practice, after Ashlee was born and school had let out for summer, Indy was practicing to her favorite album, Disco Duck. Mid-phrase TOE BALL HEEL STAMP, she lost her balance and fell. Her right arm instinctively shot out. The loud snap of her wrist sounded like a particularly sophisticated tap dance move.

Her wrist did not even hurt. Her hand hung at an angle that made it look like she was trying to touch the inside of her wrist.

Indy feared so deeply being in trouble for getting hurt, she stayed in the basement for hours trying to straighten her wrist. She pressed it to the cool concrete floor that had broken it, trying to flatten it out. But as the wrist swelled hotly to the size of a grapefruit, she saw sparkles and had to sit down for an unknown amount of time. When she roused, she found her mother, who was changing Ashlee's diaper, and simply held her right arm up in front of her mother's face.

Indy had been very curious and attentive when her wrist was set and cast in Owen Sound. Her mother had stopped at McDonalds to get them both burgers. The burgers made the bone doctor say the word fuck because he would not be able to give Indy any drugs to make her be still while setting the arm for fear she'd choke and die on her own puke. Indy, drug free, had nonetheless remained entirely motionless throughout the entire process. She was too busy paying attention to the doctor setting her arm to barf.

Indy gathered the supplies she would need to set Brian's leg.

It had hurt when her arm was set so Indy looked for painkillers.

Since there was no bathroom, she figured the kitchen would be where Magic kept his Tylenol. After rummaging through every cupboard and even the propane fridge, all she had were sacks of sprouting potatoes, a pair of coal miner's shoes, a dozen jars of plum preserves, and several jars of pot.

People like Magic only believed in one kind of pain relief: marijuana. How on earth could she make the boy smoke something when she'd never smoked anything herself? Indy emptied a jar of pot on the kitchen counter and crushed the sticky flowers up between her fingers, as she had watched her stepfather do for as long as she could remember.

She could not bring herself to roll the stuff. She decided it would be easier to make Brian drink a tea of it. After stoking the fire to boil water, made pot tea. Gingerly lifting his head, she wiggled under the boy so he could rest against her as she eased him up to a sitting position. The boy resisted drinking the tea at first. Indy had heavily sweetened the tea with sugar packets she found strewn around the dining room table.

C'mon, Brian.

Indy helped Brian sip the hot drug tea.

Brian. I have to ready things to fix your leg. Don't move.

With hooded eyes, Brian smiled.

I just got a little kid high. Indy was disgusted with herself. Not for moral or legal reasons but because it was her stepfather's nectar of ambrosia and the air freshener of her old life. If it was packaged and sold as a car air freshener, the image would be of Dana and the scent would be called Tara.

Indy stepped out of the cabin, listening. Hearing nothing, she sprinted back to Magic's workshop. She'd decided the best thing to set Brian's leg was also probably the worst thing.

Indy emptied a few of Magic's burlap sacks of human pipe

129

material. She sorted through the sacks, separating skulls from arm bones, tibia from fibula, until she had amassed a half dozen of the shortest femur bones. She filled a sack with her chosen bones and hefted it over her shoulder.

What better way to set a human femur correctly than with other human femurs?

Picking her way around the alarming number of bones she had dumped out onto the floor, Indy crossed back to the cabin. The rage that helped to kill Magic was gone. The hangover leavings of it were turning her muscles to jelly. Her eyes ached alarmingly.

Brian needed her.

In the cabin, she yanked down several strands of Christmas lights. Taking a deep breath, she sprinted upstairs. In the context of the apocalypse, it was not irrational to be afraid Magic would be back. She searched the room for attack or cocoon. Instead she saw Andrew's split and crumpled corpse sailing a dark lake of blood. Scooping up a sheepskin and her Levis, Indy spun around to the stairs.

Fully equipped and at Brian's side, she stared down at the boy.

I'm going to set your leg now. I'm sorry.

Don't be. You are wearing balloon underwear.

Indy blushed. Like her own doctor's nurses did, she neatly arranged her materials so that once she had pulled Brian's leg straight, she could rapidly and tightly bind it up.

I'm going to count to three and then I'm going to jerk your leg so very hard. It's going to really suck.

Brian giggled and rubbed his lips. Indy stood over the boy and leaned down, encircling his ankle with her long fingers.

One.

Indy yanked.

Brian screamed.

Sliding a sheepskin lengthwise under his leg, fur side in, she set to work on his human leg-bone cast.

Hands and fingers flying, Indy wrapped Brian's entire leg with sheepskin like a present. She lined up two femur bones on either side of his busted leg. Finally, with light strings, she bound her work together, wrapping it all slightly less tightly than she could. She stepped back. Brian had a new sheepskin appendage girded by bright white human bone. She wondered what it would look like lit up.

Sweat beads dotted the bridge of Brian's nose.

Careful not to disturb his leg with more side to side or up and down than necessary, Indy shimmied a leg bone under the Christmas lights at the front. Gingerly, she guided Brian onto his good side so she could fit a final bone splint in at the back of his leg. The fit was so tight Brian gasped. Indy whispered under her breath, and finished the job by rolling the boy gently over so he was lying flat out on his back again. She smiled as cheerily as possible.

Done.

Can I see?

Since he would soon have to try walking and, given their predicament, running on it, Indy helped him lift himself up onto his elbows so he could see his newly splinted leg.

He laughed, delighted.

I look like a cave man!

Indy had to agree.

Indy was barely able to get caveman Brian back to their car. It seemed impossible to dampen the boy's spirit. He had a puffy welt on his head and he would probably never walk properly again. Such a crudely fashioned cast was better than nothing, but Indy was no bone doctor. Half carrying the boy as he hopped along on his good leg prevented them from taking food from Magic's cabin, but she did manage to drag Magic's very own maul – a weapon both he and Indy had wielded to tremendous damaging success – by looping the head in a strand of Christmas lights and tying it onto herself. She had also managed to bring a jerry can of gasoline she'd found in the generator shed. She used it to balance the weight of Brian. The load made her gait silly.

After re-arranging the car and tragically tossing out a box of bottled water for Brian's comfort, they continued towards Detroit. Indy packed Magic's maul so the handle was in easy reach beside her seat.

Road conditions funneled them towards the downtown border crossing. The Rabbit was so small and maneuverable Indy was able to get around all but one, most certainly purposeful, obstacle. At the mouth of the tunnel to the American border and Detroit, someone or something had built a beaver dam-like structure out of prone and unmoving 'dillos. The pile was at least six feet high and thick. It completely blocked their passage.

Indy could see glimpses of the tunnel over and through the 'dillo dam. It had been entirely cleared of cars.

Don't move.

Indy stepped out of the car dragging Magic's maul behind her. The 'dillos in the dam were different. There was no evidence of any human remains inside them and they were in broken up pieces. A shell torso here, a carapace limb there.

Someone was shuffling up behind her. Indy swung around, maul raised.

What did I tell you?

I'm sorry. I had to see.

Brian was oily with sweat. He grabbed onto Indy's arm and leaned heavily.

Indy stood for a few moments in perturbed awe at the dam, Brian catching his breath beside her.

Who would do this? And why?

Why not? There's no TV anymore. A person has to fill a day.

Brian grimaced.

She looked behind, watching for movement, mulling over what to do.

Back in the car. I'm going to find a way around.

Indy watched Brian limp back to the Rabbit. Approaching Windsor's newest downtown attraction, 'Dillo Mountain, she tested its firmness by swinging her maul at it. A few 'dillo parts tumbled down the back of the mountain. She took a few more serious swings, gradually knocking off enough parts to carve out a side breach big enough for their little car to squeeze through. Indy strode back to the Rabbit. She enjoyed the sound it made as she revved the engine. Imagine, Indy thought, just over a week ago I couldn't even drive and now I'm stunt driving through obstacles. She let go of the brake and slammed into the side of the mountain. 'Dillo parts flew in all directions, raining down after them on the other side like the wrongest, worst hail ever. The carapaces were heavy, but not enough to dent the car.

Safely on the other side, Indy and Brian high-fived and entered the Detroit tunnel towards Brian's grandfather. Indy felt good. Having survived Magic, nothing could stop them. Perhaps they were on a roll.

Brian saw it first. Exiting the tunnel they rolled past the deserted Canadian border station. Indy made the turn towards America. Silenced by terror, Brian could only point out the passenger side window, frantically.

Perhaps because they stood so still it made them seem like a wall. Indy had failed to notice and now they were surrounded. Hemmed in. Indy had no idea when they had appeared but, looking in her rearview mirror, she saw they continued along both sides of the road as far back as the tunnel: 'dillos of all sizes lined the border road, undead sentinels welcoming them to America.

Hundreds of pairs of rotting eyes clocked their progress. As if responding to Indy's gaze, all jaws creaked open in unison. Lined up as far as she could see along the road, 'dillos chomped air hungrily, awaiting some signal to launch themselves at Indy and Brian.

Indy's throat tightened. She gripped the maul handle hard enough to turn her knuckles white. Could the Rabbit take such an onslaught?

Brian was no longer pointing to his side of the car. He was pointing ahead. Marching towards them in military formation was a midget army. Twenty or so little people, dressed head to toe in black. Even their tiny heads were covered in tiny skullcaps. One regular-sized person – also wearing black – brought up the rear. They were heavily armed with various normal-sized rifles and machine guns, dwarfing them further. Indy was tempted to put on the brakes to stop moving towards them. But then the deadly wall that surrounded them might descend and rip them apart. So she compromised and slowed down.

As the midget army got closer, Indy saw she was wrong.

Not midgets.

The midgets were children around the same age as Brian. Except for the tall boy bringing up the rear who seemed to be about Indy's age. The tall one raised his fist all the way in the air and brought it down to shoulder height. He yelled HALT. The children stopped.

Indy, knowing she should not, but unable to plow through a group of children, stopped, turning off the Rabbit so as to not waste gas. The children dropped to one knee and took aim at Indy and Brian as though they had been soldiers since birth.

The tall one, his teenage voice cracking, raised his rifle.

GET OUT OF THE CAR OR WE WILL ATTACK.

Seeing no other option, Indy opened her door and stepped out of the car, silently thanking herself for strapping her diving knife to her calf beneath her Levis while they were packing.

My friend can't get out by himself. He's injured.

The tall one marched to Indy, rifle aimed at her head. He was wearing Oakley Frogskin shades, the black ones she had always wanted but could never afford. Indy could see, peeking out from under his woolen skullcap, that he or someone had carved a crude backwards letter N in the exact same place that Charles Manson had carved his swastika: in the middle of his forehead. The children all had exactly the same letter-shaped injury in various stages of healing, some scabbed over and some fresh.

Tall Boy stopped a dozen feet in front of Indy. She stared into her double reflection in his Frogskins and contemplated how

136

lopsided and disgusting she looked with only one ear and the shape of Magic's hands bruised into her neck.

Tall Boy fired his rifle directly at her.

Instead of falling back as she expected, Indy remained standing. Oddly, she felt no blossom of heat or pain. Her hands flew to her neck.

Indy collapsed onto the 'dillo-lined road.

***

Indy awoke gagging on her own vomit. The dart she had been shot with carried drugs that made her sick. Rolling over to her side to clear her airway, she fell off the cot she was on. Once she had finished vomiting foamy bile, she sat up. Looking around she realized she was in a prison cell the same size as her bedroom in Tara. In lieu of faux oak paneling though, were three walls of cinder block painted dehydrated urine yellow, and a fourth wall made of bars. It was all the same to Indy.

BRIAN!

Indy got shakily to her feet. Her boots were gone and her bare feet were freezing. She called for Brian again and instead Tall Boy appeared. He unholstered his gun and unlocked her door. Pushing her out in front of him, he prodded her to an empty interrogation-type room with one mirrored window that Indy assumed was one way. Who or what, she wondered, was on the other side?

I want to know how my friend is.

Tall Boy pushed her to the corner and leveled his gun at her. Ignoring her question and releasing the safety on his gun, he asked his own.

Do you believe in God?

Indy stared blankly at him and thought of Tiff and Eldon. Recent events could make anyone get obsessed with any number of surprising things. But, at the same time, she had no idea if this guy was happy or angry with God in his obsessions.

I don't care. I was raised by people who kept me away from questions like that. Either way suits me fine.

Indy squeezed her eyes shut and waited for another dart or perhaps a bullet to rip through her skull. Nothing happened. Opening her eyes she saw Tall Boy still pointing his gun at her but looking at himself in the mirror.

Do you love America?

Tall Boy tried to but was unable to hide what was clearly a smirk making the corners of his mouth creep up.

I'm Canadian.

A knock at the door interrupted the bizarre interrogation. Tall Boy backed away from Indy, keeping her in his sights, and opened the door. To her abject horror, a 'dillo that used to be a very fat person, entered. The human inside had once been female. The human breasts the shell had formed around were decomposed and rested flaccid and dark inside their previous bulbous shape, like empty sails. The room filled with thick odor. Indy bent and wretched dryly.

When she recovered enough to stand, she saw she was now alone in the room with the shell creature. It was not moving towards her, it was not trying to tear her apart. Its jaw did not chomp. The eyes of the human inside stared flatly at her. It was not moving, yet it still cracked and creaked. Perhaps it was breathing somehow. Or maybe it was just the sound of its body settling, like an old house settles into a foundation. Indy pretended to need to vomit again and bent to unsheathe her diving knife. Praying to a god she did not believe in, she sunk her knife deeply into the sweet weak spot, the G-spot Magic had shown her, right at its ear lump. In a chorus of crunches and groans the 'dillo fell over, like a stumpy crabapple tree.

Planting her bare foot on the thing's head by her knife, Indy yanked it free. She went to work on its arm at the elbow joint, prying back and forth and then hacking with high arching blows through the carapace until she broke through to the other side. Holstering her knife back on her calf and planting both feet on the 'dillos upper arm, she separated the things claw from its body.

Indy faced the mirror. She looked filthy, starving and completely mad.

She swung the 'dillo claw high overhead, smashing it into the one-way mirror as hard as her hostility and hunger allowed. Glass exploded, revealing a large unlit room. Indy scanned the room and saw a person, dressed in black, cowering in the corner. The person had their arms thrown protectively over their own head. He sat up. Indy was bathed in light, as though someone had turned a floodlight on her. Squinting against the light by holding one arm up to shield her vision, Indy tried to see.

The light was not coming from a floodlight. It was not from any sort of electric light at all. The light was coming from the person's eyes.

As quickly as the light appeared it was gone. The young man with the floodlight eyes had put on sunglasses. Indy dropped her arms and found her knife. The young man stood. He was wearing Ray-Bans. This boy was even taller than Tall Boy. He had five o'clock shadow on his upper lip. He too was sporting a black skullcap and a backwards N on his forehead. His N was long healed, the scabbing replaced by taught fresh flesh. Pulling himself up to full height, he towered over Indy. Yet he somehow still seemed small. He was more pudgy than strong looking, but not fat. He looked soft. He smiled nervously, and Indy could see that his teeth were broken and filthy. He stepped forward to the hole that had been his one-way spy

139

mirror. He put his hand through it, palm out in a familiar gesture.

I'm Trent. I've been looking forward to meeting you.

Not knowing what else to do, Indy switched her knife to free up the proper hand and met his gesture. They shook hands. His felt as icy as her bare feet.

Where is my friend?

Trent's smile widened.

He's eating. What's your name?

Indy's stomach rumbled audibly.

Trent's head bowed briefly towards the felled 'dillo creature.

Would you like to join him?

Indy paused, not knowing if he meant Brian and food or head-stabbed like the 'dillo she had cut down only moments before.

What are you?

I don't understand.

I mean, are you alive or dead?

That is a meaningless distinction. Those categories are no longer mutually exclusive. You must be starving?

Not waiting for an answer, Trent stepped clumsily through the broken mirror, overly careful about the broken glass, and held out his arm in a gesture that said 'after you.' Gripping her unclean diving knife in one hand, Indy opened the door with the other and proceeded down the hallway with Trent behind her.

She found Brian feasting on stew with the child army. They were using cups to scoop and eat from a giant pot. The sweet smell made Indy's stomach growl again. After days and days of Snickers and Hostess Chips, this was the first meaty warm food Indy had seen in ages and her mouth watered. The pot was on a metal desk, the kids arranged around it. Their mouths were smeared with dark gravy. Brian, his caveman cast replaced with actual plaster like a hospital would use, grinned at her from a wheelchair. He presented her with a cup of stew proudly.

Where were you? Look! I kinda miss being a caveman though.

Indy smiled and rested her hand on his head, flattening his coiled hair. She took the offered cup. Sipping and chewing blissfully, she thought, this is not bad. She noticed Trent had chosen to sit far off in the corner of the room, in a crappy office chair. He was not eating. He was leaning forward and cracking his knuckles rapid-fire, back and forth methodically across each joint in both hands. His knuckle sound was disturbingly similar to the movement sounds of the 'dillos. He pivoted his head stiffly towards the eaters, cracking his neck. A soft glow sneaked out around the edges of his Ray-Bans, reminding Indy of his weirdness that lurked beneath.

They were inside the border station she had seen when Tall Boy shot what she assumed was some sort of tranquilizer dart into her. Much to her relief, there were no signs of 'dillos in the makeshift dining room. Someone had scribbled black marker all over President Ronald Reagan's photo hanging on a windowless wall. The tattered and burnt remains of an American flag hung beside Reagan, held in place by a bowie knife. The windows on the other walls were so darkened with char and filth, Indy could not see out of them. She and Brian chewed and chewed. An involuntary shiver ran along Indy's spine. She could *feel* Trent watching her even though he did not have eyes.

Trent stood. The children stopped eating, enraptured and gravy-smeared. Indy and Brian chewed on.

141

Welcome to our guests. You are the first Canadians.

Trent punctuated their nationality with a knuckle pop.

The children clapped, resumed eating.

Indy suctioned gravy greedily off her fingers and wiped around her mouth with the back of her scabby hand.

Trent removed his sunglasses and turned towards the window.

Indy felt lulled by a meat-fed sense of contentment. For the first time in days, pangs of hunger were not pushing out contemplative thoughts.

Trent's eyes were merely another disturbing thing the world had thrown at her. Her whole life there had been obstacles. And the recent ones *had* slowed her progress towards Las Vegas, and *should have made* giving up seem an easier choice than finding her father.

Never.

Indy would never give up. She would find her father. Beyond that, she was unsure, but nothing else mattered and that much was fact.

Trent was talking to her. About food.

Huh?

Brian tugged at her wrist.

He asked if you liked your meal.

Brian held up a bone that he had just finished gnawing on and handed it to her. He had cleaned enough of the meat and gristle off for her to recognize it. It was a familiar and disturbing bone to be eating off of.

Trent smiled. He stood up and removed his glasses. Pam-like, he dropped his jaw and called out one pneumatic note.

Fuck, Indy thought. What do we do now?

One by one 'dillos arrived through the same door Indy had used.

As the room filled with monsters, Indy and Brian watched as one of the smallest children reached into the pot and pull out a gravy-caked ball, about the size of a Nerf soccer ball. It was just slightly smaller than the eating child's own head. The child licked hungrily, poking his tongue into the grooves he found on the ball. He was able to clear out first one, and then another, hole. He lowered his tongue and licked clean a row of perfect, tiny white child's teeth.

Brian vomited in his own lap. Indy got behind his wheelchair, dizzy, and swallowed hard.

Trent had shut up and replaced his sunglasses but was beaming nonetheless. He spread his arms wide and gestured beatifically to the creatures surrounding him.

Meet my friends!

The room filled with window rattling reverberations. Indy and Brian covered their ears.

You see, we're equals! All ages, skins and sizes! As soldiers or sustenance, we all are important!

Dizzy and confused by her own inability to cope with both imminent physical threats and questions about who she had been enthusiastically eating only moments before, she drew down and back to the Christmas when Dana told her nine-year-old self that her mother was dead.

She had spent almost an entire day drinking more and more
NeoCitran, trying in vain to block out her racing anxiety, or at
least blunt it. Or maybe, bluntly wanting to die too. She had
looked to her baby half-sister and known she could not
abandon her to this villain as she herself had been repeatedly
abandoned by the adults around her. She had vomited up the
last dose of NeoCitran and hid in her room covering her album
jackets with writing about the life she had and how she would
one day change it by finding her father. She'd dressed in her
snowsuit and ran to the Arran Township salt dome where
winter salt stores were piled high. She stood in the center of the
dome and screamed and screamed and screamed until the
pigeons wintering at the apex flew out into the December blue
sky. It had saved her.

Again, now over 'dillo monsters instead of the mounds of
Arran Township road salt, she screamed and screamed and
screamed.

The 'dillo call stopped. The border station was quiet except for
Brian's hiccupping sobs.

Despising herself for being tricked by Magic and now detained
and turned into a cannibal, she stared down at Brian knowing
she would not abandon him.

Where's your restroom?

Trent was taken off guard. He stopped cracking his knuckles
long enough to point past the defaced Ronald Reagan behind
Indy. She rolled Brian's chair away from the cannibal table in
the direction of Trent's finger. There were three doors, one
read MEN, one WOMEN, and one a wheelchair symbol.
Fingers, eyes and mind crossed, she pushed open the
wheelchair door. She locked it immediately behind her.

It was there.

It was high. Maybe six feet off the ground. Too small for a big
person. Maybe two feet high and three feet long. Luckily, she

and Brian were small. Pushing Brian's chair under the window, engaging the chair brake, she balanced her feet on the armrests. Indy stretched up and tested the window.

It had a small padlock on the lever keeping her from opening it.

Unsheathing her diving knife, Indy worked away at picking the lock to no avail. She had no idea how to do it. Like so many other things, she'd only seen it on TV. Hopping down, she turned on one of the taps full stream and clambered back onto the chair. Using the heavy gauge steel hilt of the knife as leverage, she pried the shank from the body of the small lock. Grunting, sweating, and finally hanging most of her weight off the knife handle, the lock finally popped open, taking Indy off guard. She lost her balance and crashed backwards off the wheelchair. Cracking her head against the tile made her see stars but did not knock her out. She climbed back up and opened the window to freedom.

In the distance, she could see their Rabbit.

Indy jumped off Brian's chair and hoisted him in his arms. He was heavy. The stinking pile of human meat vomit ran off his lap in rivulets. Awkward yet balancing on the seat of the chair, Indy lifted Brian up by his hips, his bright casted leg knocking into her bruised neck.

Brian could reach the sill but was not strong enough to pull himself up and out.

Brian this will hurt, but I think if I use your cast I can shove you out.

A terrified expression on his face, Brian nodded.

Squatting on the wheelchair and centering his thickly casted foot on the top of her head, Indy stood. Unable to see what was happening, she listened for protest but heard only her own groans of effort. Before Indy was standing all the way up, the weight of his leg was off her head and she heard Brian scrambling outside.

I'm out!

Make your way towards the car. I'm coming.

Her own face flushed, Indy wrapped her hands around the sill and hoisted herself up, kicking her legs like she was swimming, her bare feet seeking purchase on the slick painted cinderblock walls of the border crossing station.

Someone knocked at the door.

Anything the matter?

It was Trent.

Hanging onto the window, Indy took a deep calming breath and turned her face to the door.

No-ope. Just hard to deal with his cast. Be right out!

You don't need any help?

Indy could hear him rattling the door trying to gain entry.

Oh, no! Just washing up.

Taking a deep breath, Indy heaved herself up and halfway out the window. Brian had not done as he was told and was leaning on his good leg waiting to grab her hands and help her the rest of the way out.

Skinning her shins painfully, Indy was finally free of the Detroit Border Station-cum-Cannibal Cult and 'Dillo Army Headquarters. Dragging Brian along, they hobbled the three hundred or so feet to their baby blue Rabbit.

Brian got into his seat. The keys were miraculously in the ignition. Indy took another deep breath. The Volkswagen turned over. Remembering to put it in D, she mashed the accelerator and, according to the big signs overhead, turned towards downtown Detroit.

Indy checked the rearview mirror for 'dillos, cannibals, child soldiers, Trent. At first, the coast ahead and behind was clear. Trent was hopefully still waiting for them to come out of the bathroom.

But as Indy turned onto Jefferson Street and away from Trent's headquarters, she took one last look in the mirror. Trent was standing on the centerline of the road behind them, all alone.

Indy looked over her shoulder to get a better look at what exactly he was doing.

Horrified at first because she thought Trent was pointing, as if to direct his armies. But then she saw he was not pointing.

Trent was merely waving.

He looked so lost.

Indy tilted the mirror so she could look in her own eyes. Still there and green.

Brian pulled out the map to his grandfather's house. Indy turned onto what Brian said was the main street, Woodward Avenue. Together they looked for any signs of life, danger, or food, in no particular order.

Brian's grandfather cleaned for the Detroit Institute for the Arts. As janitor, he was given a cheap place to live in one of the school's unused buildings on Ferry Street.

Stay on Woodward, and I'll keep watch for Ferry Street.

Indy felt lost. She hoped Brian was good at map reading because she had never been to America. Or anywhere besides Tara really.

The boy was giddy. Indy guessed it was because he missed his family. She tried to remain hopeful about unloading her now-damaged charge, but as they drew closer to the address, her hope drained away. Detroit exemplified devastation. Abandoned cars had been pushed off to the side of Woodward Avenue, implying intelligent life had been there. But it had probably only been Trent and his minions. Other than the partially cleared road, there was no sign of life in this once magnificent city, its monumental buildings and broad streets emptier than the Canadian countryside.

Turn here! Here!

Indy made the turn onto Ferry Street.

Again! Right here, turn right here!

Indy entered a wide driveway between two massive red brick century homes. They were vacant looking. Behind the houses, Brian showed her where to park.

I *remember* coming here.

Memory overpowering reality made Brian forget his shattered leg. He opened the Rabbit door before Indy shut off the car and tried to run to the coach house they had parked beside. He tripped over his casted foot, crashing to the gravel driveway.

Indy shouldered her loaded shotgun and jogged to the fallen boy.

Goofball! Wait for me next time.

That's where he lives. There.

Indy opened the weathered screen door. She rapped her knuckles on the solid oak door inside and peered through the stained glass on the top half of the door. All she could see was a distorted view of an empty hallway.

Impatient, Brian leaned his shoulder on the door and used his cast to thump at the bottom loudly.

Grampa! It's me. Me, Brian.

Indy, feeling the hair stand up on the back of her neck, swung around and scanned the parking lot. Still empty. She felt someone watching them. Indy tried the knob and it opened.

Indy and Brian tiptoed together into his grandfather's house. Brian clung to the waistband of Indy's Levis, his fingers hooked there, his cast scraping along the quartersawn hallway.

They walked with Indy's shotgun aimed ahead of them at darkness.

The heat hit Indy like a fist. It was not a temperature. It was heat from an odor so spicy, smell was superseded. Eyes filled with tears, she sped up, dragging Brian with her.

Brian sneezed violently.

At the end of the hall there was a kitchen lit by a tiny window.

Indy stopped so suddenly Brian fell into her. She caught him with her free arm.

The kitchen was clean and normal, except it looked like a horror film scene. Someone had decorated this normal kitchen with dozens of ceiling to floor streamers made of chunks of meat. The meat streamers had been hung from the ceiling by nails and reached all the way to the floor. These gory decorations were the source of the burning air.

Indy yanked at one of the strings. The chunks were two-inch squares of meat cured in red paste. The meat in her hand made her skin burn. Her stomach, still full of Trent's borderland child stew, crumpled in on itself. Had Detroit become a city of cannibals? It didn't really matter. Her priority was Brian's grandfather, not moralizing over cannibalism. Indy let the meat streamer swing away and pushed another away with the barrel of her shotgun. The places on her skin where meat lightly grazed tingled.

Did your grandfather like spices?

Brian wiped a drip of clear snot from his nose.

The only way to proceed through the kitchen and not get hurt by meat streamers was to get onto the floor and crawl under them. Indy helped Brian down to the floor. He hung onto her pant leg as she shimmied across the kitchen on her stomach towards the next room, her shotgun held out in front of her like the bow of a ship.

The hellish meat décor tapered off at the living room. Photos filled the living room walls. Some Hudson's Bay blankets were balled up in the corner of a large bare mattress beneath the photos. There was something attached to the ceiling made of brass and not meat: a pole. A pole Indy recognized immediately from her second favorite movie, Flashdance. It was a stripper pole.

Indy did not bother asking Brian if his grandfather was a stripper.

Helping Brian to get into a comfortable sitting position, Indy searched the photographs on the walls for the boy. A girl who appeared to be ninety per cent hair appeared from nowhere, sliding down the stripper pole. Looking up, Indy saw that she had pulled back a tile in the drop ceiling and used the stripper pole like a fireman to enter the room. She landed gracefully, considering her high-heeled clear plastic boots. Her feet inside revealed the boots to be at least three sizes too big. She stood over Indy and Brian, holding a green Polo cologne spray bottle a few feet away from their faces, menacingly.

Indy tried and failed to suppress a giggle. Brian joined her.

The girl sprayed them. Their giggles turned to chokes. Instead of a Ralph Lauren cologne, they had been doused with homemade hot pepper spray, undoubtedly from the same wretched batch anointing the kitchen meat streamers.

The girl smirked and struck a Wonder Woman type pose.

Through her tearful burning eyes, Indy saw the girl couldn't be much older than Brian. Nine, maybe ten years old. She was wearing a fluorescent pink plastic bra loosely over non-existent breasts that were somehow even smaller than Indy's. The too-big bra sagged low, revealing her nipples and creating more the effect of sails at half-mast than a functional article of clothing. On her bottom she wore black baggy panties that had a small Calvin Klein label on the hip. Her waist length hair appeared to have been half-heartedly put into dreadlocks. Complementing all this were false eyelashes hanging slightly askew, thick black eyeliner on her inner lower lid and heavy brown lip liner filled-in with frosty pink lipstick. The finishing touch was a bright white fur hat with a patent leather peak. This girl was obviously the stripper.

As if reading her mind, the girl returned to the pole, wrapped her legs around it and shimmied up to the top of the pole, plastic boots squealing. At the top, she put the ceiling tile she had come out of back in place and, her thighs gripping the pole, arched over backwards and slowly, erotically sunk to the floor.

Indy, feeling annoyed but safe, put down her shotgun and used her shirt to wipe the Polo pepper spray from Brian's eyes, hoping his tears had obscured the disturbing child stripper show.

Indy took the largest photo off the wall. It was a family portrait, very different than the airbrushed one that hung in Kris's house. In it a silver fox had his arm wrapped around a much younger Asian woman who was wrestling a toddler onto her lap.

Indy wiped pepper tears from her own eyes, and showed Brian the family portrait.

Your grandfather?

Brian, looking away from the girl, held the photograph.

Yes! Where is he?

The girl's pout was amplified and made clownish by the horrible make-up.

They never come home. I made spiced pork though.

Brian looked from the photo to the childish stripper girl and back, tears returning to his eyes as his relationship to her dawned on him. She was his aunt. He held out his arms to her from the floor, leaning over his casted leg. After hesitating long enough to piece the familial blood logic of it all together, the girl dropped into his embrace. Her white fur hat fell off and Brian scooped it up and placed it on his own head.

I hid in the ceiling waiting to be saved. I never knew it would be by my own nephew!

How Brian's aunt had survived this long on her own in such a poor survival costume was a mystery to Indy. But survive she had. Brian could stay here with her and heal, and she could come back for them once she'd found her father. She'd done her job. Brian was with family. He would learn to like spicy food.

Huh, Indy?

Brian had asked her something.

She stared blankly at him.

I'm always repeating myself around you. Can Aunt Jenny come with us?

Indy touched her missing ear. This was not a good question. Detroit was supposed to be where she unloaded her child burden, not multiplied it. Under the wall of happy family photos, she struggled for the right answer. These two, who had never met, felt an immediate and close bond. A fast and total bond Indy had only ever felt with one, long lost, person. She did not belong here. Her bond with Brian would not ever be as strong as what he instantly, and for no real reason, felt with this Jenny girl. She felt the child stew bubble acidly into her esophagus.

As hard as it would be to get to Las Vegas and find her father with one crippled kid, how hard would it be with one crippled kid plus one stripper kid?

Are you alone here?

I'll show you!

Jenny dropped heavily to the floor off the stripper pole and clomped like a horse away through a doorway. Indy, not wanting to leave Brian alone in a strange place, helped him up so they could follow.

Jenny led them to a room containing furniture piled ceiling-high against the back door of the coach house. A large, solid wood bookcase loaded with Encyclopedia Britannica was pushed up against what was, Indy assumed, another doorway. Leaning vertically against the bookcase was a black leather sofa. Against the sofa were two more mattresses and buttressing these were a mishmash of cushioned kitchen chairs, coffee tables, and chests of drawers.

Someone broke off the back door. Furniture is the new back door.

Indy frowned. The child couldn't weigh more than sixty pounds. Embers of hope for Brian's grandfather glowed inside Indy.

How did you ever move all this?

Jenny was about to answer when someone spoke from behind them. In one smooth movement, Indy bent and pulled her diving knife from her ankle and turned to meet her latest attacker.

So focused on defense, Indy heard nothing. Her own furious eyes met one eye the same green hue as her own. The person's other eye was hidden under a black pirate patch. Indy looked to the patch wearer's hands, half expecting a sword or other piratey high seas type weapon, but his hands were empty and rising into a sign of surrender.

Patch Boy held his hands high. While his one eye was the same color as Indy's, his skin was not. Her skin was peachy beige that tanned well and flushed easily. His skin was the same tone as the cinnamon sticks Indy used to flavor the tasteless Mott's apple juice that came in tins and sold for forty-nine cents at the Knechtel Market in Tara. Most importantly, his skin was not mineralized or glowing. Desperate not to repeat her past Magic and Trent mistakes, Indy remained ready to stab out his remaining eye. What was he hiding, Indy wondered, under that patch?

Who are you?

I just said. I'm the one who helped Jenny move all the furniture. I'm Napoleon.

Indy said raised her knife into striking position.

And I'm Joan of Arc.

Jenny jumped in front of Indy waving her arms in defense of Napoleon.

He brings me water and sometimes stuff in cans. He beatboxes. Please don't.

Napoleon was laughing and unafraid.

Ever so slowly, more because she felt like everyone was laughing at her than because she felt safe, Indy lowered her knife.

She's Indy. I'm Brian.

She's making fun of my name?

Indy picked at her earscab.

It's Indiana.

That's so much better.

Napoleon stepped forward and, in a move eerily similar to Trent's, held out his hand. Unlike Trent, his hand was warm and rough with the scabs and calluses of someone who has been using them for more than knuckle cracking. Hands that had been worked. While his body was not much broader than Indy's, his arms were made of thick ropes of muscle and veins.

155

Oddly, he was wearing old tuxedo pants, black with the ribbon down each side and a threadbare tuxedo shirt, the sleeves ripped entirely out to make a muscle-type shirt. On his feet he wore burgundy suede Bally shoes, the texture matted with layers of what Indy easily recognized as congealed 'dillo gore. His hair was wavy and short.

Napoleon swung a World Famous backpack off his shoulder and asked who's hungry. He kneeled and emptied the contents onto the floor. Jenny rushed to examine what he had. Brian looked plaintively at Indy and so, slowly sheathing her knife, she helped him over beside the bounty Napoleon had brought.

Indy did not eat and did not even look at the food. She kept her eyes anchored on Napoleon.

Napoleon leaned against the stripper pole holding a bowl of Jenny's spicy meat close to his face so he could shovel it in.

Indy regarded him silently. A long moment passed between them, with only the sound of Napoleon slurping and chewing. Indy broke silence.

Why are you here?

Napoleon stopped eating.

He placed his half empty bowl down at the base of the stripper pole and folded his arms.

You are a real hard case, huh? Ear gone never mind. Kid with busted leg, keeping on.

Indy hated her non-ear but would not give him the satisfaction of touching again the scabby space where it had been before her stepfather removed it and her mother ate it. Instead, Indy answered him by finally picking up her own bowl and, using chopsticks instead of a spoon, artfully lifted a spiced chunk of meat into her mouth.

One second later she was choking. The intensely spiced meat was lava in her throat. She chewed on, swallowing with difficulty and coughing continually, her eyes watering again.

Napoleon passed her a can of Dr. Pepper.

Indy cracked the pop open and swallowed deeply from it. Her eyes never leaving Napoleon's one good eye.

I'm just here. I'm just me, nothing special.

How do you know Brian's aunt?

Aunt, huh?

He paused to bend his head and run both of his hands slowly from the back of his head to the front in a vain attempt to understand everything better. Or maybe just tidy his hair.

He returned Indy's gaze.

Your parents?

Yours?

They shared another few moments of silence, staring at each other. Surprisingly, Indy thought, comfortable.

Without breaking eye contact with Indy, Napoleon pulled off his patch.

This is what you're worried about, right?

Indy stared into the empty eye socket and was reminded of Pam. But that is where the similarity ended. The eyeball was missing. Unlike Pam, he had no strange glow-parts or anything else inhuman-looking inside. His hole was simply an empty sightless socket.

Napoleon dropped the patch back on, repositioning it just so, and carried on like nothing had happened.

That's one weird looking knife you got. I never seen anything like it.

Napoleon leaned over and touched her calf beside where the diving knife was sheathed. Indy shivered and yanked her leg back protectively.

It's a diving knife. Made for cracking crustaceans off reefs and prying them apart from each other.

Appropriate.

Indy nodded as she cautiously lifted another chunk of prohibitively spiced meat to her mouth. Better than eating child. Or nothing.

Indy wiped the burn off her lips with the back of her hand. She managed to finish her second piece of meat without coughing, by chasing it immediately with the rest of the Dr. Pepper. She was sweaty.

Napoleon slurped up the last of his suicide meat. As he stood, the coach house shook with a loud boom.

Indy jumped up and went for her knife.

It was just thunder.

Napoleon shuffled over to the mattress and pulled an itchy Hudson's Bay blanket from the pile.

That's the first storm I've heard in a while.

Napoleon dropped prone onto the mattress and rolled over and away from Indy facing the wall. He yanked the blanket over himself. Indy could see a handgun stuffed into his tuxedo pants, nestled in the small of his back. *He could have shot me when I pulled that knife on him.*

The rain fell. Indy could not remember any weather from the last while. No room for trivial concerns. 'Dillo reports were all that mattered. And predatory survivor reports. All her exhaustion was not enough to keep at bay anxious scenarios as she listened to Brian and Jenny play checkers. Carefree children in the back room, furniture piled high beside them against all the various kinds of monsters outside.

159

Indy resented them and then hated herself for resenting them. All the resentments lined up and, like counting sheep, formed a pattern that lulled her to sleep still sitting up.

Chapter 18: Trent

Indy woke up. She had been dreaming she was sleeping safe inside the Rabbit. For some reason, Napoleon was hollering from the kitchen. Shaking her head to knock the sleep out of it, Indy got to her feet on legs numb from sleeping sitting up. Feeling around in the gloom she located the stock of her shotgun and dragged it towards her eager palm.

The sun was barely up. The kitchen meat streamers glistened as they twisted in the dawn light, sparks of chili blazing against the aging meat. Through this curtain she saw Napoleon, wearing a Hudson's Bay blanket like a shawl. He looked like a granny or an Indian. He was pointing his gun at someone standing in the open door, meat streamers arranged against his wool-protected back like Jenny's dreadlocks.

Same as she had last night, Indy dropped to crawl along the kitchen floor, gun out front. Her approach so that whomever Napoleon was yelling at would not see her coming.

Indy. Pleased you could join us. Why are you slithering around?

Trent. Indy felt her blood vessels contract sharply. He punctuated his question to her with a knuckle pop. I left the Rabbit parked outside like a beacon! Indy hated herself for thinking of it only now, too late.

Napoleon was screaming.

YOU KNOW THIS FUCKER? Why won't he take off his SUNGLASSES?

Napoleon was asking but he already knew why.

Indy stood with Napoleon at the door. She pointed her shotgun directly at Trent's shades. Meat streamers seared into her cheek, her arms.

I'm hurt.

Trent spoke softly, trying and failing to sound hurt. He worked his knuckles some more.

I thought we'd reached some sort of rapprochement.

Indy answered with a silent glare from her own as-yet human eyes.

Shooting me will only worsen your situation.

How you figure *that?*

It's so boring. If you shoot me in the head I can't protect you. You are stupid eyed. My god-eyes receive and transmit a constant stream of information. But this river flows both ways. If you cut me down, they will avenge me by ungently popping out your hearts and consuming them whole.

That makes me *really* want to shoot you.

If you only injure me, I will simply call them. Either way, you lose.

Napoleon's voice was hoarse from cursing Trent; it didn't stop him from cursing more.

Indy?

What do you want, Trent?

I want you to join me, Indy.

Indy rolled her shoulder, moving a burning meat streamer from in front to behind her.

You will join me soon one way or another. Why not prepare? Why not learn from me so that your transition will be smooth?

Who *is* this guy?

Trent popped all his knuckles once, left hand, then right, before he answered.

I, am you.

Take me, then Trent. But only if I am enough.

Trent smiled. He nodded and once more held out his too soft hand to Indy.

Indy lowered her shotgun. She let it slide from her fingers and clatter to the linoleum. To demonstrate complete supplication, she yanked up her denim pant leg and added her diving knife to her weapon pile. She glanced sideways at Napoleon. He appeared frozen, from shock or fear or both, Indy was unsure.

Indy gripped Trent's hand, hard. Trent held hers limply.

At least, Indy thought, Trent can't pop his knuckles when I have his hand in mine. And then she noticed her head was soaked. So wet that she looked up to see if it was raining in the kitchen.

Napoleon's Glock-filled hand flew up beside her in recoil. There was empty space in front of her that a second before had been full of Trent.

Indy looked down. She was still gripping Trent's hand tightly. Trent was crumpled at her feet. Tilting her head sent a bolus of glossy pink tissue tumbling off. It landed back where it had come from: on what was left of Trent's head.

Louder or perhaps not louder but maybe just denser than ever before the 'dillos called out. Mourning Trent. Indy felt like she should be able to see her breath; she felt instantly that cold.

Indy dropped Trent's hand like she had dropped her weapons. She used her newly free hand like a wiper blade to flick the worst of Trent's skull and brain matter off her face and from her hair. She was sorry he met this ending, despite feeling sure there was no other way. She shivered.

Napoleon was already retreating deeper into the house. She ran around the outside of the coach house to the Rabbit. The keys were in her hand before she sat, and in the ignition before the door closed. She drove up right beside the coach house and rolled down the window.

COME ON.

Napoleon, a terrified Brian in his arms, and a bouncy Jenny came to the passenger door Indy had already flung open. Napoleon dropped onto the passenger seat with Brian in his lap. He pulled Jenny in on top of them both and slammed the car door.

Indy made a left onto Ferry Street and a right onto Woodward. Whispering, Las Vegas, Las Vegas, as a talisman against all obstacles, she took the I94 westbound exit. The interstate was open. Wide open. She peered into the rearview mirror and saw no one, no things, mineralized or otherwise, coming after them.

Napoleon screamed.

He was pointing out the windshield.

It was a barricade. A familiar barricade. Another 'dillo mountain, this one higher and wider than a tractor trailer. The entire interstate from curb to curb was blocked.

Napoleon and Jenny were pleading with her to stop. Jenny was maybe crying.

Brian was saying no. He was looking at Indy, from under Jenny and in between her dreads, with tear-filled eyes that said no more. He reached out and hugged onto his aunt's shoulder to protect her from impact.

Indy pressed the gas pedal all the way until the sole of her boot touched the floor of the car. The Rabbit was shuddering against the speed. Something under the hood smoked. The air filled with the sickeningly sweet smell of burning candyfloss.

The shellicade was five hundred yards away. Four hundred. Three hundred.

The Rabbit hit the 'dillo barricade at eighty miles per hour.

Shells flew. The Rabbit pulled right, but Indy held the steering wheel tight, shunning the brake pedal.

They broke through to the other side. And the other side was thankfully clear, or they would have crashed into whatever was there. Indy slowed down by removing her foot from the gas pedal.

Brian was the first to shout his relief. He held his hand up, catching a dreadlock, to give Indy a high-five. And then they were all high-fiving each other awkwardly in the cramped space.

They got out of downtown Detroit alive.

Indy asked Jenny, who was sitting on the edge of the passenger seat between Napoleon's knees, to get the paper map out of the glove box. Napoleon tilted his head.

Do we know where we are even going?

Las Vegas.

Bright orange flames licked up and over the front of the car. It was too smoky to see the road ahead.

Indy hit the brakes, stopping the Rabbit in the middle of I94. Napoleon carried Brian while Indy dragged Jenny to a safe distance away from the burning car. The teenagers hurled two boxes of food and water from the car's stocked hatchback. Indy stuffed all remaining ammo in her pockets and took her hatchet and Magic's maul. Brian was sobbing and pointing, so Indy took all that was left of his mother: her shelmet.

Underneath the rising sun they watched the Rabbit burn. It was slow at first. Finally, the car exploded into complete and utter uselessness.

On the outskirts of Detroit what was left of the Rabbit smoked blackly. Indy and her three new fellow travelers stood stranded on a bare section of I94 that seemed entirely industrial, save for the Ford drive-in in the distance.

Brian hobbled on his broken leg back to the exit they had just passed. Indy watched him and thought about yelling at him to come back but instead followed behind. Jenny, who seemed entirely unable to sit still, was balancing on one leg in some sort of yoga/stripper pose. She was wearing a white nightgown so big that it billowed around her in the morning breeze. Her dreaded hair was safely out of the wind, stuffed into and entirely filling Brian's mother's shelmet. It sat high on her head like a shiny hairball crown.

Stranded in the Motor City – *without* a car.

Napoleon seemed to find this funny.

Like, all the cars in the country are made here and we don't got one. Good pick on the shitty car, by the way.

Indy stopped following Brian and spun on her heel so she could respond.

Leave it to the white chick to pick a German car. Turn us into zombie suppers.

Jenny lost her yoga/stripper balance and fell over, her hair crown protecting her head from the I94.

Indy opened her mouth to speak, and closed it. She turned her head to check on Brian and saw him disappearing around wreckage on the curve of the exit. He could really hustle on that perfectly casted leg now.

167

Indy swung her attention back around to Napoleon and let out what she had been holding in since she had dropped Trent's dead hand to the coach house doorstep.

We would not be in this predicament at all if it weren't for *you*. You three would be safe and sound with food and water and shelter if you'd just let me go. Maybe Trent could have taught me how to use his communication stuff, only I'd use it to make all the 'dillos run into Lake Michigan and float away.

Or, Indy thought to herself, in case my dad is a 'dillo I'd be able to call him. It had been a back-up plan she had been forming since she'd seen what Pam could accomplish with her powers. It was a plan B.

It was Napoleon's turn to stare at Indy. He quickly closed the several feet between them. He lifted his finger to her face.

I saved *you*.

Indy took the deepest breath her tight throat allowed. For some reason, she had to blink back tears. She thought, *Las Vegas*.

Brian's shout broke the moment. Indy's heart flipped. How had she let him go off on his own? What was wrong with her?

Brian shouted again but it was clear this time it was not from fear, but joy. They followed his voice and found him at a car dealership off the exit he'd hobbled down. It was a massive lot of hundreds of brand new, dusty cars.

Indy grinned. Unfortunately for Napoleon, it was another German car dealership. It seemed they'd be driving yet another German car. But, Indy thought, I somehow doubt he'd complain about driving one of these cars.

It was a Porsche dealership.

Indy, Napoleon, and Jenny hovered in the driveway of the dealership looking at millions of dollars' worth of cars, apocalypse-free for the taking. All it took to buy a car now was survival.

Brian was frantically limp-hopping up to each car. They were all locked.

Napoleon ran up to the closest Porsche and slapped his hand on it.

The keys will be in the showroom offices somewhere.

Jenny pumped her arms in the air like she was fighting an invisible enemy.

Napoleon scooped Brian into his arms and the four made their way across the Porsche-filled parking lot to the glass showroom. The building's windows were mostly intact, but the door had been completely sheared off its hinges. Inside, they spread out, looking through offices and desk drawers. Their search disturbed papery pod remnants, silently explaining the fate of the salesmen who had once worked there.

Napoleon found a huge combination safe under one of the desks. Both he and Indy tried and failed a few times to open it.

Indy picked at her ear. Keys jingled.

Jenny was holding keys above her head and shaking them rhythmically from the back of the showroom. She disappeared behind a door. Scooping Brian up again, Napoleon and Indy followed.

Behind the showroom was a small, covered parking area. Jenny was hanging out of a car parked there, keys dangling from her fingers.

I found them in the ignition!

Relief flashed across all faces except Napoleon's. His face fell.

Leave it to us to come to a Porsche dealership and drive away in *that*.

Indy smiled. Napoleon had used the word *us*. She got in the car Jenny had found. She grew up driving around in shitboxes and didn't care either way.

They would be leaving a Porsche end of the world fire sale in an early '80s Honda Civic that was either orange or a sun-faded red; it was so old it was hard to tell.

Chapter 20: Ashley

It took twice as long as it should have, but the Honda made it to Ashley, Indiana before sunset.

Ashley, like my sister's name but with a *y*, Indy thought, as she drove her new companions into the desolate village.

They were forced to get off the I94 after escaping Detroit because the interstate was no longer clear of crashed cars. Taking small roads that always headed south and/or west and were clear enough to pass had brought them to Ashley.

Indy and Napoleon had decided to avoid big cities in case dangerous urban survivors, like Trent with armies, were a rule not an exception. Indy did not speak about her time in the small, yet dangerous-as-Detroit, Owen Sound. There was no way to avoid all human civilization and still find enough to eat and drink, so there was no point in freaking everyone out. Napoleon strangely had not questioned her decision to head for Las Vegas. He had instead been entirely on board with the trip. He asked no questions, only made zombie jokes and even funny raps about what they were driving past on the back roads. He did say that he wanted to go south before winter hit, so maybe he simply liked the direction. And he said he'd never seen the desert.

Indy pulled into the parking lot of a 7-Eleven gas station in downtown Ashley. If you could call it a downtown. Smiling painfully thirty feet over them like a false sun was a humungous yellow happy face. An industrious Ashleyan had painted the water tower mustard yellow with a gigantic grinning face on top, turning it into a gigantic smiley face. What was once a happy roadside attraction now mocked survivors from above. The smiley no longer welcomed families needing to stretch their legs. Instead, it welcomed new breeds of tourists: 'dillos looking for someone to kill and looters, like them, desperate for something to eat. Hello! Welcome to the Apocalypse! Have a nice day!

Jenny whined and asked why they had not brought at least one suicide-hot meat streamer.

Everyone's stomach rumbled. Indy's eyes watered.

The gas station was surprisingly intact. Cautiously, shotgun raised, Indy took the lead to the station store. It was unlocked.

The store was familiar even though Indy had never been there, because every 7-Eleven everywhere is the same. The apocalypse made it darker. Indy sniffed the air. There was a rotten milk smell but nothing else.

Indy called out to the empty store.

Nothing answered.

She gestured for Napoleon to bring Brian and Jenny in so they could all shop. The floor was clear and the aisles tidy. Indy reached for a handful of 7-Eleven shopping bags from behind the cashier counter and noticed that someone had smashed the register and removed all the cash. Stupid. The money-hungry idiot had meanwhile left all the food and water. As quietly as possible, given Brian's limp and Jenny's creepy stripper exuberance, the foursome moved towards the back of the store where the coolers were. Napoleon opened the first cooler. The stench of failed dairy and long warm meat closed their throats. Indy guarded, her shotgun raised towards the door as Napoleon filled his knapsack with cola from the upper shelves. Jenny and Brian filled shopping bags with water from the lower ones.

Napoleon squeezed his backpack so he could zip it shut.

So fast it was a glowing streak, a small thing launched from the 7-Eleven cooler, attaching itself to Napoleon's cheek just below his only remaining eye. It held a mouthful of his face flesh tight between its jaws.

172

Napoleon's groans of agony were drowned out by Jenny's wild shrieks as she cowered below his thrashes. Brian hugged Jenny to him, trying to protect her, or maybe shield her so she would not witness Napoleon lose his last eye.

Napoleon, good eye squeezed shut, was hammering uselessly on the thing's armored skin, his fists glancing off as its prickly limbs sliced at his face like X-Acto blades

With her shotgun, Indy felt powerless. If she shot the animal 'dillo now, she'd blow it off Napoleon for sure but she'd put a hole in his head too.

Acting instinctually and without pause, Indy reached her right hand towards the thing's mouth and inserted three of her fingers inside, encircling its un-armored lower jaw. Stiffening her arm, she fell back, using her body weight to snap the small monster's jaw clean off. She stared at her right hand, gory and still gripping the lower mandible of a cat. She'd saved Napoleon.

Without its lower jaw holding it to him, the zombie cat dropped off and skittered noisily down the gum aisle.

Napoleon pulled Indy up. His grip was tight. Under his good eye, a flap of his face the size of a baby's tongue hung down towards his nose. His eye patch had come askew revealing his empty socket.

Thanks.

I guess I owed you one.

Indy grimaced as she pulled the 'dillo cat teeth from the holes they had made in her hand. The punctures were like the ones she used to get climbing thorny crabapple trees looking for robin nests. Deep, red holes. Very little blood.

Napoleon examined her injured hand, taking it into his own.

173

After filling the Civic with Pepsi, Slim Jim, Twinkies and water, Indy drove what she was coming to accept as *her friends* along an Ashley side street. They searched rundown houses hoping to find suitable and fortifiable shelter for the night. No one liked the idea of everyone sleeping stuffed in the Civic.

Indy had never belonged to a group before. She had only had her one best friend Tammy. Indy's own family had been merely a collection of humans with whom she lived and had to cautiously navigate around when she could not possibly physically avoid them. She had never spent this much time with three other people who made her feel good. Of course it would not last. Given the deadliness of almost every other living or, if not living, moving thing, it was stupid to think it could. It had not even been realistic in the pre-'dillo world, so how could it be now.

As if to confirm her worries, Napoleon pointed to a trailer exactly like the one she grew up in. He wanted to stop for the night there.

Instead, Indy pointed across the road from the trailer.

There, that's where we will stay.

Napoleon followed her finger.

But, there's nothing *there*.

Nothing but a banana-yellow toaster-shaped van.

Okay. A van. Cozy.

They parked behind the van. Napoleon peered inside. It was a '64 Ford Econoline. The kind with the engine between the front two seats like a third loud passenger. There were at least a dozen syringes tossed around the back of the van, a couple used condoms and some bits of shopping bags shredded up. Someone or something had been using it as a toilet too: there

174

was a mound of feces in the rear corner. But the doors were open and the keys were in the ignition.

Napoleon climbed into the driver's seat.

Wow. Three in the tree.

Napoleon did not look concerned by his discovery.

See, we can live in here. It's perfect. We won't need to stop and find a safe place to sleep anymore.

Napoleon put the van into first gear with difficulty, having to mash both feet into the clutch before the tree would shift. He turned the key. The toaster roared to life. He grinned.

It looks like we have just found our next shitty vehicle.

Indy and Brian cleaned the human feces because Napoleon flat refused. Needles fine, condoms sure, but shit was not his bag, he explained. He took Jenny across the road to the trailer he'd pointed out to shop for food and a mattress.

Brian was useless carrying anything, so Indy put him up front in the Ford on watch, her shotgun across his lap. Indy put on her shelmet, hoping it would mute the stench of scooping up the feces with a folded piece of cardboard. She used one of the 7-Eleven shopping bags as a glove to pick up needles and condoms.

A scream, not a needle, pierced the late afternoon Indiana silence.

Indy pulled the bags off her hands.

Stay here.

Indy slammed and latched the van's back doors shut behind her to protect Brian. She sprinted across the road and into the trailer house Napoleon and Jenny had disappeared into. It was almost exactly like the trailer she'd grown up in. She ran down the dark hallway, diving knife in hand, calling out until she heard Jenny's sobs. She found them in a bedroom. A child's bedroom. Jenny was bent over a crib. Napoleon comforted her, his hand rubbing her back.

She thought it was a doll.

In the crib was what at first appeared to be an ugly doll. But detail gave away to truth quickly. The ugly doll was really a withered human infant. It looked intact and unbitten. Maybe it had starved to death when its parents died then came back to life very disinterested in caring for it, forgetting it even existed.

If it had even lasted that long. Indy put her knife back on her leg.

Her sister Ashlee had been so sweet when she was that age.

It took half an hour for them to drag a double mattress to the Ford and load their supplies in the space between the mattress and the back doors. Napoleon tore off two lengths of chain link fence from a nearby yard to fortify the windows at the back of the van. They held the fence in place with stacks of food and water. It was indeed a cozy set up.

Sunset was about an hour away when Brian spotted something in the sky that may have been a cloud of 'dillo bugs.

Everyone got in the van to get ready to sleep. Except Indy. She did not feel sleepy.

I don't think we should ever all sleep at once.

How about just tonight?

You sleep.

Indy supposed the last time she'd had a good sleep was when she'd been hit with that dart in Detroit. Did drugged count as rest?

Napoleon shrugged and returned to arranging the pillows in a way that he, Jenny and Brian could be most comfortable on the van bed.

You sure you don't want to join us?

Napoleon was splayed out parallel to the windshield right behind Indy, his head behind the driver's seat so he could watch her in the passenger seat. Brian was at the end of the bed, his casted leg elevated on a pillow Indy had carried from the dead baby house just for him.

177

Indy scanned the landscape beneath the smiley water tower, shifting the 12-gauge on her lap to optimize her grip.

Jenny plopped down on the mattress beside Napoleon and begged for a bedtime story.

Napoleon sat up and folded his knees to sit cross-legged. Jenny mirrored him, clapping. Indy readied herself to hear some inane Disney prince rescue story. Her mother had never told her any bullshit bedtime stories.

Instead, Napoleon took a deep breath and quietly rapped.

Indy kept her focus on the world outside the windshield, trying to maintain disinterest overtop the discomfort she was feeling. Napoleon finished his song.

Jenny clapped loudly and Brian asked if he was a famous rapper.

Napoleon shook his head.

Indy was unable to contain herself. Her explanation for why she loved rap music so much spilled out so fast she couldn't stop them if she tried.

My stepdad went to college to be a '70s rock DJ. He ended up working at a nuclear power plant instead, but he kept all his records and loved them like children. Or at least more than me. I heard a stupid Who song or The Eagles every day. I was never allowed to touch those albums. But he hated rap records. He said it was just a fad.

I never heard of a farm girl who liked rap.

Indy returned to scanning the night for movement. Her voice became unstable.

Not a real farm. We had forty or so chickens. But only to hide all the marijuana we were growing.

Napoleon said nothing. Indy bit her lip and stared into the night wishing Napoleon would say something so she could stop talking.

My real dad was a drug dealer too. Or at least, I think so from what I can remember about him.

Indy looked down to the shotgun in her lap.

Napoleon stared at her and remained silent.

I was a kid, but I took care of the plants. And the chickens.

Jenny flopped down on the bed, bored.

Napoleon pulled his tuxedo shirt off over his head. A thick gold chain hung to his navel. He folded his shirt up neatly beside him and finally spoke.

I was doing pretty much the same thing, only the Detroit version.

Napoleon rolled up behind Jenny and in short minutes everyone, except Indy, fell into the heavy rhythm of deep sleep. Indy cried silently.

***

Indy lowered her head releasing her neck with a pop. Dawn was breaking beneath the smiley face water tower. Through the night, her imagination forged 'dillos out of spicebush and dogwood. The sound of a far off engine, or maybe just thunder, almost caused her to wake everyone up. Through the night, she wore her hyper-vigilance like a shining scar.

She had stayed awake by worrying about food and Las Vegas.

Napoleon's hand fell on Indy's shoulder. She had failed to notice Napoleon get up behind her and it made her jump. He loomed behind her, his shirt still off. Despite the fact that none of them had bathed properly in days or longer, he smelled good.

Good morning.

Napoleon's voice cracked from sleep and adolescence.

Indy blushed for no good reason. Napoleon probably thought she was scrawny and disgusting. He sat down on engine beside her. She shifted her head away from him to resume her watch. Napoleon reached his hand across and gently, with his fingers, turned her head back and up to face him. This touch made Indy feel the need to explain herself.

I know I'm gross. I've got one ear, I haven't really bathed since a baptism pool and I've got chicken legs, big feet. I'm ugly.

Napoleon chupsed, sucking his lips in.

Who told you that?

Need a list?

Indy turned from Napoleon to stare again out the windshield. A poker chip sun slid further up towards the water tower.

Napoleon dropped down into the driver's seat. They were now on the same level.

Like, you could use some meat on you. I can't put it all together for you like an argument or anything. But you are not ugly. And—

Napoleon stopped because he had to catch his breath, not because he spoke quickly but because it had become ragged from emotion. Indy's pulse raced like when she had last run beyond her limits to keep up with Kris. She couldn't think of a time in her life when she had ever been complimented about her appearance. Ever. Her school work by teachers, sure. The best she'd ever had was tall. But the compliment did not make her feel good; it was uncomfortable. Not ugly wasn't a real compliment, anyway.

I woke up just now and watched you.

Napoleon leaned way over so he could reach across the engine towards her lap. Indy's legs ran slack like water from a tap. He brushed his hand across hers, still tightly gripping her shotgun. He pulled it from her grasp slowly.

Sleep for a couple hours. I got this.

Indy tried to take a deep breath and picked at her itchy non-ear. Wondering why Napoleon seemed to just accept Las Vegas like it was set in stone, made it itch. It was her leading all of them on a futile and selfish mission to find her dad, who was most certainly dead and a monster who would only try to eat them. And here this strange boy was being so nice to her.

Almost as if he could read her mind, Napoleon smiled and shook his head.

Don't worry. Everything is going to be okay.

Despite the twin facts that most certainly everything would *not* be okay and that Indy was dying to kiss him, she scrambled back over the engine onto the van bed and fell sound asleep.

The van engine, two feet away from Indy's head, roared angrily to life. It took three heartbeats for her to remember where she was. *One:* find my dad. *Two:* in our van. *Three:* Napoleon.

The van was bouncing and rolling with Brian and Jenny asleep beside her.

Where are we going?

Napoleon screamed his answer and scowled at his side mirror.

If a pack of white kids point at me and yell nigger, I don't ask permission from the captain to take off.

Captain? Indy thought, bracing herself against the engine as she got back in the passenger seat.

I'm *not* captain.

Napoleon did not respond. They drove off the gravel lot they had found the van in and back onto blacktop. Indy stared out her own side mirror at eight white kids chasing them until an arrow shattered both her view and the mirror.

Indy called out in surprise.

Jenny appeared beside her and leaned on the warming engine.

Napoleon grunted from using his entire body weight to depress the van's sticky clutch so he could move through all three gears.

Turn here. West.

Napoleon turned. The road ahead was blocked by something. Not cars, not 'dillo people.

Indy grabbed Napoleon's arm and told him stop. He pulled over.

Ahead of them about half a mile was a herd of apocalyptic longhorn cattle. No longer edible, they were monstrous corpse steers wearing giant mineralized bodysuits. Their already lethal horns had gained the width, weight and girth of extra armor. This heaviness caused their heads to bob up and down, like bobble heads, as they struggled against gravity to keep their burdensome skulls horizontal.

Scraping and clacking against one another, they were at least fifty strong, forming a solid moving wall of crunchy meat. There was no way their Ford toaster van could break through. Maybe, Indy thought uselessly, if we had a snowplow hooked to the front. As they watched from the safety of their Ford, a rib rattling low tone, like a rusty foghorn, rose up from the steer wall. At tank speed, they groaned slowly forward.

Napoleon turned off the van.

I think it is my turn.

Before Indy could ask for what, Napoleon was leaping over the ditch between the road and the field and running diagonally into the pastureland of Indiana, back the way they had just come from Ashley. When he was a few hundred feet out, he screamed and jumped and yelled, trying to get the attention of the herd. The moving wall of meat continued towards Indy and the kids in the van, undeterred. Napoleon whistled loudly at the dumb beasts. He hurled insults at them, calling them assholes and pigs.

Only, Indy thought, would someone from the city, call a herd of cattle *pigs*.

Indy shifted around in her seat so she could see Brian and Jenny.

Jenny, I need you to run out to Napoleon right now, I'll be right behind you.

Jenny nodded solemnly and poked her filthy knees out from under her grungy Barbie Doll nightgown. Indy climbed into the back and smiled at Brian. He held out his arms.

Indy helped Brian to the driver's seat and Jenny sat on the engine. Shouldering her shotgun, Indy ran around the outside of the van to the driver's side and let Brian climb on her, piggyback. Over her shoulder, she saw that the cattle had quartered the distance between them, slowed by the periodic fall of one of their number causing an obstacle for them to crunch over and around.

Brian. Wrap your arms around my chest and hold on. Jenny, *run.*

Jenny sprinted, flying like a hair-winged bird across the field towards Napoleon. He was screaming no. Indy, burdened by Brian, ran as fast as she could after Jenny, pushing hard for each step until she reached Napoleon.

It's not ... our voluntary noises. It's our ... involuntary—

Napoleon had scooped Jenny up onto his hip.

You *are* crazy. You gotta let me help, too.

Your plan isn't working. I don't think they listen to our talking or shouting. They are dead and don't hear the way we do.

Brian leaned over Indy's shoulder so he could be heard from her back.

My brother Paul said the blood pumping through our veins calls to them. He told me quietness, even silence, won't save you from their attention. Only death.

And here they come.

Napoleon pointed. The dead meat wall had changed course. It was crunching and bobble-heading in their direction.

Napoleon swung Jenny onto his back mirroring Indy and Brian.

We need to lure them out here off the road and circle back to the van. Now.

Each teen, loaded down with a kid, ran hand in hand as fast as they could, further away from the safety of the van and veering deeper into the field. Twice Napoleon caught Indy, made clumsy by her Brian load, as she tripped on a furrow. At the stone fence line they put down their loads and caught their breath, watching the monsters correct and move towards them once again.

I knew I hated farming.

Me too.

Indy managed to smile at Napoleon through gasps for breath.

Napoleon nodded and they began the final leg of their race: the life or death one back to the van. They made it to the ditch and Indy tripped again over a half buried stretch of barbed wire. She landed flat on her face. She was sandwiched between road gravel and Brian. Stinging, blood filling her mouth, she felt the earth vibrate through her face as the zombie cattle bore down. She tried to get back up but Brian, who weighed only ten pounds less than her, had her pinned. The first 'dillo steer were breaking out from the front of the pack. Brian's weight lifted off her. Napoleon had him. She took Napoleon's hand and kept hold of it even though blood ran from her smashed nose staining her shirt as they raced the last few feet to the van.

They piled inside their Ford. Napoleon fired the engine, shifting into first and they rolled forward. Jenny and Brian crawled onto the mattress in the back. Indy was halfway through a blood and snot hork when the van was shoved several feet to the right, so that it was driving on gravel shoulder instead of road.

Jenny cried out.

A pair of 'dillo steer horns had pierced the driver's side of the van. The monstrous tips were less than a foot from the heads of Brian and Jenny. Napoleon reversed. Indy reached over to the steering wheel and yanked it hard to the right. Everyone winced at the sound of sheering metal. The side of the Econoline was opening like a sardine can as the van pulled away from the horns. Napoleon yanked the wheel back so they would not drive into the ditch and shifted rapidly through to third gear, flooring the old van. The unwanted steer passenger, still attached to the van, gradually lost purchase on the highway, unable to move its armored limbs at thirty miles per hour. It bumped along for a few seconds, slowing the van. The engine whined. Napoleon dropped down into second and began crisscrossing the yellow line to shake the 'dillo off. Indy watched as the rip in the side of the van narrowed out and finally broke off with a final metallic bang. The steer rolled like a bowling ball wielding a van-made scythe into its herd, taking a dozen of them out.

Their newly modified Ford Econoline now boasted a driver's side, lightning-bolt shaped, three-by-five-foot-glass-free window.

Brian and Jenny clung to each other, huddled against the back of Indy's seat. Jenny's dreadlocks were whipping violently around in the wind. Indy turned around to look out the windshield and saw a sign that said:

GOSHEN DAM POND.

Indy yelled clearly over the engine and wind noise.

Let's go there!

Napoleon answered by turning left, as the sign directed. He followed the road to PUBLIC ACCESS and parked beside a long, groomed stretch of sandy beach on a man-made swimming area, cordoned off by orange and white buoys in the water. The water was mirror calm. Jenny finally let go of Brian and looked out the new van window.

Can we swim?

Indy peeled a small scab from her ear hole.

We can get cleaned up. But we can't be sure about what's *in* the water.

Brian made a frog sound.

Jenny folded her arms and pouted.

They were not the only vehicle at the beach. Kitty-corner to their Ford was a burgundy Goldwing motorcycle. Indy rummaged around in the thing's massive panniers and found four balled-up vinegar scented t-shirts with huge grinning cats with Elvis pompadours on the front. Wrapped up in the middle of one of the shirts was a Skor bar, Indy's favorite. She ripped into it, downing it in two wide, selfish bites.

On the beach, Napoleon volunteered to take first water watch while Indy and Jenny bathed. He rolled up his jeans and took off his socks and shoes so he could wade in, shotgun cradled. Brian, because of his cast, was marooned on the beach.

Jenny, unsurprisingly comfortable with nudity, lifted her nightgown over her head and strutted naked up and down the beach. Indy was not so eager. Her gold shirt, leprous with fresh face blood from her latest disaster, dropped to the sand. Wearing only her Levis and undershirt, she paused.

I'm too busy looking for freaky fish to stare at you.

Napoleon's head confirmed his statement. It was tilted down so he could see through reflections for any movement beneath the surface.

Indy had never been intentionally naked in front of a guy before. It was Scott and the baptismal pool all over again. Her breasts didn't exist. It was so embarrassing. Napoleon, meanwhile, had probably seen a million boobs and asses, all bigger and less weird than she'd ever have. Sighing, Indy unbuttoned her jeans, peeled them off, and shook them out. Wearing her filthy balloon underwear and gack smeared undershirt, she waded into the water up to her knees and sat down about four feet from Napoleon, facing away. The water was cold, but the cold was right because it sliced through the grodiness she felt from not bathing and wearing dirty panties day after day. Indy dipped her face into the water to clean the blood and gravel that her trip onto the road had implanted. Under the water she felt for that spot where her right ear used to be. It would have healed to a series of thick numb scabs if she could stop picking at it. She could not remember what having an ear there was like. She sat up, flicking her hair back, blinking water out of her eyes. She looked over her shoulder.

Napoleon was looking at her, shotgun gripped tightly. His eye shifted back down to the water.

They had no soap so Jenny was squirming around beside Indy trying to agitate herself clean like a Maytag. Her shamelessness held Indy's attention as did her tiny child breasts. They were about the same pathetic size as Indy's own.

We are in *Indiana*. And I *am* Indiana.

Jenny squealed with delight.

188

I'm in Indiana swimming with Indiana!

I'm in Indiana watching for some weaponized zombie fish so they don't *eat* Indiana.

And I'm waiting on the shore hot and itchy on the sand in Indiana wishing Indiana would hurry up and help me clean up, too.

Indy splashed water at Brian with her hands. But then Napoleon's hands were under her armpits, lifting her up and pushing her forward, out of the reservoir.

He was screaming, *Out*, over and over and over.

Indy and Jenny by Brian, dripping. Napoleon returned to the water. He bent over, peering into it closely. Indy's breath hitched in her chest as she watched him. He reached into the water up to his elbow. Indy could hardly watch. His submerged arm jerked as he grabbed something. Jenny took Indy's hand and squeezed it hard enough to hurt.

Napoleon had plucked a crayfish from the water. A normal, not dead inside come back to life covered in glow-exoskeleton monster, but what appeared to be just a normal pre-apocalypse everyday crayfish. Indy was so shocked she stated the obvious.

A crayfish.

Napoleon tossed the thing on the sandy beach. They watched it skitter away. Brian licked his lips.

They are delicious.

The crayfish returned to the sanctity of the water. They watched as it disappeared below the surface. Before they could talk about what the crayfish meant, Napoleon screamed again.

The air had filled with glittering thumb-sized silver daggers. A weapon blizzard. A school of 'dillo minnows had risen from

189

the Goshen dam reservoir as a simple crayfish had held their curiosity.

A tidal wave of daggers several feet wide rose and pierced everything in its path. Napoleon, closest to the water, was hit first, his entire back their pincushion. Now a wretched version of a porcupine, he helped Indy grab the kids and race for the van while the wave of minnow knives crested upon them.

They made it back to the van. The Econoline van with the new huge glassless window.

Napoleon tossed Jenny through the lightning-bolt hole in the van. She bounced like a rag doll on the mattress, wailing, the side of her head riddled with silver daggers. Brian had escaped without any because Napoleon caught the wave headed towards him while Indy had thrown herself over him and rolled them both out of the way, saving them from the worst of the onslaught.

Napoleon leaned forward, chest pressed against the steering wheel to avoid driving the minnow daggers in his back deeper into his flesh. He started the van and treed into reverse. The beach where they had been joking and cleaning themselves seconds ago was sparkling with lively daggers. A second wave bounced onto the sand and redirected itself towards them. Indy pulled herself out from under Brian and joined Jenny on the mattress.

She screamed at Jenny to get into the front. Lifting the mattress up vertically, Indy slammed it over the hole in the van and held it up with her fists as Napoleon drove them from the dam. Like hail, 'dillo fish rained against the van. Indy felt the muted impact of them puncturing the other side of the mattress.

Returning to the road that had brought them there, they came to a new turnoff. Without asking, Napoleon took the southwest road. He coughed thickly, and spat blood onto the floor of the van.

No offense to you, Indy, but I really I hate Indiana.

Napoleon was in no shape to drive out of Indiana as the bleeding human porcupine. Indy leaned Brian up with his back against the mattress to keep it blocking the hole in the van. Jenny helped as best she could given her restless squirmy nature. Indy watched Napoleon sweat, bleed, bleed, blink, sweat and drive. Finally, Napoleon pulled over, turned off the engine and rasped, *Help me.* He collapsed forward, over the steering wheel then slumped slowly over onto the warm engine towards Indy. She caught him carefully, wary of driving the silver thumb quivers deeper into his skin. She pulled him partially out of his seat, chest down. She plucked one 'dillo fish from his shoulder blade.

Once it had been a harmless, boring minnow. Indy had used them many times for bait as she fished off the oxidized bridge over the Saugeen River. This zombie minnow was encased in iridescent plates as thin and as sharp as razor blades. They were weapons. The ones she pulled out were wearing a slimy coat of Napoleon's blood. The stench of rotted minnow wafted from the thumbnail-shaped inch-deep wound in Napoleon's back. Indy yelped as the thing bit into her. She dropped it to the floor of the van. She rolled down the window, struggled to catch the minnow as it flopped around, and finally flung it out. She had to get the remaining daggers out of his back. They were not done hurting Napoleon. They were boring tiny minnow-mouthful after tiny minnow-mouthful deeper and deeper into his flesh.

Using her thumb and forefinger like precision tweezers, Indy pulled the undead minnows out of Napoleon's back and hurled them from the van as fast as she could. Their bodies sliced into the pads of her fingers. Napoleon's blood mixed with her blood, making the job maddeningly slippery. Brian, wearing his mother's too-big 'dillo shelmet, hobbled from the van and began popping the discarded minnows like zits with the heel of his cast. Jenny helped by sitting, still naked and hugging herself, in the side doorway of the van and pointing to still flopping minnows. Napoleon groaned.

Don't sit up. Almost done.

Indy thought about AIDS and wondered if Napoleon had it. He didn't seem gay at all. If you were gay in Tara you better hide or someone would beat you. Indy was often accused of being gay because it was such a popular insult. He did carry himself like he knew a lot about sex of all kinds. I suppose, Indy thought, I'll die long before AIDS gets me anyhow. I guess I'm free to have reckless sex with anyone now.

There.

Napoleon sat up and slightly back, but not enough to touch his gouged out back against the Ford seat. He was free of minnows. He looked stricken.

Are you gonna faint again?

Napoleon chupsed. He moved his torso enough so he could pull his torn and bloody tuxedo shirt off. He handed it to Indy. She wiped her hands with it and looked down at her own nearly bare body. Indy grabbed one of the t-shirts with the catheads on them from where she'd stashed them at her feet. She tossed one at still naked Jenny and another at Napoleon. Pulling one on, she stared at her bare feet. They had left their shoes at the beach. How could she run away now when something chased her?

Cat shirts?

Napoleon held the shirt up. Jenny pranced around the back of the van in hers. It hung down past her knees.

It's the Stray Cats. You know, Rock This Town was their biggest hit, I think.

Oh.

Indy smiled.

Can I have one too?

Indy tossed Brian the remaining shirt as he slammed the van side door shut. His cast stunk. Napoleon put his shirt on and pulled back onto the road. Brian put the clean new shirt on overtop his old filthy shirt. He grinned.

We are like an official team now, with a uniform and everything.

Napoleon laughed.

Or a gang.

Yeah! Or a gang.

Indy nodded. She turned away from watching a pleased Brian to watching the empty road to Illinois and felt like she belonged.

***

Indiana's newest gang, the handicapped Stray Cats, crossed over into the land of Lincoln one hour before sundown. Gas was low. After refueling with one of three remaining jerry cans and checking Napoleon's clotting minnow wounds and only eye for abnormalities, they continued wordlessly west into the night.

Indy could see Napoleon straining to stay awake. He blinked for longer and longer intervals. He was unable to lean back because of his wounds. Jenny and Brian slept curled up as close as they could get to the front seats. Over the rumble of the engine between them, Indy started a conversation. She, at least, couldn't wait any longer.

Don't you want to know?

Know what?

Napoleon's gaze stayed fixed to the small off-center patch of light the vintage circular high beams threw on the road ahead.

How come you don't ask about Las Vegas?

I was hoping you knew something I didn't know.

Napoleon's skin glistened in the dark. The steering wheel had so much play in it his hands moved continually just to keep them driving in a straight line.

I've never been out of Detroit. I don't know anything about anywhere. I figure, you come all the way from Canada, you got more mileage than me.

I've never been to Las Vegas either.

Okay.

Indy stared at Napoleon. He stared at the road.

You just seemed real fixed on it and I'm not one to cause trouble without a good reason. Now you seem eager to tell, so tell it.

I'm not eager. I just don't want to drag you somewhere under false pretenses like a land of salvation or any real kind of plan.

So you have no plan?

Not a real one. I've got one that's hard to figure.

Napoleon ran his right hand over the back of his neck. His hand came away sticky with blood. He wiped it on his gang shirt.

Thinking the word made Indy squirm. She said it anyhow.

195

Father. I'm looking for my father.

I'm sorry if you two were close, but you know, unless we cross some sort of equator where every living thing, except for some asshole kids, has not turned into hard zombies, I don't think you're going to see your dad again.

Some old people, too.

Huh?

Some really old, like in their eighties, they survived too. I know because I killed one.

Napoleon smiled.

Also, it won't be "again."

What won't?

I mean, I have seen my dad but don't remember it so it is not really seeing him again. Last time I saw him I was three, I think. I guess. I don't remember what he looks like and I've never seen a picture. Only thing I think of is the ship on Molson's Canadian beer. You probably don't even know that beer. I used to hold it for him while we drove across Canada. He kidnapped me when my mom took me from him and we lived in the back of a truck. Like we are now. Only this is a Ford van and that was a Datsun pickup with a cap on the back.

How come you got no pictures?

My mom destroyed them. She believes if you think someone doesn't exist they don't. I tried that with my stepfather, but it didn't work, he didn't disappear. Until now, but that wasn't from thinking.

So you want to go to a city you never been to find a man you don't remember who most likely is dead, and even still is

196

walking around anyways and will want to eat you when he sees you?

That's exactly right.

Okay.

Okay? It makes no sense.

Makes perfect sense.

Explain it to me then.

You must know. You been waiting with all your might to make him real, all obsessed like, and just because the world ended doesn't mean you can stop.

Indy blinked; glad it was dark inside the van.

Napoleon touched his foot lightly to the brakes, shifting, slowing the van down to a roll.

Lucky for you, I got no specific designs or obsessions for the end of the world besides trying to see more of it before … well, before.

The van rolled to a stop and he turned to look at Indy. He shut the engine and the high beams off. Everything went black. In the darkness, Napoleon felt around for Indy's hand. He squeezed.

Indy and Napoleon fell asleep like that, in the front seat of the van, holding hands. Indy slumped sideways with her head resting on one side of the pleasantly warm engine cover and Napoleon folded over on the other side, the tops of their heads touching.

***

Jenny woke them at first light.

197

Look.

Jenny pointed across the pale unharvested cornfields.
Something moved deep in the middle, making the husks rustle.
It was clear from the movement of the corn, it was moving
towards them.

Napoleon let go of Indy's hand to start the engine. Indy placed
her hand once again around his and whispered *stop*.

Indy had heard it first because of her hyper-vigilance. Finally,
they all heard.

JUST KILL ME.

Someone was hollering from the cornfield. Words, not a siren.
A naked boy burst out of one of the rows. He was filthy. His
flaccid penis flopped around some dark but sparse pubic hairs.
Indy's second real-life penis sighting. So much less terrifying
than Magic's. The boy had dark red gouges in his shoulders.
His feet were wrapped in husk. In each hand he held a cob of
shucked corn either for eating or perhaps for hitting, maybe
both. The boy did not break stride as he emerged from the field
but ran right for them.

Kill me. Kill me. Kill me.

The Kill Me boy was out of the corn stalks, but the cornhusks
moved still.

The Stray Cats gang watched as a six foot tall 'dillo lumbered
from the field. Husk and corn silk, like bicycle streamers,
floated from its joints. The jaw chomped like a piston.

Kill Me Boy ran onto the road in front of their van and hurled
himself against the grill, his eyes and forehead high enough
that they mashed into the windshield. He kept his eyes open,
even on impact.

Kill me.

The Stray Cats watched.

Kill Me Boy bounced off the flat front of the van and landed a few feet in front of it, on the ground.

Kill me.

Indy felt Napoleon's hand tense inside hers. She let it go so he could start the van. The 'dillo reached Kill Me Boy and fulfilled his wish. In one wet bite.

The 'dillo, eating a skin and gore neck sandwich, stood and stared at them through its carapace with swollen dead eyes.

Napoleon shifted into reverse, making good use of the van's tight turning circle, and headed back the way they had come.

The pneumatic air raid whine trailed after them. Brian tapped his head anxiously on the back of Indy's seat. They backtracked a dozen miles and turned south, everyone straining to hear if the zombie call was fading or growing over the roar of the engine. They drove like that for hours.

Stop.

Napoleon slammed on the brakes.

Drive to the tree.

Indy pointed ahead. In the middle of a dry mud field was one lonely tree, laden with some sort of fruit.

Napoleon rolled to a stop near the tree. He turned to Indy, completely unable to hide his confusion as he held up his hands to say *what gives?*

Indy answered his hands.

199

It's a shoe tree.

Napoleon leaned forward so he could better see the tree through the windshield. His expression changed from annoyed confusion to horror. His eyes never left the tree.

Does this mean that the plants are changing now too?

His voice sounded, for the first time since Indy had known him, hoarse with fear.

Indy laughed. Brian joined her.

Silly, a shoe tree is man-made. It's normal.

Napoleon pointed at the tree.

You are telling me *that* is normal?

Yeah. It's a thing people spontaneously do. I don't even know why. It probably started with one person throwing a couple pairs of shoes up in the branches for kicks. Then someone saw it and stopped, and threw theirs and so on till you get this, a magnificent shoe tree.

The tree, once a simple old oak, was dead yet overripe with shoe fruit. Undead, Indy supposed, in its own harmless way. Hundreds of pairs of shoes dangled by laces from its branches. More laceless kinds like sandals and flip-flops, were piled in heaps around the base.

Napoleon shook his head.

You white folks have x amount of tricks up your sleeves.

This is a trick we can use.

Jenny bounced from the van squealing with delight.

The variously handicapped gang, walked bare-footed over the cracked earth of the dry mud field. They got to work finding shoes. The sizes and varieties were ample. The hard part was finding a pair of anything in good enough shape to bear running and kicking. Most of the shoes were left because they were very worn out. Except the kids shoes. The small ones were in better shape. Jenny found a dozen pairs she wanted, and Brian, who had taken the shoe off his one good leg at the beach, hunted anyway, for fun.

Napoleon had the worst time. He had never worn used shoes and was complaining so much Indy felt sure he'd rather face another school of flying minnows than wear used shoes. He informed his gang he would only wear certain brands and to please watch out for them.

Indy was incredulous, but too busy working on her own shoes to watch what anyone else was doing. She tossed another pair of navy blue Keds away because she could not cram her whole foot into them.

Certain *brands*? I need something that fits my size 10 feet.

Napoleon sighed angrily at a pair of no-name white canvas sneakers, in his size, that Jenny hand delivered to him. She was wearing her prized find: black velvet Chinese slippers. Indy would kill for a pair of those.

She watched as Napoleon's defeat switched to victory. His green eye locked on a position almost at the top of the huge shoe tree. He walked towards the trunk of the tree and wrapped his hands around the lowest branch. In two swift moves, the first being a chin up and the second a heave of his torso over the branch, he was sitting in the tree.

Indy could see, along with the definition in his forearms and the pump in his biceps, dark patches opening up all over the back of his Stray Cats t-shirt. If the shirt had been white, she knew the patches would be blood red.

What are you doing?

I found my shoes.

How many trees have you climbed?

None. What are you, tree police?

He hugged the trunk of the tree weirdly.

No. But, I am a tree-climbing expert.

When I was in grade 8, I did my science project on ornithology. I started climbing trees and collecting nests a whole year before, along with drawing and coloring scale model birds to fit into the nests. Since most birds use old nests for parts the next year, I put them back where I found them in the spring, after I won the science fair.

Napoleon stood up on the first branch.

Indy walked under Napoleon and gazed up. A drop of his blood fell on her cheek. She backhanded it off, leaving a wide blush-like smear.

If you show me the shoes you want, I'll get them for you. This is my territory.

Napoleon looked down at her, beads of sweat popping out on his forehead.

Okay, you win. Look out.

Napoleon jumped off the branch and landed hard but evenly on his bare feet. He walked away from the trunk and pointed up, using his other hand as a shield from the afternoon sun.

It's those. The Filas.

Indy gazed up. Three-quarters of the way up the tree. He was pointing at one of the highest hanging shoes. They were shiny white with a glossy black trim. She could just make out what might be a Fila symbol on the tongue. She took a deep breath and began her first tree climb ever that was not for birds.

Napoleon pulled his Filas on.

DO THEY FIT?

Indy stood on a branch sixteen feet in the air. The Filas had been hanging fruit-like from it seconds before.

The laces are jacked!

Indy looked up, soaking up the small fashion victory and taking in her surroundings. She saw no people or 'dillo anywhere. She could see fields of raggedy corn, roads empty of anything except the odd crashed car. She counted six silos, two steel barns and one tidy red brick farmhouse with a pickup truck in the driveway. And not just any pickup. She was no vehicle expert, but she knew this Datsun instantly because she had lived in one just like it with her dad. The only difference was his truck had been mustard yellow. This one was white. Otherwise, they looked exactly the same.

In the front yard of the Datsun farmhouse, in between punctuation clumps of peony shrubs, were letters about six feet high made of what looked like flour or salt. Something white, like the truck. From this high and far it was hard to tell.

Indy watched the farmhouse for movement and, save for an aluminum screen door that was tap-tapping against the brick of the house with the breeze, she saw none.

She stared at the letters beside the Datsun. They spelled HEL. A lost fourth letter had become just a snowy tinge on the grass.

Indy shivered. She was standing two stories up in nothing but a t-shirt just long enough to cover her ass. She had scraped her inner thighs on the climb up. Napoleon was yelling at her.

Are you ever coming off that thing!

This *thing,* Indy thought, is a shoe tree.

Indy lowered herself carefully down onto her branch, her toes gripping monkey-tight. She was terrified of heights. But she was more afraid of unsolvable things. Her fear of heights, like her fear of 'dillos and Dana, were solvable, short term, and thus completely tolerable forms of terror. Comfortable, soothing even, in a way. Fixable fears were fun.

Indy dropped and swung down the branches as modestly as she could. Napoleon was more interested in spit polishing his Filas than watching her. Probably he only watched her go up to learn some tree skills.

She dropped from the final branch and had to steady herself against the branch above her head because she landed on an upside-down shoe. She flipped it right side up and saw it was a Weejun penny loafer in size 10. Her foot slipped in like a glove. It even had a penny in it. A Lincoln penny. With her newly shod foot, she kicked around in a pile of sneakers searching for its mate. Jenny joined her in releasing the rank odor of moldy rubber and vintage foot sweat as they sifted through the pile of laceless shoes.

It's like Easter! Only like Easter *at the mall*!

Napoleon, Filas gleaming, dropped to his knees to help. He reached under a matted Garfield slipper, its plastic half-mast eyeballs cracked and faded, and produced the match to Indy's Weejun. He crawled over to her and presented it for her to try on. Indy's foot fit perfectly, again. Jenny, overcome with joyful emotion and Disney sentiments, cried out.

It's like Cinderella!

Indy walked back to the van shaking her head.

Napoleon swung up into the driver's seat and turned the key. The motor remained silent. There was no meaty roar, just a tinny click. He tried again. Nothing.

Jenny offered her ideal solution.

Maybe we should stay here at the shoe tree forever!

I need some kind of drugs or booze for my back. And I need something real to eat besides Twinkies and candy bars.

Indy, who had lived most of her life on Fruit Loops and Orville Redenbacher's Nacho Flavored Popcorn because her mother's cooking was poisonous, didn't miss real food. But Las Vegas.

I saw a house.

NAPOLEON

Indy was not lying. But she was not telling all the truth either when she told them what she saw from that cracker art shoe tree. She was an open book to him.

When I was picking your Filas from the tree, I saw a farmhouse about a mile away. There was a truck in the yard.

She paused and picked dried crap off her missing ear.

It's likely the battery, but we've got nothing to jump it with.

Indy didn't even seem to hear him.

Well, we can't just sit here. Let's go.

Napoleon could be gentle to keep the peace and not push. His mom got furious with backtalk. He'd get one warning from the back of her hand. And a serious tongue lashing. Her favorite insult was one-eyed devil. If he defied her further, she'd tie him to a metal kitchen chair with her bedtime bras and cook up voodoo stew. All ingredients could vary depending on what was in the fridge except one. Usually they had leftover goat roti, chicken feet and okra. To that she'd add a spoonful of one essential ingredient: either fresh or preserved menstrual blood. When she got her monthly she caught as much as she could and cooked it down to a jelly with pectin, strained it through her pantyhose and kept it in an old mayonnaise jar marked with a red X. This voodoo stew will get in you, she'd say, shoveling it fast into his face like when he was a baby and couldn't use his hands. He'd turn away and spill as much as he could. By the end, he'd have equal amounts of period blood voodoo stew in his lap as in his stomach. He couldn't probably taste her blood in the stew, but at the same time it was all he could taste. Sometimes, mostly when he was younger, he'd vomit it up. She'd catch that in the same bowl she was feeding him from and, screaming devil, stir it all together – vomited stew and not-yet-vomited-stew and force him to eat this even more wretched voodoo/vomit stew mix. He supposed it worked though, her voodoo stew, because it had taught him infinite patience.

Napoleon was sure Indy had her own white version of voodoo stew but was not yet sure where she kept it or how it was getting in him.

***

They moved across fields in the direction of the tiny brick farmhouse. It was Jenny who pointed out the giant H through some fence line sycamores.

They reached the trees. Indy lowered Brian from piggyback onto a rock pile and gave him her shotgun. Indy held her maul by the head and glanced at Napoleon.

Ready?

Born.

Napoleon peeled Jenny off his legs and returned her hug with a pat on the head.

Do what Brian says. Don't go anywhere.

Jenny nodded solemnly and plopped down on the rock pile in front of Brian.

Tracing the shadow line of late afternoon trees, Indy and Napoleon approached the farmhouse. They stopped at a huge boulder at the bottom of the yard. They could hear the taptaptapping of the screen door. They had a clear view of H E L letters, and the front door. And the Datsun truck. Indy dropped to sit in the lee of the boulder and pressed her back to its coolness. Napoleon had his shoulder against it so he could face her on his haunches. He deftly snuck his hand around the nape of Indy's neck. Burying his hand into her hair there, he used it to pull her lips up to his. His tongue circled over her closed lips, so lightly it tickled. Shocked, Indy responded for two heartbeats before yanking her head away from his grasp. Undeterred, Napoleon traced his hand down around her remaining ear.

Relax; it's just for luck.

Napoleon strode over the letter E, smudging it. He made it safely and quieted the tapping front door of the farm. Indy, in kiss shock, wobbled after him. She wasn't sure if she hated it. The yard letters, she could now tell, were not composed of one thing but were an amalgam of household stuff. Most of the H and the vertical line of the E were white paint. The E vertices were heavy gritted stuff, like coarse salt or sugar and the L was a mixture of eggshells and finer powder, maybe flour. It had begun to blow away like the P.

The front door was locked. Napoleon slammed a Fila'd foot into the old wood and it cracked away from the jam. They were in. The original residents of the house had had their own personal apocalypse years before the current 'dillo one. For years, plaster had been peeling away in huge curls from the living room ceiling and breaking off onto a tweed sofa that sagged preposterously. The baseboards were missing, as were the light fixtures. Bare bulbs were screwed into all the sockets.

Napoleon rushed Indy again. He pressed her against the wall beside the front door. His hand found her nape again and his tongue her lips, but this time he split them apart and sank deeply towards her throat. Indy groaned. She could feel his penis through his jeans, against her hip. He smelled familiar and sweet, like fresh topsoil warmed by the sun after a rain when she re-filled the emptied marijuana pots with new soil after harvest. Napoleon spoke evenly into her ruined ear.

I want you. But I want you to be ready. You have to ask me, you have to tell me when.

Napoleon released her and left the room. Indy's mind blanked. A clear image of her mother eating her ear shot across that emptiness. Her ear scabs ached and that ache spread like

209

morning light. She was fully awake. When words returned, she wondered, how could he think she would ever know when.

Kitchen's got lots of food. And one of those country stoves you probably know how to use.

Indy could hear canned food being slid around.

She joined Napoleon in the kitchen.

That's not a country stove. It's a wood cook stove.

Napoleon clunked a can of chunky beef stew on top of the stove and stepped back.

Tell me you don't know how to use it.

First, you need some wood.

***

Wood was plentiful and kept in a tin lean-to outside the kitchen door. There was no sign of recent life other than the H E L sign, so the sign had either worked well and fast or, not worked at all, still fast. Mostly importantly, the farm was 'dillo free.

Indy heated four tins of childfree stew on top of the cook stove: one each. Jenny and Napoleon dragged wool blankets and drool-stained ticking pillows into the kitchen so they could all be together, by the fire. Brian fell asleep literally in his bowl of stew after consuming most of it. Jenny laughed and then did almost the same thing. There were no bandages, but they did find a full bottle of Jack Daniels and some duct tape, and with that Indy went to work on Napoleon's ravaged back using only the light of the fire to inspect the wounds for pus or worse.

Napoleon lay down on his stomach and Indy kneeled beside him, the wood cook stove open in front of them to cast maximum light. The thirty or so minnow entry/exit wounds gaped like hungry open mouths. The puffy red-rimmed sores

210

were surely infected. Indy leaned in close over Napoleon's back to see if she could smell infection. All she could smell was him.

Indy unscrewed the lid on the Jack Daniels.

Napoleon answered by sucking in and holding his breath. Indy poured. The familiar sweet smell filled the kitchen. Jack Daniels had been the only thing her stepfather Dana drank. Indy covered every wound and the booze pooled up in the small of Napoleon's back. He glistened in the firelight. He let out his breath and craned his neck around, arching his back so he could look.

It'd be a shame to waste that.

Indy used what smelled like a clean flannel bedsheet to soak up the Jack Daniels pool.

I don't drink. Never have, never will.

Never is a big word.

Napoleon flipped over, grabbed the Jack Daniels and downed the rest in three long pulls. He flipped back over, sliding the empty bottle away from him along the kitchen floor. It came to a stop under the cook stove. Indy returned to drying his back, massaging softly, too slowly, between the wounds. I am ridiculous, she thought. We are barely alive and fighting to stay that way, so we can get to Las Vegas. But instead I am enjoying this.

Indy swung her leg over Napoleon and straddled him like a horse. She dropped her tongue down between two wounds on his shoulder blade causing Napoleon to flex away in shock. She maintained contact and lightly tasted her way up to the nape of his neck, licking through his minnow sores. Words were forming on her lips when a hairy shroud encircled her, small teeth clamping cruelly down on the base of her skull.

Indy could see the Jack Daniels under the stove and, stretching down over Napoleon, she grasped the bottle's neck, taking a swing at the thing on her back. Napoleon flipped over beneath her and stopped the arc of the bottle cold, yanking it from her hand. Face to face now, so close she could feel the force of his breath, he could surely see the hurt spread upon her face. Napoleon slipped out from under her and snatched the thing off her back. Freed, Indy gained her feet to unsheathe her diving knife from its home on her calf.

Napoleon was holding a hysterical Jenny in a bear hug.

She was eating you! KILL HER!

Indy took a breath. Napoleon laughed, Jenny was clamped tightly in his arms so her swings at Indy could not connect.

Calm down, calm down. She wasn't eating me.

Brian was awake too.

We were just playing, right Indy?

Indy hated bullshitting kids.

Yeah. We were sort of making out, I guess.

Jenny was still whining but had stopped swinging her arms.

Take a look; my sockets still have eyeballs.

Napoleon let Jenny go and she stepped forward to look into Indy's eyes. Her anger dissolved as quickly as it had arrived. She danced, pressing her fist into her crotch.

Okay. You guys play weird. I gotta pee.

Indy lifted a Mason jar from a shelf.

It's safer if we stay inside. Do you think you can pee into this?

If you help me.

Indy nodded. The two girls went to the room where Napoleon had pressed Indy against the wall and whispered instructions.

Okay, I'll hold it upright. Just use your hand to wipe and we'll wash it off after.

Indy turned away and listened to Jenny pee, reliving what had happened against the wall. Jenny once again interrupted her.

I'm bleeding! I'm bleeding!

The little girl was holding her hand up in the firelight spilling in from the kitchen. Surely, Indy thought, she was just freaked out. Or maybe while Jenny was attacking her she had cut herself. Taking the girl back to the kitchen, she examined her hand in front of the cook stove's light.

Jenny's hand was bloody. Napoleon took it, flipping it this way and that, looking for injury. Her hand appeared uninjured, without even a small cut or scrape.

Are you hurt? Where does it hurt!

Nowhere, nowhere but I'm bleeeeeeeeeding!

Napoleon hugged her close and tried to quiet her, all the while feeling around her body for the source of blood.

And then Indy knew. She ran to get the jar Jenny had peed in and saw a blossom of blood in the urine, slowly diffusing the dark yellow to ochre. She checked Jenny's bedclothes and these too were bloodied at the spot where her bottom was resting.

Despite her age, Jenny was doing something that Indy had not yet begun to do herself.

Jenny had begun to menstruate.

They were always prepared, as one of the quaint chroniclers of the time phrased it, to 'explain hell to the savages.' – *Mark Twain, Life on the Mississippi*

She's fine. She's not hurt. It's normal.

Indy held the jar of Jenny's pee up to the firelight for everyone to see.

Napoleon was still pressing around Jenny's abdomen and still asking her where it hurt.

Jenny, is it your first?

My first what?

Napoleon's pained expression dissolved. Then reappeared.

She's too young, isn't she?

Napoleon looked like he was going to throw up.

No. My best friend was only twelve and her cousin was ten.

What should we do?

Indy opened the woodstove door wider.

Bring Jenny by the fire.

Jenny let Brian study her eyes. He looked back and forth carefully and then backed away clumsily, nearly tripping on his own casted leg.

Indy took Jenny's head in her hands so she could see for herself. In Jenny's right eye a clear spot had appeared, the

215

same vertical shape as a goat iris, but off center and thinner. If Jenny were a pencil drawing, it would be as if the white, iris, and pupil of her eye had been removed with an eraser, revealing the blankness beneath. Napoleon took his turn looking and then he hugged Jenny close again. Indy helped Brian back into his blankets.

What now.

The same thing we been doing. Following you to Las Vegas. Being careful.

Napoleon pulled Jenny even closer. Indy shook her head. Napoleon's words made no sense.

If we were *careful* we would not *pretend* she is not dangerous. Any second she could summon an army to murder us.

I'm not pretending. You or me or Brian, we could change any second. Why you so hung up on Jenny?

Indy called forth her condescension so it could froth up and ooze from her voice.

Let me explain it to you. Boys get puberty later. That means Brian is no risk and you, you don't even have facial hair. Your voice is high. Like a girl. I might be the biggest risk, but I am not even close to bleeding. Look at me. But mostly, I trust *me*. To take off or at least tell. But Jenny, I don't trust her. She's too childish. Flitty.

Napoleon leaned towards Indy, holding Jenny tight, the firelight bouncing off his bare skin, slick with hostility.

So your answer is what? We leave her? We chop her head off?

Jenny squeaked, squirmed out of his arms and ran – flitted, Indy thought silently – from the kitchen. They could hear the clacking footfalls of her Chinese slippers on the stairs.

216

She's changed. Brian saw the same thing happen in his brother's eyes.

Indy looked to Brian for confirmation.

Brian nodded.

In three days his eyes were gone. He tried to fight it, but when I took his head off he was a monster just the same. You think that girl can fight it, or tell us when it is too late? She can't even sit still for five minutes when we ask her.

Indy turned to look in the direction Jenny had run, away from the firelight and Napoleon and Brian. Indy tried to summon confidence, but her voice had weakened to a whine.

I have to get to Las Vegas.

Nothing, *no one*, else matters. Right?

Indy winced and stared at the floorboards.

All this is sidetracking. I don't know how I got here.

You don't know?

Napoleon glared at the back of Indy's head.

Brian cleared his throat.

We might be all that's left. We might be it. The last people.

We can't be. There were the kids in Detroit.

Brian touched the supper bowl he had fallen asleep in.

Those kids are stew by now.

There were the racist kids too. For all we know, we'll walk out of this.

Do you really believe that?

No one spoke. Brian sniffled. He was crying.

Should the last people be fighting like this?

Yes! Indy thought. She lifted her hand to pick her ear and stopped herself.

Okay.

Hope shone from Brian's eyes, bright as firelight.

Okay, what?

Okay, of course we can't just kill her. Maybe leave her?

Napoleon growled.

That would be the same thing. Let's just take turns with her. Always watch her.

Then what?

Let's all decide together at the time, when we reach it.

Indy nodded quietly, screaming LAS VEGAS at the top of her lungs, inside. Bottled up, it banged at her ribs like a fist.

I'll go get her.

Napoleon pulled on his shirt. Indy could see his wounds had not re-opened despite hugging Jenny.

Indy shook her head and stood, too.

No, no. I caused this. Let me fix it.

From the bottom of the stairs, Indy could hear Jenny's dismal sobs. She sounded like her baby sister. How much longer before she could get to Las Vegas?

By the light from the stars, Indy found Jenny huddled and quivering in a corner of what was once a master bedroom. Now it reeked the cinnamon odor of rot. The detritus of a decade of abandonment marked the room: rodent droppings, a rusty headboard and a half-full bottle Karo syrup. Thousands of tiny Styrofoam pearls used in the 1960s to add insulation moved around the room in the slightest air current, no one predicting the mess they'd be when they leaked out of every crevice and crack. The drifts of insulation beads looked like snow in the pale light. It was as though Jenny's misery had caused an alternate climate within the house. Indy's shadow fell on the sobbing girl.

I'm sorry, Jenny, please. It's okay now. Come back downstairs. I was worried or confused or something, but I'd never hurt you.

Like a faucet, Jenny turned the sobbing off. Her breath wore the hitches of deep grief. She did not look up, her mounds of dreaded hair shrouding around her. It reminded Indy of Kris, and how his hair would hide his face when he was both really happy and really sad so you could not tell the difference.

I have *hitch hitch* a message *hitch* for you.

Jenny's hand slunk down her legs to her ankle.

Jenny, please. Come downstairs.

But I said I have *a message.*

Jenny stood and lifted her chin, her face tipping out from both her hair and the shadow Indy's body cast on her. Indy took a step backwards so Jenny's face could be in full light.

Indy could not see where Jenny was looking. But no longer because of hair or shadow. She could not see where Jenny was looking because one of her eye sockets was completely empty, absorbing all starlight like a black hole, and the other wore a wide strip of light swallowing blankness right across where a pupil had once been. Indy's entire body clenched in time with her breathing. She was breathing hard enough to spin insulation pearls around her feet wildly.

Jenny tilted her head as though trying to understand something, like a dog sometimes does when issued a new and strange command. She explained herself.

I have a *message,* and it is from your *father.*

Jenny sprang. Indy realized too late she had been coiled not huddled in the corner of the dilapidated room. Coiled to strike at her.

Jenny flew into Indy's face. Indy managed to bow her head down so instead of nose or cheek, Jenny got a mouthful of Indy's hair. Her hands clawed at Indy's neck, her feet struggling to grip onto the older girl's narrow hips. Indy pulled back both her arms and slammed her fists into Jenny's chest.

Jenny flew back and down, stripping out a clump of Indy's hair from the crown of her head, bloodied roots and all. Now Indy knew how her bully Laurie Courtan felt when Indy had finally retaliated. Jenny wiped Indy's hair onto the cat face of their gang shirt and lunged again.

Indy was ready. She had her knife. The two girls connected mid-air, Jenny's emptying eye met Indy's well-used diving knife. Indy drove the knife in hard as she could, burying it to the hilt. A red surge splashed Indy's face. Their combined efforts toppled them both to the ground, Indy on top, still gripping her weapon.

Ruhhh was the final message Jenny delivered before she took what Indy hoped was her last breath. The room stank, not just

220

of emptiness, but now of battle. Indy dislodged her knife, wiped it across the shoulder of Jenny's t-shirt and took the stairs down to the kitchen three at a time.

What did you do? You *liar?*

Indy stood before Napoleon wearing a mask of Jenny's blood, gesturing sadly upstairs. He pushed past her, ignoring her. Indy looked to Brian but found no solace, only an indictment of grief. Before Napoleon could come downstairs to avenge Jenny, or Brian could make up his own names for his disappointment in her, Indy grabbed her maul and bolted from the house into the clear, still warm night.

PART II: August 1988

APOCOLYPSE: HAPPY ENDINGS

What I have in view is a much humbler, though perhaps, in the present state of science, not less useful object. I have desired, in fact, to show how the careful study of one of the commonest and most insignificant of animals, leads us, step by step, from every-day knowledge to the widest generalizations and the most difficult problems of zoology; and, indeed, of biological science in general.

– Thomas Henry Huxley, The Crayfish: An Introduction to the Study of Zoology

Tumbleweeds were all she remembered about Oklahoma. As she crossed it on Route 66 towards Amarillo, they had been terrifying. The worrisome things looked to be a heretofore unseen expression of the armored living dead apocalypse. There were no tumbleweeds in Tara. Indy resolved her tumbleweed concerns by boldly smacking into one with the Datsun truck she took the night she lit out and away from her Stray Cats gang, so she could get a closer look.

Ah-ha, she had realized, feeling like a dope, this must be the thing called tumbleweed. She had seen them in Wile E. Coyote cartoons. Pulling branches out of the Datsun's grill, she scolded herself for being afraid of a dead plant after successfully slaying hundreds of undead everythings from human to rat. Texas was stupid with this goofy rolling weed, herds of it caught up by their sharp stiff parts on the fences. Indy wondered if fences in Texas were to keep cattle in or if they were merely tumbleweed nets. That got her to wondering if she could build a similar net to catch 'dillos.

Indy puckered inward. She hated how Brian's word – 'dillo – had come to be the name she called the carapaced predators that had superseded humanity, or at least all of it in the six states and one province Indy had been through. She scratched her ear; the final scab gave way and she flicked it to the floor of the Datsun. She had abandoned Brian after impaling Jenny through her empty eye socket. Her actions, though defensive, burnt out all the warmth Brian and Napoleon had for her. As tragic as it was to lose the closest friends she had on Earth, and maybe the closest she had ever known in life, it was a comfort. She was no longer waiting for the other shoe to drop. She hated thinking of shoes now too because it reminded her of the Filas she had plucked from the shoe tree for Napoleon. He had convicted her so easily and in a way that was all too familiar.

By luck, the Datsun truck Indy had seen from the top of the shoe tree was unlocked. Better luck still, the keys were in ignition. The upside of how quickly the apocalypse killed everyone was that no one had time to put their keys away. The residue of the Datsun owner's chrysalis puffed about when she sat down behind the steering wheel. Since Indy had lived in exactly the same model vehicle with her dad when he kidnapped her, she knew just where to flick on the headlights – that had been a job he gave her to make her feel important and needed. The Datsun started immediately. She drove over the fading H E L sign on the lawn, and never looked back. Not even in the rearview mirror.

Indy had lost track of everything except tumbleweeds and that included the count of days. She knew it had taken more than five and less than twenty before she had reached Texas. During the uncounted days, she had managed to make the Datsun homey. She had found a black and white suitcase somewhere. The clothes in it were very large men's clothes, but there was one navy sundress with spaghetti straps and it fit her perfectly. Eager to rid herself of her ex-gang shirt, she had stepped into the dress immediately and had not taken it off since. She tossed the Stray Cats t-shirt out the Datsun window at the tumbleweeds. There was also a pair of black army boots that were about one and a half sizes too big for her, and far too wide. But she had to get rid of her shoe tree nostalgic Cinderella loafers. They gave her blisters anyway.

She remembered Missouri because it was there she found the final thing needed to make the Datsun home. As she drove watching for 'dillos she also looked for yellow clapboard houses. That state was full of painted wooden houses and, while whitewashing aging wood seemed to be most popular, she guessed it wouldn't be long until she saw a yellow one. Just south of a town called Lebanon she found it. A typical box style farmhouse with a plain Jane wrap-around porch and a driveway long enough to park ten trucks in. The house had a fairly fresh coat of mustard yellow paint. Pretty perfect. Indy parked at the end of the driveway and turned off the Datsun.

She settled in to watch, stakeout style like they do in detective shows. She ate wine grapes as she waited, seeds and all.

Thirty grapes in, the yellow clapboard house had remained silent and unremarkable. Indy drove up the driveway and once inside she located the basement door (under the stairway to the second floor) and, using the Bic she'd found in the Datsun's ashtray, lit her way down the dark cellar stairwell.

She saw them immediately. Glidden house paint, three cans high and as many deep. More than enough. Rooting around for a brush or some kind of rag to paint with, she found more proof she was on the right track: a fancy box containing an old revolver and several boxes of ammunition. There was even a tube and rag that Indy assumed was for cleaning the gun. The rag was too small to paint with, but the foam packed around the gun to keep it safe was made of sponge. Perfectly adequate to use for painting!

That had been some number of days ago. Indy feared the house paint would not dry right. Or would smear when she drove while the paint was still wet. But her fears had been unfounded.

She was finally at home, living and driving west across Texas in what was nearly the vehicle she had lived in with her dad: a mustard yellow Datsun. She popped more heat-softened wine grapes in her mouth and chased it with hot Pepsi. Texas was hot. Hotter than the hottest day in Tara, and hot all day long and into the night.

Heat rippling across the blacktop made it tricky to distinguish tumbleweeds from 'dillos. It confused her eyes and made the road look as though it was dissolving into parched Texas sky. That's how she nearly ran over the hitchhiker.

Indy slammed on the brakes locking eyes with the hitcher as his face flashed past her windshield and side window. Heat weak tire-rubber smeared into gooey Texas blacktop.

The Datsun screeched to a stop diagonally across the road. The hitchhiker braced against the side of the truck, hands out like a human umlaut. I wonder, thought Indy, choking on the sweet smoke of rubber and road, if there is any tire left. She pulled the yellow clapboard house revolver from under her seat and drew down on the hitchhiker, hoping she'd taken the safety off right so she could fire this old gun.

Get lost.

What fuck is this?

The hitchhiker spoke with an unplaceable accent. He looked petrified.

I never meant this.

You never meant what? Trying to crash and kill me or trying to crash me and failing?

No.

He carried a burlap feed sack, round with something. His feet were bare and black with filth. He smiled with yellow teeth.

I'm meaning to arrive with you.

The high solemn bell of shoothimshoothim clanged Indy's head so hard she had to give it a shake. The hitchhiker turned, and she appreciated the shirt he was wearing.

What's your name?

Grinning like a fool, as though the world were not apocalypting, the boy spoke nonchalantly.

Boaz. Only going to Grand Canyon this time.

What was it last time?

The hitchhiker did not even smile. Indy caved.

Her head continued to ring but the boy was just a smidge bigger than her, so surely not much stronger. His deep-set brown eyes were puppy dog miserable and joyous at the same time. Mostly what convinced her was his Public Enemy t-shirt. Boaz stared at her in disbelieving joy, then at the truck, swinging his burlap sack over his shoulder to climb in. No longer alone, Indy once again set off across the top of Texas.

I need to get Grand Canyon.

Boaz opened his sack and produced a glass jar of water. He unscrewed it and took three long pulls. He put the cap back on. Indy stared longingly after the water, momentarily ignoring the boy's obsession with the Grand Canyon. All she had was pop. He re-opened and passed her the jar.

You like it?

Indy took it and, keeping her eyes on the road, gulped a mouthful. The truck swerved on the road. She choked on the liquid fire as it burned all the way down to her gut. She recovered enough to pull the truck back in line with the road. She had never *felt* the shape of her esophagus before, but now here it was on fire each inch all the way down inside. Indy spat and dropped the jar. Boaz deftly grabbed hold of it mid-air, spilling only a little of the noxious liquid on the bench seat. The sharp smell of alcohol polluted the cab of the truck.

Are you still trying to kill me?

Boaz answered by taking another long drink.

Indy had no interest in drink. She had entirely avoided it. Until now. A goddamned hitchhiker had broken her perfect streak of non-drinking. She contemplated ramming her fingers down her throat to puke it up but decided it would still count against her.

227

Boaz used the edge of his Public Enemy shirt to wipe up the spillage on the seat and dab spray from Indy's gagging off the dashboard. He sucked on what his shirt had soaked up.

I love America sceneries.

Let me guess, like the Grand Canyon?

Somehow he looked surprised she knew.

I don't think that stuff is meant to be had like water.

Sure, yes, of course it is.

To prove his point, he took another massive swig and tried to pass the jar over to her.

Indy shook her head. She smiled at the next thing he pulled out of his bag: a cassette tape. He popped it in the Datsun's tape player, and for the first time in ages Indy was listening to music.

It was music she'd never heard before. It was punk but then it strangely had a rhythm like reggae at the same time.

Boaz bounced on the seat, pouring moonshine down his throat.

Indy racked her mind for where he might be from. He had dark hair, darker eyes. Even his skin was a deep gold.

Spanish?

No way, Johnson!

It's Jose.

Indy laughed as the Datsun smacked another tumbleweed. Boaz looked confused.

It's 'No way, Jose,' and not Johnson.

Right. Keep more guesses.

Egypt or some Arab country?

Boaz's formerly bouncy friendly expression vanished. His
forehead creased between his generous eyebrows. He finished
his liquor.

Arabs are pure fuck!

Indy did not interrupt Boaz's tirade. He ejected his tape and
held it to her face, gesturing wildly with it. Over radio static,
Boaz continued his diatribe.

My hate makes all this death right. Does that frighten you?

Having come to appreciate the upside of this apocalypse
herself, Indy had no problem whatsoever with Boaz's position.
She smiled and shrugged. She was about to tell him when the
radio static crackled and spit out a female voice.

Stay tuned for more news.

Indy mashed her too-big boot onto the brake pedal, stopping
the truck so that no road noise would interfere with her
listening. She twirled the radio volume to its maximum and
held her breath. Boaz looked as though he was about to speak
so she pressed her fingers to his lips and shook her head in case
he didn't understand that gesture. A familiar song began to
play. The audio quality was poor, like it was being played off
an old, scratched record.

The record skipped a couple times. They could hear the sound
of the needle scratching as it was lifted from the vinyl and
reset. The sound was instantly recognizable to Indy. Her
stepfather had been anal and obsessive about his records.
Despite and because of Dana, she was insanely acquainted with
the proper treatment and use of record albums. Finally, the
album played. It was the American national anthem.

Should we get out and do the stand with hands and hearts?

For all his strange tantrums and goofy accent, Boaz had proven himself an amusing passenger. Indy smiled and met Boaz's drunken red eyes.

Nope. Neither of us are American.

Boaz put his empty moonshine jar in his sack and produced a Polaroid camera.

Indy was transfixed by the radio. Could the 'dillolypse really be regional? Did a radio station mean her father was normal and alive?

The song ended. A voice, the same female voice, returned.

Water water everywhere. Water water everywhere.

Boaz pushed the big red button on his Polaroid and the sound of the film ejecting from the camera body drowned out radio lady.

Don't you want to hear what she's saying?

Indy knew those words; her mother used to recite them, more of her made-up nonsense she would tone-deaf sing whenever Dana wasn't around, like in the checkout line at Steinacker's. Boaz pushed the red Polaroid button again.

I know what she's saying.

Boaz joined radio lady, somehow reciting in unison the words *her mother made up* in the checkout isle:

Water water everywhere, nor any drop to drink.

As suddenly as it began, the static swallowed the radio lady and filled the cab of the Datsun.

Who are you?

Indy slid her hand between her seat and the door to where she had stashed the old revolver. Could Boaz be yet another kind of abomination? A mind reading monster? Had he somehow drugged her with his booze so she was now hallucinating? Indy stared hard into his as deep and brown and normal-as-ever eyes, looking for holes.

I'm Boaz, I said already. It's the Rime of the Ancient Mariner, obviously.

It's the what?

A poem about a stupid sailing ship.

Do you communicate with that radio girl?

Boaz dug through his sack again until he found a beige plastic box slightly larger than a pack of cigarettes.

Yes and no. She tells me this Ancient Mariner through my transistor.

He flicked on the box and its static sung alongside the static of the Datsun.

She has my ear, but I don't have hers.

Boaz's eyes flicked guiltily to Indy's missing ear.

This Rime ship is a famous thing?

Of course. It's not your favorite?

Indy did not know how to answer.

It's good, but not so good that this radio girl should repeat it much, so I'm afraid she's down a sick brain.

231

She doesn't say anything else?

Just all day with this poem.

Indy scanned the horizon for radio towers, 'dillos, or anything else to ground her and found instead the tumbleweeds and the fences hunting their progress. The sun was closing in on the chimera that was the Texas horizon. Indy sighed. She started her truck.

Grand Canyon now?

Boaz was absently scratching at the painted glass that divided the truck cab from bed with his thumbnail. The yellow paint prevented passengers from seeing the truck's payload.

Indy simultaneously pressed her foot to the gas pedal and her finger to the tape she had reinserted in the player.

Far ahead in the scrubby tree line a few 'dillos were tottering. Bored, Indy commanded Boaz to stay put before she took off after them. Boaz followed her.

Indy admired the curved knife in Boaz's hand. She had never seen such a weapon. The stupid zombies chewed the air in anticipation of their living blood-pumping flesh.

Ready?

Boaz gracefully flipped the sickle in his hand. They jogged towards their enemy. Indy filled her hands with 'dillo defeat, sinking her knife into their fontanel G-spots, ending one creature after another. Boaz's sickle neatly removed the jaw of first one, and then another 'dillo, disarming them so Indy could drive her knife home.

Boaz was brave, Indy saw, as he barreled into a 'dillo. He leapt onto its monstrous chest between snapping arms, sliding his sickle neatly under the thing's neck joint, and then falling sideways, hard, using his body weight as leverage while maximizing the force of his weapon, so it could rip through the layers of armor and rotting human brain. Mesmerized by his grace, Indy let a 'dillo fall on top of her. Agony cut across her bare shoulders and thighs. She cursed the heat that transformed a skimpy sundress into logical clothing. She wiggled out from under the 'dillo, its armor skinning her back. The thing was so close she could feel the air displacement from its chomping jaw. She squirmed out, her scrawniness an advantage. Unfortunately, she escaped into a tumbleweed. She mistook its sharpness for another attack and stabbed at the fragile assembly of thorns. It disintegrated in her arms and she hurled it back towards the last moving 'dillo. Tumbleweed bits stuck to the thing's head like an outrageous British fascinator. Laughter, pure and relieved, burst from Indy as she attempted Boaz's technique and barreled into it, only to bounce off because she was too light and too amused to knock it over. Boaz brought his sickle down deep into the 'dillo's head, spilling the soupy human contents out. The final monster crashed to the ground.

I wish, Indy thought, we had not ruined so many heads.

They walked in silence back to the Datsun. Indy ran her hand down the back of her neck. It was wet with sweat and blood. At the truck, she found her wolf beach towel and wiped herself clean.

Boaz leaned beside her, against the Datsun. Again, with his thumbnail, he picked at the paint on the truck, this time making tiny Xs in the drips he found.

Indy held out her towel.

Can you get my back?

Boaz took the towel.

Do you say that those things we attack is murder or what?

I say killing something already dead can't be murder.

Indy turned her back to Boaz so he could clean the blood from her shoulders.

But isn't dead that moves?

Indy stiffened with pain as Boaz absently mopped blood off her back. Before he could finish, Indy turned to face him. Her lips held an inch from his, she whispered, *you say too much,* and allowed their lips to touch. She licked his teeth. He tasted of mountain dew and dead sea.

Boaz fell forward into Indy's mouth. Clumsy with eagerness, he collapsed forcefully onto her with his entire weight. Indy caught hold of him by bracing herself against the truck. His mouth opened to speak so she filled it with more tongue. Pulling back, she yanked his Public Enemy shirt almost over his head, stopping short of removing it. Instead she lifted it only to his cheekbones, turning it into a blindfold. Taking his hand, she guided him to the rear of the truck and lifted the yellow painted-out window of the truck cap and lowered the DATSUN tailgate. He jumped from the sound of metal on metal. He shook his head back and forth as stink hit him.

Indy positioned Boaz with his back to the bed of the truck and guided him down over it, one hand protecting his head from hitting the roof, and the other pressing his chest down. He reached out behind for the metal of the truck bed, but instead hit something not firm and flat, but lumpen and rounded. His hand movements became frantic for purchase because Indy was pushing him down. He faltered, fell on top of whatever it was. Indy balanced precariously over him. Her bony knees searched too for balance so her palms had to take most of her weight.

Inside and lying down on something uneven and unknown, Boaz reached for his Public Enemy blindfold/t-shirt. Indy stopped him by swallowing his reaching fingers into her mouth. It was the only thing free; she needed both her hands to

234

keep upright. She suckled his fingers, using no teeth. Mouthing his hand, she delicately lowered her head like that, towards his groin.

The boy's chest was soft and hairless. His nipples were intriguing and dark. He was wearing track pants.

Indy released his hand from her tongue and lips. She grabbed hold of his elastic waistband with her teeth.

Boaz used his free hand to pull one eye clear of the t-shirt.

Indy let fly his waistband from her teeth. Boaz could now see the truck bed was lined one head deep with harvested and poorly rinsed 'dillo heads. The very rear of the truck was stacked three and four heads high. Still glowing and emptied of the worst of their human remains, they created a romantic candlelight-like ambiance in the darkness of the capped back of the truck.

Boaz struggled to move away from Indy. He tried to sit up. His hands and feet and ass slipped through the slippery heads and he was unable to. He fell back down but continued to struggle to get back up. Knowing of only one way to stop him, Indy reared up precariously on her knees and yanked his pants down with her hands, far enough over his hipbones so they stayed down.

Indy was giddy. He was entirely hairless, his small flaccid penis more closely resembled a cocktail wiener than Magic's angry cock. Indy thought of all the hotdogs she had succeeded in not wasting back in Tara.

Chew chew chew.

Indy's stomach growled. Her hands on either side of Boaz's groin, she swallowed his small penis, gumming it urgently to life. Boaz groaned with an accent. She felt blood slowly swelling him.

He is so hairless, she thought. She spat his penis out and raised her head so abruptly she almost crashed face first into the 'dillo head architecture. I wonder, she thought, if this might be against the law in Texas.

Silly! But now there *were* no laws.

She returned to working on stiffening his child-like penis. Boaz pushed her away briefly, but then soft groans of pleasure displaced all struggles.

Once he was entirely hard, Indy searched his face. He still had one eye covered by the Public Enemy blindfold. This entire operation had so far really been as much of a surprise to Indy as Boaz. She did not find him the least bit sexy. But looking at him that way, one eye covered and one not, she finally felt a strong pull from deep inside her own genitals.

Artfully, Indy rebalanced so she could fuck him. She lifted one foot forward at a time, each sole atop a 'dillo head on either side of Boaz's now sweaty, perplexed face. Only in this way could she keep her hands where they were so she could lower herself onto his erect penis.

It felt weird, resting her entire weight on top of him with this small appendage of his inside her. Her weight joining his on top of the 'dillo heads was too much and the space between the heads where his ass had been resting widened. The heads re-arranged around them, squeaking and cracking protest as they were forced closer together. It sounded like an attack. Indy quickly raised herself off of his penis so they didn't drop down to the metal truck bed and get trapped between heads. As she lifted herself off his cock and held herself aloft above him, a dollop of blood oozed out of her. It landed on Boaz, mostly in his navel. At first she was relieved (my period!), and then alarmed (my period!). Then she realized it was just her virginity. Boaz gasped. His hands had somehow found their way around her hips and he was guiding her down again, urging her to finish what she started. Indy allowed him to pull her gently down onto his cock, but she was too wet with blood and the thing missed her orifices entirely. Boaz grabbed his cock and inserted it inside her. She looked at him and saw he was still looking at her with only one eye because of his t-shirt.

Napoleon.

Boaz ignored her word and rocked his hips up into her, causing a symphony of crackling to erupt from the heads beneath their hips, hands and feet. What's going to happen now? Indy wondered. Can he ejaculate? The thought of it ripped through her. Indy pulled her hips up and off Boaz and crab walked back, shuffling her hands and feet so she could get out of the truck as quickly as possible. She watched as Boaz showed her that he could cum, he knew how, his hands making a frothy soup around his cock, of her hymen and his semen.

His hands on his cock slowed down, stopped.

Can you help me get those heads now?

Indy used the wolf towel again for this different mess on her thighs and butt. Boaz nodded. He picked his way over the heads out of the truck leaving a handprint trail of pink semen.

Boaz' sickle was perfect for crudely emptying the worst of the human remains from the heads. Silently, they retrieved six of the heads Boaz had not carelessly destroyed during battle. Indy put them in the back of the truck where they belonged. She was surprised when Boaz didn't climb into the passenger seat beside her. Instead, he shouldered his burlap sack filled with sickle and moonshine, and stood on the shoulder. Indy nodded without looking at him and pulled away. She saw a sign for Dimmit, Texas.

She turned the knob on the radio to make sure it was off.

Lights.

Indy had been watching these lights for two days as she drove, never sleeping, across Nevada, arriving, finally, at Las Vegas. The lights near as the sky turned violet behind her. The desert made it hard to tell exactly how long it would take her to walk to them.

The Datsun had no more gasoline.

Captivated by their lonely brightness, she ran through all possible explanations for the lights. Silliest was the lights of Vegas had gone out on the day when everything died, grown chrysalides and hatched with glowing exoskeletons, visible to her now as 'dillo lights. In other words, she was seeing zombie lights. Somewhat more likely was that Vegas had some smarty-pants survivor kid gang or a palsied but wise old electrician who knew how to rig up generators. But her favorite possibility was Vegas had not been touched by the apocalypse so her dad was down there, waiting with the lights. Her mind kept trying this possibility on and running it far and away from reason.

Indy's chest bones had never felt so loose and warm. She bent to retrieve her revolver from under her seat. Her elbow dislodged a 'dillo head, part of a new pile that had overflowed from the rear of the truck. The entire pile tumbled down onto her.

She'd been busy. In New Mexico, skirting Socorro, she'd been nearly overtaken by 'dillos and had only escaped by flooring her Datsun and smashing through a herd of northbound beasts. Another night, looking down desert as she peed in the sand, Indy had seen far below her what had at first looked like a glowing river, but what was actually a legion of 'dillos moving in tandem like a school of fish. A million chitinous skin articulations filled the arid night, sounding more like the crackling of a sap-rich forest fire than dead on the march.

She had made it this far and now gasoline stopped her. She fashioned a 'dillo head into a basket using coarse twine pulled from a longhorn gate lock and stringing it through holes she had made with her knife. She put her last Twinkie, meat stick, and a Pepsi in her basket along with her revolver. Indy set off, the rising sun's heat pushing on her back.

Any other time, this would be dangerous walking. The desert had been punishingly dry and picked clean at every rest area and gas station. Each store in Boulder City had empty shelves, not even crappy candy like Popeye Cigarettes or Macintosh were left. All she'd found were two dented tins of Dinty Moore. But what this wasteland gave was the priceless gift of perfectly unobstructed views, making up for everything else. No 'dillos; no one could sneak up on her. At that moment, she could see nothing but emptiness save for those somehow-still-on Las Vegas lights. She felt safe.

Indy stood before the grill of her Datsun, let her eyes play along its golden yellow exterior. The paint was streaky and drippy and was probably not exactly true to the Datsun color she and her dad had lived in, but what her three-year-old mind had recorded was *yellow* and this felt more than close enough. Indy touched her hand to the hood, wanting to absorb the feel in case she never saw it again. The post-apocalyptic plunderings she had observed these last few weeks lent credence to the idea that there were active survivors afoot, putting her Datsun home at risk from looters.

She would miss her home. When she and her father were on the run together from the law with nothing but caught fish and Flintstones Vitamins to eat, she'd felt a part of something important. And what was a home if it wasn't feeling a part of something? In Tara, with her mother and Dana, the apex of good feelings could best be described as confused. When she and her mother were watching All My Children after school, she'd felt sort of comfortable. But as soon as the footsteps in gravel alarm announced Dana home from the nuclear power plant, her mother would twist off the TV knob and fill the kitchen with busy work. She was a terrible cook, so it was never cooking she was doing. She'd gaze at Uncle Ben, flipping over the box of what she called his perverted rice. Or she'd stir a pot of frozen peas that had been boiling for so long the water was nearly gone and all that remained was something between baby food and mucilage.

Indy lowered her mouth and kissed the hood. She had never felt safer than she had on the road in this truck. The feeling that other kids got when they walked up their driveways after getting off the school bus, she felt this now. In her Tara driveway, she'd felt like running back on the bus. By the time she was twelve or thirteen, she'd grown numb. It was worse to be numb. Numb emptied her out and left her to search the patterns in the faux wood panels of the living room trailer for meaning. Or to watch television for hours, yet not know who won Bowling for Dollars or notice The Littlest Hobo was long over and the channel had gone off the air and been replaced by a test pattern.

Indy blushed, thinking how dumb it was to kiss a truck. Then she kissed it again because it wasn't dumb too. Growing up, her stomach had lurched when she'd seen Datsun trucks because it made her think the word *home*. This was normal.

Just two years ago, her mother had been in her Aunt Jane's kitchen and Indy had overheard them. They thought she was outside. Dana called Jane and her husband fucking losers every Christmas after he was forced into their proximity in the Christmas Shed. That day in the kitchen, Jane had asked her mother if she had ever told Indy about what had happened. The answer had been silence, but Indy knew it anyhow.

Indy smiled. It was funny how they acted as if her time in the Datsun had been the bad time. Indy stuck her fingers through the grill of the Datsun and squeezed the metal there, a truck hug. The worst pain she could imagine was the pain of enduring the endless agony of not knowing when she would fuck up by running past the record player or get caught talking on the phone too much. *Not* living in a truck with her dad.

She dropped her hand from the grill. She turned to face her Las Vegas, the impossible lights winking at her. Precisely two weeks before the day she'd found Dana slumped in the yard she had begged him to punch her, hit her, had in fact said *Please! Give me a heartpunch so that everyone can see what it is really like to live here.* He had chased her through the trailer doing the living-room-kitchen-hallway-living-room steeplechase until Indy had tripped over her own Bozo feet, collapsing backwards onto the gold shag. She had begged *punch.*

Dana, if he had not been taken by that first apocalyptic die-off, would not have survived now. He was a man who could not stand the sight of a droplet of his own blood from a tiny cut, or endure the pain of hitting his funny bone on a table at Burger King. Indy had watched him faint on both such occasions.

Indy endured. Dana had sliced off her ear, 'dillos had scraped off yards of her skin and she'd received blows to almost every part of her body. She'd even survived being tied up and mostly raped. She had not only endured, but she had *thrived.* And that was because all of this apocalypse bullshit was a cakewalk compared to life in the trailer in Tara with Dana and her mother.

Thanks, Dana, for preparing me for the end of the world.

Indy's voice echoed against the desert dawn, her over-big boots kicking up Nevada dust as she began her descent into Las Vegas. She cut a clear silhouette against the rising sun as she marched towards fraught lights and her father in whatever form he was waiting for her.

It was far.

The desert sun had swung around and Indy had to squint to see where she was going. She used her homemade 'dillo head basket, now empty of food and drink, as a metronome, swinging it with each step. She had been counting for a while, but stopped when she reached five thousand six hundred and four at the Henderson city limits. If she remembered correctly, Las Vegas was still another fifteen miles. She was going to have to find shelter for the night. The zombie desert cockroaches were vicious, as she had discovered one night when she had sleepily gotten out of the truck to pee. One dove right into the meat of her calf, deftly burrowing down to bone, its ass sticking out of her flesh like a Japanese throwing star. It had embedded itself so deeply into her tibia, she had almost decided to leave it there. But the thing chittered constantly, threatening to summon more. She had searched the glove box and under the seats in a vain attempt to find pliers or something to grip the thing with, and yank it out, or pop it, and in the end she had resorted to chewing it out with her teeth. The taste of her mother's Shake 'N Bake burnt on the outside, raw in the middle pork chops mixed with cod liver burst into her mouth. Oily residue clung to her mouth and withstood repeated Pepsi rinsing. She could taste it still, if she closed her mouth and sucked hard enough against the grooves of her gums and teeth.

The setting sun and her intense focus on the rhythm of the basket metronome prevented Indy from noticing an electric golf cart trailing behind her into Henderson.

Hey, Chicken Legs.

A boy's voice broke Indy's trance walk. The moniker, so familiar, stopped her like a brick wall. Shielding her eyes from the sun with her hand as if saluting, she turned in the direction of the voice. Two boys, about Brian's age, smiled at her from a beat up golf cart. On Indy's first day of high school a pasty-skinned girl named Sarah, who herself was very unpopular, had screamed the same insult at her across the lobby: LOOK! IT'S CHICKEN LEGS!

Indy stared at the boys with pure hatred. They had stopped beside her, only a few feet away.

Are you a moth'r?

A *what*?

The golf cart driver tried to clarify.

You got a clean head there. We don't see many girls tall as you.

The passenger boy looked at the driver with disgust.

A moth'r, you know, brings in moth money.

Indy lifted her 'dillo head basket up towards the boys.

You mean this?

In unison, the boys confirmed.

Indy took a deep breath. It was a relief to have a Brian-free and thus guilt-free name for the zombies, even if it was senseless. Indy shrugged.

The passenger boy held out a bottle of water to Indy. She took it and drank it down in one chugging gulp. He was eager to explain.

They went into cocoons, like a butterfly, but then, you know, came out all ugly and stupid. Like a moth.

Indy swiped a hand across her mouth. She handed the empty bottle back to the boy.

Exoskeleton instead of wings, then sure, why not.

So are you?

The driver boy was wearing a police badge around his neck on a bathtub chain, like the cops sometimes did on TV.

Am I what?

A moth'r – a moth collector? I'll trade you. Me driving you wherever you're going for that head there.

Indy thought about her compulsive moth head collecting in concrete terms for the first time, counting what she now understood, thanks to these boys, as bounty. Previously, she had felt compelled, but worried she'd gone mad. Brian had given her the idea, of course, with his shelmets. At best it gave shape and purpose to her travels while providing an homage to her long lost charge she had failed so badly. Now her work took on real, material meaning. It made her some sort of modern apocalypse coureur du bois. A trader. Indy wondered if Native Americans felt like this when the skins they collected for personal warmth and tradition turned into money under their colonizers' regime.

Yeah. Yes. I'm a moth'r. I got more where this came from. But I'm headed to the lights, looking for someone.

That's where everyone wants to go when they first get here. Get in.

Indy climbed onto the back bench of the golf cart, the back of her thighs so sunburnt that the seat felt like sandpaper. Indy passed her moth basket, now a form of currency, to the passenger boy as the driver flicked the cart to *on*. They whirred towards Las Vegas proper. Passenger boy jumped up on his knees and laid a switchblade against Indy's cheekbone.

Nothing personal, but I have to take a look.

The boy pressed the blade hard enough for the tip to draw a tiny bead of blood. He leaned forward, close enough to bite. Or kiss. Indy's hands balled up in her lap. She did not flinch.

The boy examined Indy's eyes. She stared back. He smelled of Old Spice and grape Bubble Yum. He sighed and sat back down.

Geez, you're the oldest clean girl we got. Tallest too. You know what they say, girls are either gone or are on their way. Some luck finding you.

Indy watched blighted low-rises roll by. It was nearly magic hour so every hue bloomed importantly. They crested a long grade and Indy could, for the first time, see Las Vegas.

What the hell happened to your ear? That's messed. I'm Kiko.

The driver rolled his eyes, centered his police badge.

Indy. Who runs the lights?

Wouldn't *you* like to know.

Indy wrapped her hand around the handle of her diving knife. She had adapted it recently to her Le Chateau sundress by wearing it up higher, the holster strapped tightly around her upper thigh. It felt really good there and was invisible under the skirt. A current of fear crackled down her spine. Trent or Andrew all over again. At least these two were no Dana. Scenarios of being imprisoned and made to tiptoe around record players and never create or leave any disorder or mess anywhere, ran through Indy's head. She smiled.

WELCOME TO LAS VEGAS.

Indy giggled. She was here. She felt her father's nearness like wet Sauble Beach sand stuck to her skin. Gritty, real and familiar. It was as though all her relaxation pressure points were being triggered at once.

Kiko wanted to know what was so funny.

They were in Las Vegas. Indy imagined what her dad looked like. His hair and eyes.

The golf cart cut carefully across a wreckage-strewn roadway. They were on Las Vegas Boulevard. Massive casinos rolled past, one after another, some were on fire, or at least smoking. Her asymptomatic eyes throbbed. She squeezed back tears of joy.

Cocoon city down there. Cocoons to the *max*. It took the moth'rs until just a few days ago to clear.

So how many are left?

Phfff. Guess.

The driver finally spoke.

We've got people from Los Angeles, El Paso and people like you, from east.

North. Canada.

Kiko held up his hand to high-five Indy. She kept her hands in her lap.

You see any grown-ups there?

Sure. Really old ones.

Did I say old bags? I mean, like your parents. You seen any of them?

No. They all died. For a while.

Kiko laughed.

Why do people come here?

Same reason as you.

I doubt that.

You shouldn't. Everyone is looking for something. No parents to tell you what to do.

Stop!

Indy clamped her hand down on the quiet driver's shoulder. He slowed but did not stop. She pointed at a phone booth.

There. Can you stop there?

Uh, hate to tell you, the phones totally don't work.

They nevertheless stopped at the AT&T phone booth. Indy checked up and down the empty street, and entered the tagged and abused booth. For kicks, she picked up the receiver and held it to her ear and then out to Kiko.

It's for you.

Kiko rolled his eyes and crossed his arms.

Indy opened the black plastic case hanging from a steel cable in the phone booth. Jackpot, she thought. She took either side of the spine of the Las Vegas & Clark County phonebook in her hands and dropped her entire weight on it to loosen it, falling back onto her haunches inside the booth. The phonebook spine pulled apart, causing her to fall the last few inches down onto her bum. The booth would be keeping the front cover and some of the Yellow Pages, but the bulk of the book and the entire white pages section had been freed into

Indy's hands. With the book in the crook of her arm, Indy returned to her seat in the golf cart.

The cart rolled past empty housing tracts before swinging with a barely audible whir into a cul-de-sac composed of six houses huddled in a cozy circle. And from each and every window, bright light shone. *The* lights. They were far less impressive up close.

Each lit house, Indy noted, had rooftop solar panels like the ones she had seen in The Environment chapter of her Science and Mankind textbook the previous year. They parked the cart in the driveway of an unfortunate brown and white aluminum-sided '70s split-level. They parked only halfway up because the driveway was filled with renovation detritus. Sections of wall, moldy pink fiberglass insulation and rolled up pet-stained bundles of green shag carpet filled most of the driveway. The door opened. A driving beat filled the air. A pretty girl in pigtails, about six years old, appeared.

You've brought someone.

Having made her observation, she disappeared back into the split-level. It wasn't until she turned to go that Indy saw she was wearing a plush dinosaur tail. It bumped the ground behind her.

Kiko disappeared into the house with Indy's moth head. Indy got off the cart, annoyed that her bounty had disappeared. She was not at her final destination.

You're on your own. I got errands.

Indy watched the driver boy zip around the cul-de-sac and disappear down the road they had come in on. Indy took a deep breath and walked to the front door. It was amazing the effect the electric lights had after sitting in the dark at night for so long. It felt warm and welcoming. The trailer in Tara had never been this bright because her mother hated overhead lights and, after all, electricity was expensive. Indy felt herself being lulled into a groundless and dangerous sense of security. She dug her fingernails into her palms and coiled her pilfered phone book as she pushed her way into the house.

Immediately, she felt dizzy. And there were no walls around her to brace herself against. It took her five heartbeats to figure out why she felt disoriented. One: is the air poisoned? No. Two: have I been shot in the head? No. Three: am I starving and dehydrated? Yes. But I've been worse off. Four: have I begun to change? I don't know, maybe. Five: it's the floor.

Yes. It was the floor. The foyer opened to the wide space of a completely gutted wall-less interior. Only the exterior framing and a staircase up remained. But it was the floor that was really wrong. It had been painted to be the sky. And not just shitty childish painting, or even furniture store art painting. The floor was a realist rendering of a blue sky with fluffy clouds so breathtakingly sky-like that Indy, upon stepping into the house, and thus onto the open sky, had the feeling of being upended, of falling upwards, while still being pulled downwards by gravity. It gave her vertigo. She took a tentative step forward, trying to step onto the clouds because it somehow made her feel safer. For her own sanity, she squatted down to touch the sky-floor. Even from less than a foot away the painting looked real. Indy leaned down lower and touched one of the clouds to see if she could see or feel the brush strokes. She could not.

Her phone book. She dropped it open on the floor and thumbed through it for the O section. With her forefinger, she ran past Oakley, O'Brian, O'Connell (so many), one Olhouser and then yes. Four Olivers. One Daryl Oliver, an E. Oliver and there it was. Seeing his name in print: Oliver, Glen. *Glen Oliver*. He was real.

Indy sat onto a cloud, floating on top of the blue sky and said her father's name out loud. She covered the name with her fingertip, making it disappear. She lifted her finger and it was still there. Nothing in the outside world had ever met her even part of the way like this. Just a name in a phone book, yet Indy had not, in her life, had validation like this. She felt like flitting like Jenny. Like hollering. She lifted the page with his name on it and sniffed.

Well I've never seen someone use a phonebook like that.

The voice was hoarse and echoed loudly across the sky-floor.

Indy looked for the voice. In the far corner, a man watched her on his hands and knees. His beard was long enough for the tip to drag against sky. It grew in white but faded yellower and yellower with each inch of length. The dragging tip was entirely blue. Sky blue. In his hand, he held a brush the thickness of one of Indy's fingers. He rested back on his haunches. His face was tattooed with a pattern of lines and circles she recognized. It was an old fashioned test pattern. In between his eyes was the racist Indian head and across the tip of his nose, the number 30.

You got ripped off. Heads're worth more 'n a ride cross town.

Maybe I'm not done spending.

Indy held up her father's phonebook page. Victoriously.

I need to go here. Now.

The girl with the dinosaur tail appeared at the top of the stairs, a few American dollar bills lazily floating behind her, several more stuck to her tail. She wrestled a fussing, chubby, chocolate brown toddler. Cornrows had been carefully plated into its hair. The girl joined the old painter, baby sagging from her arms.

The end of the world has done terrible things to manners.

The man took the baby and cooed at it.

I'm Victor, but everyone calls me Test Pattern, obviously.

The toddler grabbed onto Test Pattern's beard and yanked.

I was a set painter for soaps. I came here for a quick ceiling job and got stuck.

He put his arm around the little girl with the tail.

This is Daisy and our baby T-Bone.

Indy shivered, the toddler's name reminding her of Trent's child-as-food stew in Detroit. Her dad's phonebook page throbbed in her hands.

You got a car I can use?

Not really. But I'm more 'n happy to drive you where you need to go. And we can talk more about your moth stash.

The old man, with help from Daisy Dinosaur, got to his feet with the baby on his hip and the odd threesome disappeared upstairs. Indy waited anxiously by the door. Many minutes passed. Indy's impatience overwhelmed her. She stomped up the carpet-stripped stairs, careful to avoid nails and other long metal extrusions.

The second floor was skyless. But still not just normal. The upstairs had not been gutted; it had been turned into a Richie Rich theme park. Ankle, and in some spots, hip-deep piles of loose bills obscured the floor and trim of what at one time had been someone's family home. It was now more of a game room. Not poker or blackjack like one would expect in Las Vegas, but Atari. Two new boys were nested comfortably, joysticks in hand playing Asteroids, their heads tilted slightly to the side to mirror the slant of the RCA floor model television they were glued to because it sat askew on a money pile. Amidst the money were empty Old English beer bottles and bags of potato chips. Kiko was observing from the corner of the room on what Indy at first assumed was a white beanbag chair. But when he moved to motion her into the room, she realized it wasn't a chair, but a pile of white powder like flour.

251

When he lifted a fingernail full of it to his nose and snorted it, she realized it was not food at all.

Kiko slapped the cocaine beanbag beneath him, causing him to disappear momentarily in powder. The gamers giggled. Indy held her breath. One gamer got up, not taking his eyes off his space ship or his finger from the red button trigger. He dunked the bottom of the joystick into the cocaine chair like a scoop and returned to his money nest, tipping the coke he had scooped into his lap. He lifted a nailful to his own nose and snorted. Kiko sneezed.

Kiko scooped up a handful of coke and held it out to Indy. She watched the white powder dribble, like sand through an hourglass, from the corners of his hand onto the money below. Indy thought of the first time she'd seen cocaine. She was four years old in Toronto, or to be specific, a part of Toronto her stepfather called Bangladesh because of the dominant immigrant population there. It had been in his best friend Bob's townhouse, the nicest house Indy had ever been in until Kris's. Three stories of white on white on white. White shag carpet, white leather furniture and three white Persian cats. Bob had a glass-topped backgammon table and, at some point in the night, he had laid out lines and snorted one. At four, Indy had not known what they were doing but had been eager to join in. Everyone laughed. It had stung Indy particularly hard because she was so allergic to the cats and so sneezy and wheezy she had been hoping the sniffing powder had been brought out to alleviate her symptoms.

Indy shifted away from Kiko, almost losing her balance in the cash quicksand.

Dinosaur Daisy came into the room and slipped on the money. She dropped the toddler on her ass. Indy scooped the toddler up, worried the baby would get close to the drugs. Holding the fussing baby, Indy could hear its labored breathing. The child was wheezing.

Hey, this thing's got asthma.

Indy held the wheezing child back out to Daisy since she had righted herself. Daisy was not interested in taking it.

You know how to fix her? It's been choking and wheezing for days.

She's probably allergic.

Indy looked around the room. There were too many allergens to choose from.

You a doctor?

I have asthma.

What do you do?

Indy bit her lip and thought about it. When she was small, she would get terrible asthma attacks all the time. Especially from Bob's Persian cats. After visiting, she could only get enough air by sitting up straight as a board, making sleep improbable. Late at night and all alone with perfect posture she'd watch television up close so she could hear it with the volume way down. She could not risk waking anyone. She searched for programs to distract herself. She knew that once she started wheezing, the worst thing for it was stress because it tightened her chest more. But, since not being able to breathe itself caused stress, it was an impossible situation. Steel tight anxiety clamped down, making air even harder to sip through pinned airways.

Eventually Indy found a cure. A drug-free cure. In front of the TV those late nights she discovered her first horror film, Phase IV. It was about desert ants ganging up on people. Indy had been seeing the sparkles you see before you black out, and had been frantically clicking the dial between the only three channels when she found it. An ant mandible close up gripped her attention. An hour later, when the credits rolled, she realized she had not thought about her asthma, that she was alive, and she was breathing easily enough to lie down in bed. On other nights, with other attacks, she had found similar relief in other horror films. The gorier the better.

Distract her.

Daisy scratched her tailbone, just above where the dinosaur tail was attached.

With what?

You got a VCR?

Daisy nodded.

Any scary movies?

Daisy held out her arms for the baby.

We got Evil Dead.

Daisy plopped the baby wheezer down in front of the TV. Indy winced, listening to her try to whine through shrunken air holes. Daisy, clocking Kiko in the head with her dinosaur tail, dug around in the money pile under the television and produced a silver JVC VCR. She pulled the plug on the Atari. All the boys groaned and one of the players hurled his joystick at her. It bounced off her tail and hit the wall. Daisy deftly swapped Atari cables for VCR, and quickly the three boys, Daisy, and the baby were watching the movie.

Good. Finally. We've been too easy on that toddler. I've got a proposition for you.

Test Pattern had joined them. Indy did not think it was possible to be less interested than she was in hearing this person's plans. Being this close to her father, to where he actually *lived* and ate and *existed,* and doing nothing about it was unbearable. She briefly entertained smashing Test Pattern in the face and searching his body for car keys. But then she realized she would need a map or guide to this infernally huge city. The quickest way to her dad would, unfortunately, be through this bearded sky painter.

Okay.

Test Pattern answered quietly, just barely loud enough to be heard over the Evil Dead.

Well, you've got all those moth heads. I've got channels.

Test Pattern continued to talk over the satanic gibberish the kids in the room were listening to.

You bring me heads. I'll keep them safe. And then you get everything you ever need.

I need only one thing. One ride. To my dad. And I've already *over*paid for that.

And after? After you find him, you two don't have a care in the world with me. Give me the heads. Then the world is yours.

It was almost impossible to pay attention to Test as Professor Raymond Knowby read from the Necronomicon, ignorantly summoning the Evil Dead.

Indy thought about undead and Test Pattern's bullshit. She didn't trust his stupid tattoo face. But she also didn't care much about the heads she collected. It had just been something to do. Getting more would also be no problem if he did rip her off and she found, for some reason, she needed to use the new undead currency of Las Vegas. The fastest way to her dad's house would be to take Test to the Datsun and the heads. As a side benefit, she'd have her truck back. Her dad would really love that.

Sure. Okay. Bring fuel. Let's go.

A sweet baby snore joined all the sounds in the room.

Kiko slid off his cocaine chair onto his haunches.

I'm in.

Kiko became Test Pattern's crutch over the cash terrain. He trailed a fog of coke dust off his caked jeans and t-shirt.

Indy waded after them.

They left the toddler sound asleep, coiled around Daisy's lap.

***

Ruth's no ordinary old bag. She takes care of us. She lived through the depression, you know.

Indy nodded, barely listening, head humming. It was a mechanical hum. It was the hum of all trains of thought clicking over onto a single line: Father. Father. Father. It was ridiculously simple and more permanent than love. Forged by the irrational idolatry of three-year-old Indy then chased into a furnace and cooked by years of maternal denial, her feelings were now a monument to irrational and unfounded truth. If she could have been schizophrenic and embraced her mother's erasures she would have bought that she was magic, an immaculate conception, all memories of her father reduced to a pastiche of images easily confused with movies she had seen or stories she had heard of realer dads. She was, unfortunately, not that kind of sick. The closer she physically got to her father, the more monomaniacal his monumental hum. Going to his home, proof he lived on Earth, would unwind a decade of denial carved into her decade-long worship of a man who did not exist.

Test Pattern walked Indy to another house in the cul-de-sac. The middle house. He knocked on the pristine door. It sprang open. A withered woman, easily 80, with pin-curled dark grey hair and a terry cloth beige short-sleeved shirt carefully tucked into khaki slacks, greeted them. Her hammertoes and thickened

256

yellow nails peeked out from under the hem of her slacks. Varicose veins striped her hands and forearms. She was holding a chintz plate full of cookies with one hand. With her other hand, she adjusted the strap of a Suomi KP-31 that, despite being a smallish sub-machine gun, dwarfed her bony, shriveled frame.

Good day, Ruth.

Oh, heavens. Would you like a wheat-free cookie?

Test Pattern politely slid a cookie off the plate. He put the cookie in his pocket.

I've come to borrow the Buick again.

Ruth's well-wrinkled face grew cross, her loose jowl shortening as her jaw tensed. She looked at Indy.

Why bring one of these tall old ones?

What a funny new world this is, Indy thought, overtop the father hum. An old lady can call *me* old.

Test Pattern lifted Indy's moth head towards Ruth.

She has lots of these, so that's why.

Ruth's eyelids spread wide as if she were trying to swallow the moth head with an eye mouth. She took the head and slammed the door in their face. A few seconds later her garage door opened and Ruth appeared still with her plate of cookies. She dangled keys to the Buick LeSabre in her garage from the end of her gun.

You'll return it *as is* or pay me three more.

Is it fully fueled?

Ruth's answer was a stern stare. Kiko ran for the passenger seat.

Shotgun!

Test Pattern lifted the keys from the tip of Ruth's gun and climbed behind the driver's seat. Indy crammed seven cookies from Ruth's plate into her mouth and pockets, leaving only one, and took the back seat. A tennis ball hung from a yellow rope in front of the grill to mark the precise place the Buick had to pull to for the garage door to close. Test Pattern reversed slowly out of the garage but slammed on his brakes before they were half out.

Indy twisted around to look. Ruth was staring at her, perfectly framed in the Buick's back window.

You. Tall girl. I need you for five minutes inside. *Now.*

Kiko fidgeted with the glove box, slamming it closed and opening it. Indy sighed, but it came out as hum. She followed Ruth into the house.

Everything slowed down.

Ruth took Indy to the back of her house. She stopped in front of sliding glass doors with polyester orange drapes. A poofy valance of the same fabric ran along the top. Indy could barely keep up to the old lady she was suddenly so tired.

Ruth dragged over stepladder, the kind that is also a chair, and climbed the two stairs on it, reaching for the top of the drapes.

You see? I can't reach, even from my ladder. My grandson used to do this for me but he's all head now. I clean them every season, like clockwork. You're tall. Take these down.

She pushed the stepladder towards Indy.

Indy's hands felt like fifty pound weights pulling her arms down. She had to get to her dad. The room had no air, the hum had gone; maybe it somehow took all her strength with it. Breaking a sweat, she pushed the unneeded stepladder back towards Ruth and lifted her dead-weight hands up to unhook the curtains from their rod. It took a week. With the drapes pooled on the floor, Indy gratefully dropped her hands and, somehow unable to think of any words to say, stood silently staring at Ruth who was furiously gathering up her drapes. A string of drool slipped from the corner of Indy's mouth.

You're not done! The valance! The valance!

Indy thought it might be easier to unsnap the thin white metal bars holding the valance aloft from the stepladder, so she climbed it. If her hands were fifty pounds each, her feet were a thousand. She dragged one foot, then the other, up the three steps and stopped to catch her breath. Indy tried to speak.

What's—?

Ruth shushed her. Ruth spoke so quickly, she sounded like a 33-rpm record played at 45 rpm.

With her albatross left hand, she lifted her dead-weight right hand up and hooked it onto the top of the orange poof. Indy's eyes rolled to their whites and she toppled off the ladder to the floor, cracking her head on the steel rungs and coming to rest on Ruth's spotless cushion tile linoleum floor.

***

What kind of girl has no panties on?

Indy was not sure whether the morning light of the un-draped window woke her, or if it was Ruth's question punctuated with a kick to Indy's ribs. With her eyes slitted against the sunlight, Indy lifted her head and felt her cheek unglue from the floor. She touched it with her fingers and they came back sticky with blood.

Ruth's drapes whispered as she shook them over Indy's head.

They're clean! Ready to hang now.

She arranged the curtains over the step ladder Indy had tumbled from and disappeared with the valence around her shoulders like a boa into another room, from which Indy could hear slurping.

She sat up. Her head felt like it stayed on the ground. Getting to her feet caused darkness to bloom again. She had to steady herself against the sliding glass doors until her vision returned. She made her way to a shiny steel kettle on a counter behind her and stared into her eyes. Still eyes. Still human. What was happening to her?

Moving towards the slurping, Indy found Test Pattern and Kiko sitting across from each other at an oak dining table eating pasta from chintz. Ruth was seated at the head stuffing plastic grocery bags inside her orange valence, stopping periodically to fluff the bags inside it. She seemed intent on making it look less like an ugly scarf and more and more like a fat caterpillar. Kiko bounced in his chair.

Morning, sleepyhead!

What. Happened. To. Me?

Indy's tongue was a slab of driftwood. It splintered in her mouth with each syllable.

Test glanced conspiratorially at Indy and patted the chair beside him at the other end of the table from Ruth. Indy, using the table as balance insurance, sat down. He leaned into her missing ear and whispered.

Ruth. She *hates* drugs.

Indy squeezed her eyes shut and re-opened them again. Kiko snickered. Test leaned in again, this time so close Indy could feel his beard hairs tickle her healing ear wound.

But, she's from the Valley of the Dolls, you know?

Indy did not know. She shook her head. Test Pattern dropped his voice so low, Indy had to hold her breath to hear him. She pried her wooden tongue from her upper pallet.

Huh?

Test Pattern glanced furtively at Ruth to see if she was listening.

She pretends everything's okay. Crushes up her pills and cooks with them. I guess she figures if she isn't swallowing pills, she's not using drugs. Why do you think we need all that cocaine?

You're drug addicts, too?

Goof! She takes care of us. We don't even *have* a kitchen. The only way we can stay awake is if we balance things out.

There are noodles in front of Indy along with a strangely folded linen napkin.

Beef-a-roni?

Indy unfolded the napkin. Inside was a small cache of white powder, enough to fill a shot glass.

Indy pushed herself up heavily from sitting with her hands.

Is the water from the tap safe at least?

Test Pattern chuckled. Searching for glasses, Indy opened the cupboard over Ruth's sink. It was full of prescription bottles. LORAZAPAM. TEMAZEPAM. CLONAZEPAM. Not the size you get from Walgreens but big opaque ones the pharmacist gets from the drug manufacturer. The ones you see on the untouchable shelves behind the counter at Rite Aid.

In a world of actual zombies, Ruth was a virtual one.

The cupboard next to Ruth's drugs contained the complete Chef Boyardee product line. A house favorite, Indy supposed. The cupboards under the sink held an array of oat and rye flours, white and brown sugars, and walnuts. Too thirsty to search any longer for glasses, Indy turned on the taps. Glad they worked, she tilted her mouth to the side so the water could soothe her tongue and lips. It was glorious. She took care to actually not drink too much. Chef Ruth's entire home seemed tainted. Add to that, neglect from a now-defunct Las Vegas water utility and drinking tap water was a recipe for disaster. Indy had not come this close to her dad to be felled by cholera or typhoid.

She noticed Test Pattern was still talking to her.

Don't look at me like that, moth'r. What do you want these kids to do? Starve? I've got no time to cook. No knowing, either. My garbage truck wife left so Ruth's all we have.

Ruth held out her valance caterpillar proudly for the table to examine.

Indy was desperately trying to make enough sense of things to successfully change the subject and avoid getting involved with Ruth and her curtains again.

You were married to a garbage truck?

Kiko found this so funny he had to hold onto the dining room table so he didn't fall off his chair. He spewed half-chewed medicated Boyardee across the table. Ruth whisked her valance out of his spray line just in time.

Don't be ridiculous. Garbage truck was her nickname.

262

Although it still made no sense, Indy nodded.

She was a tolerant woman, really. You have to understand that first. It wasn't as irrational as it sounds. I have a sleep problem. I'd stay up painting sky on set for days, is what it was. And I'd sleep for days after to recover. She couldn't wake me. She'd need me to pay a bill or take out the trash or just give her some loving. She'd scream at me inches from my ear, even punch my face with her tiny fists. I'd snore. She even tried pissing on my head.

Ruth walked her caterpillar out of the dining room.

That's what broke her, really. Not the gambling. For our fortieth anniversary, I promised dinner at Aladdin. You know how it is, they march you past the slots and baccarat and blackjack to reach the fine dining. And I convinced her if I bet $40 on roulette table forty on the number forty on our fortieth, it'd be romantic. Two hours later I was still standing there with her pulling on my arm. She cracked. Stripped naked. Boasted about pissing on my head. Security pulled her off me, threw her out. That's when it went sideways.

Indy, sitting down beside Test Pattern again, was seriously considering trying some of the cocaine so she could think again. Test Pattern pulled on his blue beard tip thoughtfully.

I waited for the wheel to stop spinning, to see if I'd won, instead of following her out with security. I had her clothes, see.

You lost.

Right. I lost. I finally got outside to where security had tossed her in time to see her scale a garbage truck stopped at the lights on the strip. At first I thought it was a pink monkey. But then I recognized her screams. She got on top of the rig's cab jumping up and down, screaming let me in, I'm garbage, I'm garbage! Boys in the truck were real nice about it. I said how it

263

was my bad, so they didn't call the cops. I paid them to drive us home all slow like, her holding on up top for dear life. On the way home, they showed me how to operate the switches and the dumper and let me try driving. Said it was one of the most memorable loads they'd ever picked up.

Indy rubbed a bit of the powder from her napkin between her thumb and forefinger.

I was touching up the Golden Nugget's frescos the morning everyone dropped dead. Well, everyone save me and a night manager. He ran home to his wife and left me alone in the casino. Course, first thing I thought is I'd won the lottery. All alone in the casino! I ran around clearing out the tables. I went to Binion's, the Fremont too. Filled my van with cash. Drove out to the boulevard and saw everyone dead there. In the Sands, the cashier cage was unlocked so I went in. I saw the vault in the middle of the cage was unlocked. A cashier slumped right in the doorway, she must have been shutting it when she dropped. I looked in the vault and lost control of my bladder. So much money. And then I saw all the bricks, wrapped in beige and white and red plastic. An entire wall of cocaine. And it was too much to carry, the money and the coke, so I drove around until I saw one. A garbage truck. I dumped the garbage load right on the strip and backed it up to the Sands first, and then, compacting the cash as I went, cleared out the entire strip. I worked around the clock for almost a week gathering all the money. I'd go home and dump it on my lawn and shovel it into the house. I didn't have time to pile it up and a lot of it was wet with sludge from the garbage truck. My garbage truck wife showed up with kids she was babysitting and this old lady, asking to keep them all. They slept all the time, so I said sure.

Indy decided against the coke because the story finally made sense. She wiped her now numb finger and thumb on the front of her navy sundress, leaving two white streaks. She stood up.

The end.

Sort of. Then the moths came. The Atari generation has a head for shooting.

Speaking of heads, let's go retrieve mine.

The hum inside Indy returned and she tried to push it aside. She called shotgun this time and the first glimpse of the Datsun's roof peeking over a rockfall made her heart leap. She was pretty sure Test and sulky backseat Kiko could not see it yet. The truck's yellow color camouflaged it perfectly against the morning desert, blending with and reflecting the brightest tones. Indy glowed, too.

There.

Test Pattern, sweatbeads glistening in his beard like rhinestones, pulled over.

Test whistled as he rounded the rock fall and caught sight of the Datsun's front seat payload. He was almost, but not quite, breathless.

Now. That's something you don't see every day.

The hum in Indy woke up. She was about to blow his mind.

Oh, that? That's just the overflow.

Indy rooted around the toes of her too-big boot for the Datsun keys she'd put there for safekeeping. She unlocked the driver's side door, reaching in to open the painted-out window between the truck's cab and cap, providing a full view of her bounty. Kiko, who had been jostling around behind her trying to get a look, did not have enough time to turn completely around before puking. An arc of semi-digested benzodiazapemed Chef Boyardee sprayed across the bench seat of the Datsun, narrowly missing Indy's arm and leg.

Fuck!

Kiko whimpered through his sick.

Test Pattern backed up a step. He looked ready to produce his own barf arc.

You *drove* in there with that? That smell?

Drive? I lived. A person can get used to anything.

It amused Indy. Dudes who snorted coke after every meal thought a bad smell was something worth puking over. *Pussies*, she thought. Just hold your breath and *look*! Indy pulled Test Pattern's arm over towards the driver's seat and pointed through the cab into the back of the truck.

Test's jaw didn't drop because it unhinged. He staggered backwards before he spoke.

You didn't do all this yourself?

Do you see anyone else?

Test got carefully to his knees, pulling Kiko firmly down with him. His eyes searched out and locked with Indy's. He pressed his hands against his thighs to keep himself upright as he shook.

All my seventy-some years, I never misjudged a being as much as I have done here, with you.

Indy broke eye contact. She stared down at her black desert-dusted boots. She reached forward and wrapped her hands under Test's armpits, physically asking him to stop kneeling. It made her feel weird. All of this was a useless sidetrack. His arm bones trembled under her touch, like chickens on slaughter day. He might have even had tears in his eyes, unless it was sweat dripping from the crevasses in his forehead. Indy tried to smile by activating her cheek muscles.

It's only once I set my mind to something it comes easy.

267

She gestured to the back of her Datsun.

These can all be yours. I can get more.

We still friends?

Sure. So long as you take me to my father. Now?

Test ran, as fast as an old artist who had been kneeling or reaching to paint the floor or ceiling most of his life, can run, to Ruth's Buick, dragging Kiko with him by the wrist. He craned his neck back towards Indy as he ran.

You follow us!

He pulled the Buick up beside Indy as she sat behind her Datsun's steering wheel and gestured to make her roll down her window. Indy rolled.

Yeah?

Kiko held out a bulging beige canvas shopping tote that said REAGAN BUSH '84 in stark red and blue letters. Test limped out and filled her Datsun with fuel from a jerry can.

No. No more Ruth.

It's just some drinks. Safe.

Indy reached in the president's bag. Inside were two cans of TAB cola and one bottle of Molson's Export. The ship on the label was her dad. The label had always been, until hopefully soon, the best she could do when visualizing him. She conjured up sitting between his legs, acting as his human cup holder, as they drove around on errands and visiting people. Now Indy wedged the Export between her own legs. Test was already driving back towards Vegas.

Hum.

Indy let Test widen the distance between them as they drove back to Vegas. She watched the Nevada desert unravel. Taken in sections it was painfully empty and bland, but as a whole it was overwhelmingly beautiful. The Export bottle clenched between her thighs wept condensation, keeping that spot the only cool one on her body. The wind was hot against her brow through the rolled down window. In snow-belt Tara, she had imagined this vista but never what the air would feel like.

Out here, there was no need to follow Test or anyone closely. Range of sight stretched to the miles. Indy watched Ruth's Buick exit west, into the city. In some small amount of minutes, she would see her father. Or, Indy thought, if I'm not going to be delusional, her 'dillo/moth father. She caressed the unopened bottle between her legs. No matter what, she would walk on the floors he walked, sit on furniture he settled in, wear his shirts. She would be inside, and from inside, there would be no longer any denying his realness.

Hum.

A cramp ripped through Indy's midsection. She'd never felt anything like it. She tilted the rearview mirror so she could look in her eyes and almost missed her exit. She careened the Datsun towards it, recovering quickly and returned to making a study of her own green eyes. Still green. Still eyes. But this was a cramp, and girls in high school would get out of gym class with hand scrawled "time of the month cramps" notes. Could this be period cramping? Had she come so close to have it all ruined by this bleeding? She had to get to her father, know him, see pictures of his face, before her mind turned moth, her eyes just empty monster beacons. If only she hadn't wasted so much time with Brian, Napoleon and now Test and Ruth.

She floored the Datsun gas pedal to close the distance between her and the Buick. Test turned down a side street heading north and Indy followed as another cramp tore across her pelvis.

269

The left signal light of Ruth's Buick came on.

And they were here.

***

The house was a small white aluminum-sided bungalow. It was built far out at the end of a city road, so far out that the city road had gone to gravel and, finally, mostly dust. The house had two neighbors, both trailers.

There was a rusty blue mailbox. The gold stickers on it spelled out THE LIVE S. Down two letters. But his name, her name, right there in gold and black on blue.

The house was not so different from the trailer Indy had grown up in, except for the fact that it was clearly a house and not a trailer. Her father's driveway was empty, or it was until first Test and then Indy parked. Test stood, facing Indy with his arm's raised in a TA-DA fashion.

Between cramps and background humming, Indy had trouble responding correctly. She managed a weak nod of acknowledgement. She felt a feverish flash and plucked the Molson Export bottle from between her thighs, pressing it against her forehead. It felt good. Kiko was trying the door to her father's house. She did not want the little coke kid to be the first one in her dad's house. She ran for his door.

Test came up behind Indy, talking. She ignored him and put her hand over Kiko's on the chipped brass doorknob, startling him. He leapt out of her way. His jump looked slow, his hand floating away while his body stayed in the air impossibly long. Indy's own hand turned the knob quickly in contrast. The door opened easily and she stepped over the threshold. Inside.

The smell hugged her. She inhaled deeply through her nose and shut her eyes: beer metals, thinning flannel. Her synapses reborn in the explosion of scent memories long sought, finally

270

sated. Indy shut the door behind her to prevent the smell, the precious daddy scented air, from escaping.

The humming was the loudest ever. Indy took in the room, sure that she would see the source of the hum. She was standing in a normal foyer that was also a normal living room. Golden linoleum ran up to a glossy white baby grand piano that occupied almost the entire space. The piano was silent, not humming. The top of the piano was down. Arranged upon it were unframed photographs of various sizes. The photos were upright and facing Indy because each was leaning against something. She took a step closer. She could see the photographs were leaning against glass insulators, the kind that used to be on all the electrical poles but were now replaced. A memory of watching her father climb an electricity pole. She reached out and picked up a black and white photograph of a toddler. She stared into the eyes of a toddler with who had cut her own bangs. Her crooked bangs, her eyes. She had not ever seen a photograph of herself at this age. It was like she had grown up hundreds of years ago before the photograph or like the Mennonites next door. But now, here, on this shiny white piano was her little face. It felt anachronistic to discover for the first time her baby face because the photo of herself as a child was so brand new.

Keeping the photo of her toddler self in her right hand, she reached out her left to the pick up another. She handled this second photograph with archival preciousness. It was of a small man with a huge brown mustache and a strawberry blonde ponytail. The man was standing outside of this very house and nonchalantly leaning against a Century 21 For Sale sign with a bright orange SOLD sticker slapped diagonally across it. He was wearing a flannel plaid shirt and dark blue Levis. He was toasting the event with a Molson's Export. The photo slipped from Indy's fingers. It drifted so slowly to the floor, she was able to slip her hand under it and catch it so it rested lightly against her palm, tickling, like a feather.

Someone knocked two loud strong knocks against her father's door.

271

Hum.

The man in the photograph was evidence. *Proof.* A face, a body, a place, a hairstyle to replace the beer ship. The tickling from the photo was too much, so Indy slipped it off her palm, back on top of the piano. She placed her three-year-old self on top of it, to protect her dad.

Indy's eyes moved back to the photo/electric insulator array. Strangely, she found a very familiar, recent photograph. It was her high school yearbook photo from last year. It was grainy, as if it had been blown up from a small version and photocopied a bunch. Beside that was another yearbook photo, but black and white. The face, save for a larger nose, was nearly identical to Indy's high school yearbook photo. Same dimples, crooked teeth and cheekbones. Same, except it was of a boy not a girl.

Two more loud strikes at the door.

She looked exactly like her father had in high school. Indy's mouth formed a silent O. The efforts her family had made to erase her father had been futile. As the years passed, she had slowly turned into him. Like a bad move in Jenga, all the assumptions Indy had about herself, and how angry and hateful her mother and stepfather had been towards her, toppled woodenly apart. As she had aged, they'd needed to get rid of her to keep with the program of erasure of her father because she had *become* him. All their hard pretending work had been for nothing.

A hand fell on Indy's shoulder.

She swung around, spreading her arms out to protect the top of the piano. She came face to face with Test's ZZ Top beard, reeking of linseed and human fungus. His eyes, usually pinned and glassy, were wide and, perhaps, a little sad. He opened his mouth, but before he said anything a bullet hit the piano just behind Indy's torso, filling the room with the chords a single gunshot can play. Indy threw herself into Test's stink and beard. Her weight toppled the old man backwards and Indy floated down with him, face first.

As she was trying to sort herself out and away from Test, someone pinched the back of her neck in a dry death grip, yanking her off Test and up only to sucker punch her. Her attacker smashed a hand-sized metal object into her jaw with such force they lost their grip and it clattered against the far wall. The pistol-whipping cracked Indy's front teeth. She listened to her tooth enamel skitter across the shiny piano, hard white against hard white. Her tongue went immediately to the gap where her front teeth once were. Her dentist always said the cure for her overcrowding was to get a few taken out. She collapsed to her knees, her arms flailing. In tandem with her fall, an arm snaked easily around her throat, choking her back and up towards the face of her attacker.

Indy met the gaze of her one-eyed attacker with an asymmetrical blush of lust and agony.

Even as Napoleon pummeled her, Indy thrilled to be held again by him. She was jubilant to have him at the apotheosis of her trip. To have him truly see her face again, a face she now knew was not simply her own, but also her father's. Napoleon would now know that her cross-continent road trip had not been in vain, that she had needed to remove anything in her way to get here in time to be free. He should share her victory. Everyone had doubted she would find her father. Yet he had been there all along, shining out from Indy's own face. There was only thing left to do.

Napoleon held Indy by the hair and hammered her face with his fist. She did not fight back. She felt her nose crack and her lips rip against the crevices made by her missing teeth. Through her beating she saw Napoleon was now wearing Brian on his punching arm, weakening his punches. Brian was screaming because his mouth was all the way wide open.

The fist holding Indy's hair opened. She dropped noisily. Test's legs broke some of her fall, swelling softened the rest. Napoleon yanked his arm back from Brian causing the broken boy to teeter on his one good leg.

You killer.

Test, frozen in fear on the ground as he watched Indy get beaten, sat up. He pulled the tip of his beard. On top of him, Indy pressed herself upright and horked, flummoxed about where to spit a mouthful of blood so it would not soil her father's floor. She aimed for Test's paint-spattered Dickies. Test yanked his legs away, too late.

How did you find me?

Brian slid a beige backpack off his back and held it out to Indy.

You left this.

Indy saw that his cast was caked with filth but also tagged with street names and Sharpie drawings of sneakers. She took the backpack.

You left that after you murdered Jenny.

Indy took the backpack. It was the bag from the Alliance Church in Eldontown that she had packed with ammunition and food a lifetime ago. Before she knew who she was. Opening it she saw the bottom was still full of Twinkies but the ammo was gone. Her stomach rumbled. She hadn't eaten since Ruth's roofied cookies. She bit into a Twinkie right through the cellophane, squishing the entire contents between her swollen lips. The sugar burned a pleasure layer around her mouth. There was nothing else in the bag except a sheaf of zombie cocoon she must have picked up by accident. She looked at Brian sadly, and then Napoleon, who chupsed.

She can't even fucking see it.

She's trying.

How did I not see you following me?

Despite the roiling Vegas heat inside her father's house, Indy's fingers and toes were ice.

We've been *waiting* for you here, asshole. We didn't need to follow you.

Test grimaced and got to his feet, pulling himself up by the piano. Indy cringed at the fingerprints he left in the perfect white shine.

You want I get rid of these two?

Napoleon and Indy answered in unison.

It was Jenny or us. I did it for us. This house is everything. But I still have to try to finish, to find him.

We know exactly where your dad is Indy.

Brian spoke matter-of-factly, his face a mask.

Indy stopped talking. She looked to her hands and stopped looking at them, and looked at them again, blinking. She tried to look at Brian, into his eyes. Could not.

Let's end it.

Napoleon turned and walked out of Indy's father's house. Brian hobbled after him.

Test tried to speak, but Indy cut him off with a hand gesture. She took another look around the room, choosing photos to take with her. She decided to take her toddler self and her father and his sold sign. She placed them into her good old canvas backpack, sliding them delicately under the Twinkies.

She swung it over her shoulder, snuffling blood and snot back up her ruined nose.

Napoleon and Brian waited on a Harley. The motorcycle had studded saddlebags that glittered in the sun. The studs formed the shape of an eagle. Indy limped to her Datsun, re-piling a few mothdillo heads that had rolled onto her seat. She followed Napoleon and Brian as closely as she could without running their motorcycle off the road, fearful that they would try to get away. Brian looked funny riding, his casted leg sticking out stupidly from the bike. They turned into the desert. Test and Kiko followed, too, behind her. It's a parade, Indy thought, to celebrate finding my dad.

In the distance, an oasis emerged out of heat shimmers. Indy was certain it was only a mirage until she was almost right on top of it. How could this exist in the Las Vegas desert? Yet the lush green oasis manifested inarguably amidst the gravel yards and empty sand lots, all poplar trees and ripe grass. Napoleon directed his Harley onto a dirt road, running through the heart of the oasis, and her father parade followed.

Though it didn't seem like a mothdillo hideout or a trap, Indy unsheathed her diving knife from her thigh, just in case. Even in case she had to meet her father by taking his head.

Napoleon stopped next to a low outcropping of rocks. He helped Brian off the Harley onto the groomed grass. Indy parked beside him and got out of her Datsun wearing her backpack. She had put the now warm bottle of Molson inside just in case her father was thirsty. She had put her gun in too.

The oasis smelled dry like the surrounding desert but she could hear water. Or maybe her brain hum had simply morphed into water sounds and it was all in her head; it didn't really matter. Napoleon was scowling and Brian had his hand out towards her, saying *c'mon*.

Nothing seemed right; it was too soon. Who are these people? What am I wearing? I don't have both ears, Indy thought, as she took Brian's hand, the hand that would take her to her father. She had waited a decade, most of her life and thought at least one minute of every hour about how this would be.

Daddy?

Brian's hand was cold somehow in the Vegas heat, like hers, as he guided her back towards her Datsun, around and in front of it, and stood her some twelve feet away, two tall body lengths. He turned her so she faced away from the hand-painted truck and into the oasis. He dropped her hand. Brian pointed. He pointed, at first, at nothing. Indy followed his hand and examined the distance. It was annoying. Beyond the oasis there was only desert scrub, some distant construction rubble. Brian shook his head and pointed again, this time nodding down to something closer. Indy was surprised. The water sound was not only in her head. Brian pointed at a cast concrete statue of a naked boy perched on the edge of a concrete pool, holding his tiny concrete penis from which he peed into the pool below. Have they brought her all the way here to show her a cheap fountain that anyone could buy at a garden center?

It cannot be so. Using her fingers, she tugged at her eyelids to make sure her eyes were open and still full of eyeballs. They were.

Indy had been careless was all. Brian was pointing at a second stony form, *beside* the silly peeing fountain boy. The second sculpture was boring monolithic rock. But far too smooth, too tall, Indy realized, to be merely accidental or natural. It was the kind of rock made smooth by careful polishing so it would be appropriate to mark a place of significance. A marker. Indy approached the polished rock and ran her hand over the surface. Yes, too tall. Too much space. Something was missing. This is the back!

Indy circled around to the other side of the rock so she was now at the front of it, her Datsun in its shadow. Yes, she realized, this is the front; there are carvings here. At the top of the rock, an eagle had been carved, exactly like the steel stud eagle on the saddlebags of Napoleon's ride. This stone one did not glitter though. It was flat and grey. Beneath the eagle were the words, or not really words. Napoleon was boring into her with his one good eye. Indy could feel it.

It's his grave, asshole.

Why does this polished stone make me an asshole?

She was furious and jammed her hand into her backpack for the gun because Napoleon never ever let up. She found the gun at the bottom of her bag, beneath the papery cocoon remnant and beer bottle, and wrapped her fingers around the solid stock of it. She pulled it from her bag violently, spilling the contents as a consequence. Molson Export bottle and papery things landed at Indy's feet.

Indy. Who the fuck gets a fancy tombstone in an apocalypse?

Indy couldn't understand Napoleon, but it stopped mattering because behind him she could see into the front seat of her

278

Datsun to the dashboard and what was on it, and what was piled on the seat behind it.

Visible clearly, artfully piled on the passenger side of her Datsun, she spotted an unexpected kind of head. Reminding Indy of a pill from Ruth's cupboard in shape, it was certainly not a 'dillo head or moth head or whatever you wanted to call it. It was just plain human. There was no trace of any kind of mineralized transparent carapace. It was a normal human, if somewhat decomposed, flesh head. The longer Indy stared, the clearer it became she was looking at two human heads, chopped away from their bodies between the upper and lower mandible and then purposefully sewn together jaw to jaw with thick black thread. The left head wore a fashionable pixie cut that reminded Indy of the lady who starred in Rosemary's Baby. It looked just like the girl her and Kris had seen cutting her hair in the road before she had run away. Her upper jaw was set up against and sewn to the upper jaw of a man that could not have been but really looked like her stepfather, Dana. Somehow he was back, yet again for Winnie the Pooh Part Three. The entire effect was to create a crude yet effective four-eyed, two-nosed one gristle mouthed head that, although clearly not mirror images of each other, rotted into similarity in death: ashen pallor, collapsed sockets, black retreating lips. A post-mortem conjoined twin of hair cutter girl and Dana. Who, Indy thought, would do this? Why would someone create such atrocities?

Behind the death-twin she could now notice more heads, freed of their lower mandibles too, and somehow all without mineralized translucent carapaces. Not 'dillo just normal decomposing human heads, some twinned, some not. Had Test somehow ripped her off and replaced her valuable moth heads with this gruesome lot? What a monster. She should never have trusted him.

Indy shut her eyes and dropped her chin to her chest to listen to the peeing boy.

279

When she opened her eyes again she was facing down so she saw all the things that had spilled from her backpack. She was standing on the photograph of her father. Indy lifted her foot off the photo and picked it up, worried she had damaged it. On the ground beside the photo was a piece of cocoon. Only now, like the moth heads in her truck, the cocoon fragment had been switched. The fragment had been smoothed neatly and squared off bureaucratically. But worse still, it had words that Indy could read.

DEATH CERTIFICATE

the paper said. And her father's name. And a date of death of one year ago. Far before the 'dillo/moth apocalypse began.

Indy called something out, dropping the cocoon-cum-death-certificate. She was asking for someone to open the door. She meant to be more specific about what door, but Brian heard her and limped on his graffitied leg to the Datsun's passenger door. He opened it.

A cascade of heads, plain old human heads, if you can call human heads severed from their means of transportation between the upper and lower mandibles plain, tumbled out of the truck onto the lush Las Vegas oasis they had paraded to. It wasn't hard to pick Tiffany's head out: even long dead, her Studio Line puffy bangs were perfect.

Indy said something out loud then clapped her hand over her mouth. She hadn't meant to announce her moment of clarity to the group. She was pretty sure they knew already and she was ashamed to have been so late to the game. Was she stupid? She'd been so worried about finding enough food and monsters and racing against the apocalypse to find her father she missed the obvious.

The road was a person. The Datsun was a relationship. And the apocalypse was

Horrific. It was all far worse than she had been imagining, far too bad to face at once. No wonder she had been enjoying herself!

Indy decided to lie down on the ground, in exact alignment with the monolith and beneath its eagle and lettering. As though she were the dead body. Flat and close to the ground she felt tickled in a very pleasant way. She wanted to maximize the feel of it against her skin. She looked up and read the sign over the driveway that had brought her to her father's grave. It said CEMETERY.

At first, merely lying on his grave felt good enough but it did not last. Indy reached for the Molson Export bottle that had fallen from her bag. Using the top of the bottle like a spade, she loosened the earth under her. The grass on top was imported sod; it was a thin penetrable layer. Once the beer bottle cut through the top layer, the sod peeled back easily, like gift-wrapping. Beneath was sand, just like Sauble Beach. Indy planted the bottle, top down, at the head of the grave beneath the tombstone, staking her claim to it with her singular inexorable memory. Using only hands now, she shoveled sand, digging a huge hole rimmed by sand mountains, just as she had in her summers at Sauble after she hunted fluorescent orange salamanders and needed to imprison the pretty but slimy amphibians. She dug until her hands hurt and her knuckles bled. It was too dry. Indy stopped digging and rolled over towards the peeing boy, bathing her hands in his stream. It felt so good she dunked her face in the fountain and, safe or not, drank. Returning to her task, she dropped herself, salamander-like, into her dry sand hole above her father's grave. A grave over a grave. Grave bunk beds.

Indy's sundress stuck out at stiff angles around her prone body much like a 'dillo carapace. Except her dress was not mineralized skin, it was, she realized as she tried to press it down flat so no one could see up it, polyester hardened with dried blood and other matter. She cracked through the dress crust enough to fold the skirt stiffly down, flocking her hands in a dry red crust.

The weak sandy earth was giving way and caving in around her. She was being slowly buried alive.

It felt like a hug.

It felt like love.

One-minute apocalypse and seconds-long continental road trip.

Ashlee is six and she is babysitting. Super Fries are near burning when the mail comes. Ashlee is outside playing with the Meanos and collects it. She races back to the house, excited. A large, never before seen kind of envelope has arrived. She hands it to Indy who is straining fries and wasting all that hot corn oil down the drain.

The envelope is from Nevada. It is addressed to their mother.

Indy always opens all the mail. What else is there to do?

Her mother teaches troubled teens at a school called Pine Hill. It sounds pretty, but it is simply so remote that running is useless. You cannot possibly get away, like Tara. When their mother gets home, Ashlee wants to be important, so she tells her about the strange mail. Indy listens from the bedroom she sleeps in. She has been sitting erect in bed, gripping tightly her mother's mail all afternoon. She knows she must give it to her. It is, after all, addressed to her.

She passes through the faux wood trailer hallway to the kitchen. Her mother, spilling out of a mucosal pink boob tube grins easily from the kitchen table. The table was free. It was a hand-me-down. Her mother has opened a package of her favorite gum, Thrills. Everyone hates this gum because it tastes like soap. Everyone except her mother. She pops a purple piece of it into her mouth and chews loudly. Lavender scented breath wafts over Indy as she hands her mother the mail.

Chew chew chew.

Oh, yes. It happened ages ago.

Chew chew chew.

Remember when we changed our phone number from 2946 to 2520?

Ring ring ring.

I told you it was a crank caller. It was annoying, went on for weeks.

Ring ring ring. Chew chew chew.

It was silly.

Ring. Chew.

He was wanting to say goodbye before he died.

Indy's mother pops two more Thrills in her mouth. She was craving more soapy flavor.

I told him you were not interested. Of course you'd never want to talk to him again! I knew you wouldn't care, either way.

Indy has to nod.

Besides, it is time to go to the greenhouse to do her chores with the pot plants and the chickens.

Indy sank into her father's loving sandy embrace, eager to join him. Brian and Napoleon appear above her. Napoleon horks and lets it slide out from between his beautiful lips, never breaking the bead. A long-form insulting kiss. It lands squarely on her chest, where her breasts ought to be.

The kiss sends clarity through Indy. There is one horrendous mistake, among the thousands she had made, that she could easily fix. And should.

Her name!

Indy was a name chosen in haste. So obviously wrong! The Indy naming was a silly attempt at a naïve and impossible future. Naming herself after Indiana Jones was childish and predictable and unsurprising coming from someone running on chicken legs from neglect and abuse in a Tara. As though she needed Spielberg to become a brave and clever adventurer, handsome and strong!

She cautiously rested her hand on her missing ear, expecting it to be replaced too. It was still very sore. One tiny scab remained so she peeled it off and flicked it into the fountain. The ear hole was nearly healed. Her useful sound-channeling cartilage had been fully replaced by bright pink baffling scar tissue.

The Indiana name, sadly, would have to join the head collection in the Datsun. Another phony monster, another victim, another gruesome attempt at repair.

A second, more accurate rebirth was called for. An adult one.

It was, indeed, a question of accuracy. She hoisted herself up and out of her grave, pushing past Napoleon, his sparkling wad of spittle gliding warmly down her sternum like jewelry. She broke into a really good run. It felt effortless. Like how Kris had moved. It was easier to leave them behind, even after all they had been through together, because they never actually knew her. Not really.

Indy!

They were shouting after her now. She could hear Brian crying clearly, but she felt absolutely no obligation to stop, turn around, or respond. They were calling her by the wrong name.

And although it had been her mistake, not theirs, she sped up, leaving the oasis cemetery behind. Indy was gone too.

There was only one name she could stop and answer to now. And, like her father's face, it had been secretly with her all along, ruining things.

Indy took a deep asthma-free breath of hot Las Vegas air and screamed as loud as she could her one true and real grown-up name:

Apocalypse.

THE END